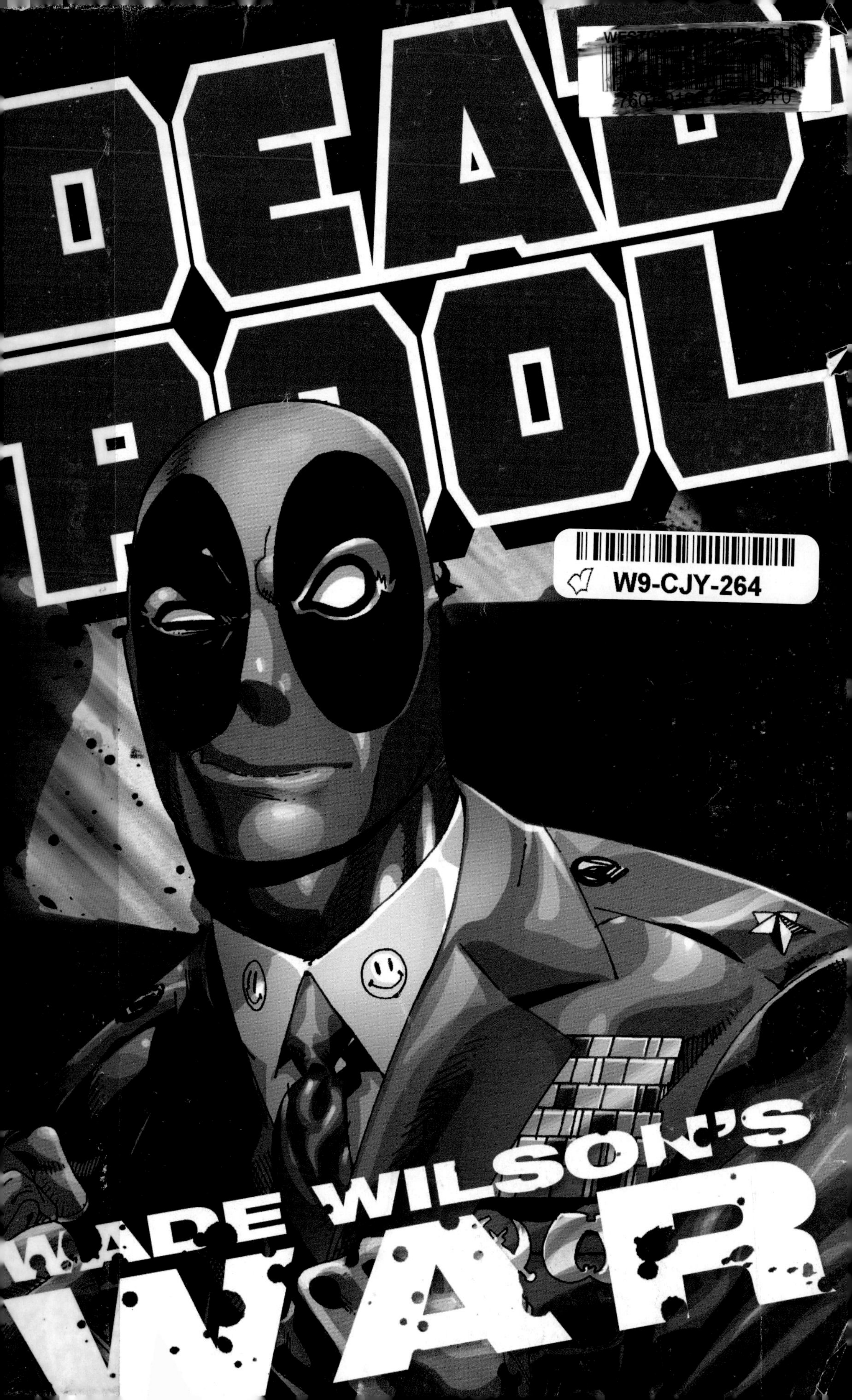
DEADPOOL
WADE WILSON'S
WAR

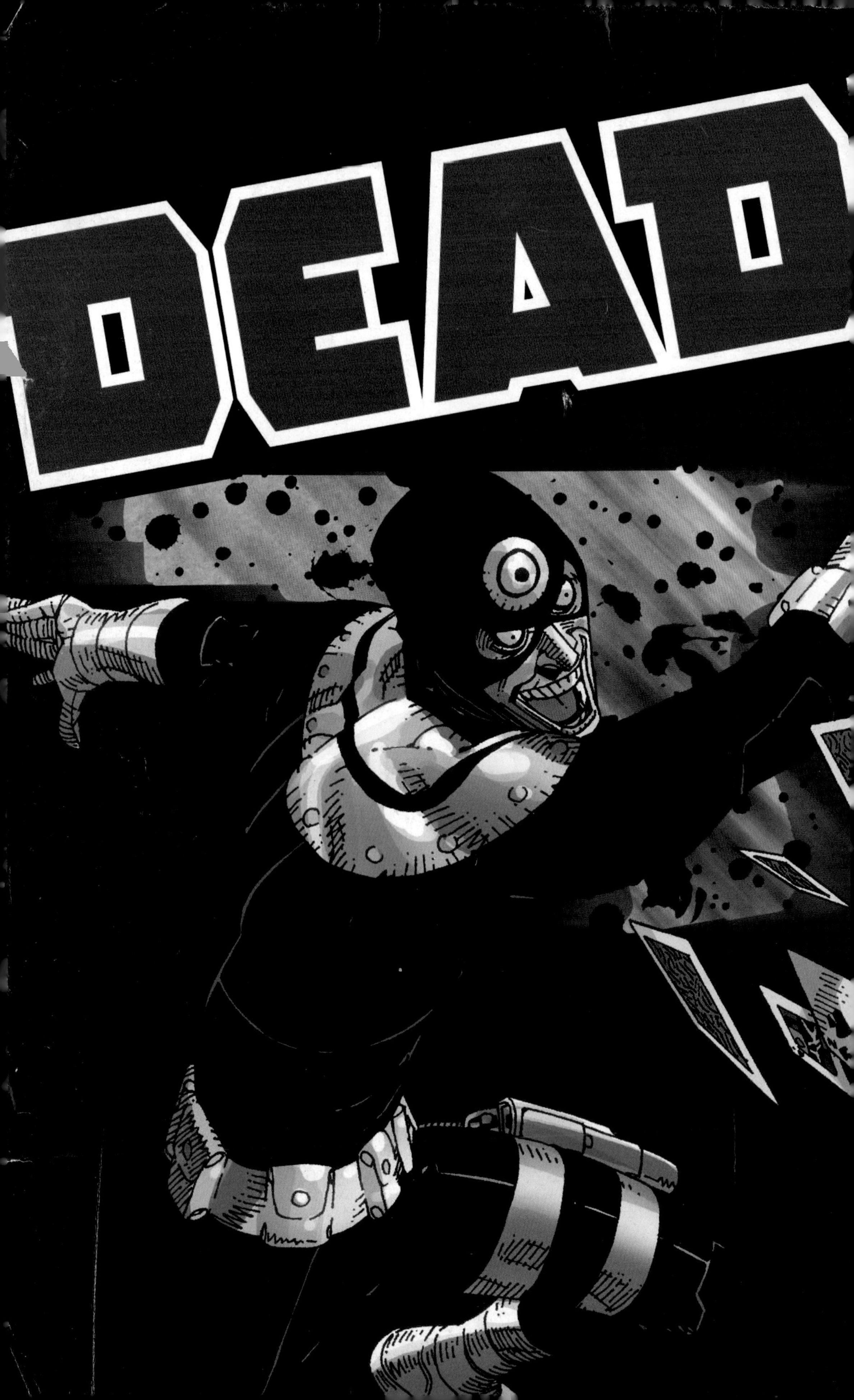
DEAD

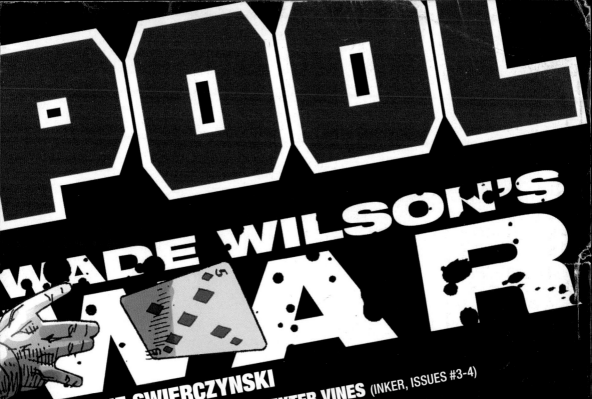

POOL
WADE WILSON'S WAR

WRITER: **DUANE SWIERCZYNSKI**

ARTIST: **JASON PEARSON** WITH **DEXTER VINES** (INKER, ISSUES #3-4)

COLORIST: **PAUL MOUNTS**

LETTERS: **VIRTUAL CALLIGRAPHY'S CLAYTON COWLES**

ASSISTANT EDITOR: **SEBASTIAN GIRNER**

EDITOR: **AXEL ALONSO**

COLLECTION EDITOR: **CORY LEVINE**

EDITORIAL ASSISTANTS: **JAMES EMMETT & JOE HOCHSTEIN**

ASSISTANT EDITORS: **ALEX STARBUCK & NELSON RIBEIRO**

EDITORS, SPECIAL PROJECTS: **JENNIFER GRÜNWALD & MARK D. BEAZLEY**

SENIOR EDITOR, SPECIAL PROJECTS: **JEFF YOUNGQUIST**

SENIOR VICE PRESIDENT OF SALES: **DAVID GABRIEL**

SVP OF BRAND PLANNING & COMMUNICATIONS: **MICHAEL PASCIULLO**

BOOK DESIGN: **RODOLFO MURAGUCHI**

EDITOR IN CHIEF: **AXEL ALONSO**

CHIEF CREATIVE OFFICER: **JOE QUESADA**

PUBLISHER: **DAN BUCKLEY**

EXECUTIVE PRODUCER: **ALAN FINE**

DEADPOOL: WADE WILSON'S WAR. Contains material originally published in magazine form as DEADPOOL: WADE WILSON'S WAR #1-4. First printing 2011. ISBN# 978-0-7851-4713-8. Published by MARVEL WORLDWIDE, INC., a subsidiary of MARVEL ENTERTAINMENT, LLC. OFFICE OF PUBLICATION: 135 West 50th Street, New York, NY 10020. Copyright © 2010 and 2011 Marvel Characters, Inc. All rights reserved. $14.99 per copy in the U.S. and $16.50 in Canada (GST #R127032852); Canadian Agreement #40668537. All characters featured in this issue and the distinctive names and likenesses thereof, and all related indicia are trademarks of Marvel Characters, Inc. No similarity between any of the names, characters, persons, and/or institutions in this magazine with those of any living or dead person or institution is intended, and any such similarity which may exist is purely coincidental. **Printed in the U.S.A.** ALAN FINE, EVP - Office of the President, Marvel Worldwide, Inc. and EVP & CMO Marvel Characters B.V.; DAN BUCKLEY, Publisher & President - Print, Animation & Digital Divisions; JOE QUESADA, Chief Creative Officer; JIM SOKOLOWSKI, Chief Operating Officer; DAVID BOGART, SVP of Business Affairs & Talent Management; TOM BREVOORT, SVP of Publishing; C.B. CEBULSKI, SVP of Creator & Content Development; DAVID GABRIEL, SVP of Publishing Sales & Circulation; MICHAEL PASCIULLO, SVP of Brand Planning & Communications; JIM O'KEEFE, VP of Operations & Logistics; DAN CARR, Executive Director of Publishing Technology; JUSTIN F. GABRIE, Director of Publishing & Editorial Operations; SUSAN CRESPI, Editorial Operations Manager; ALEX MORALES, Publishing Operations Manager; STAN LEE, Chairman Emeritus. For information regarding advertising in Marvel Comics or on Marvel.com, please contact John Dokes, SVP Integrated Sales and Marketing, at jdokes@marvel.com. For Marvel subscription inquiries, please call 800-217-9158. For Marvel subscription inquiries, please call 800-217-9158. **Manufactured between 4/13/2011 and 5/2/2011 by R.R. DONNELLEY, INC., SALEM, VA, USA.**

10 9 8 7 6 5 4 3 2 1

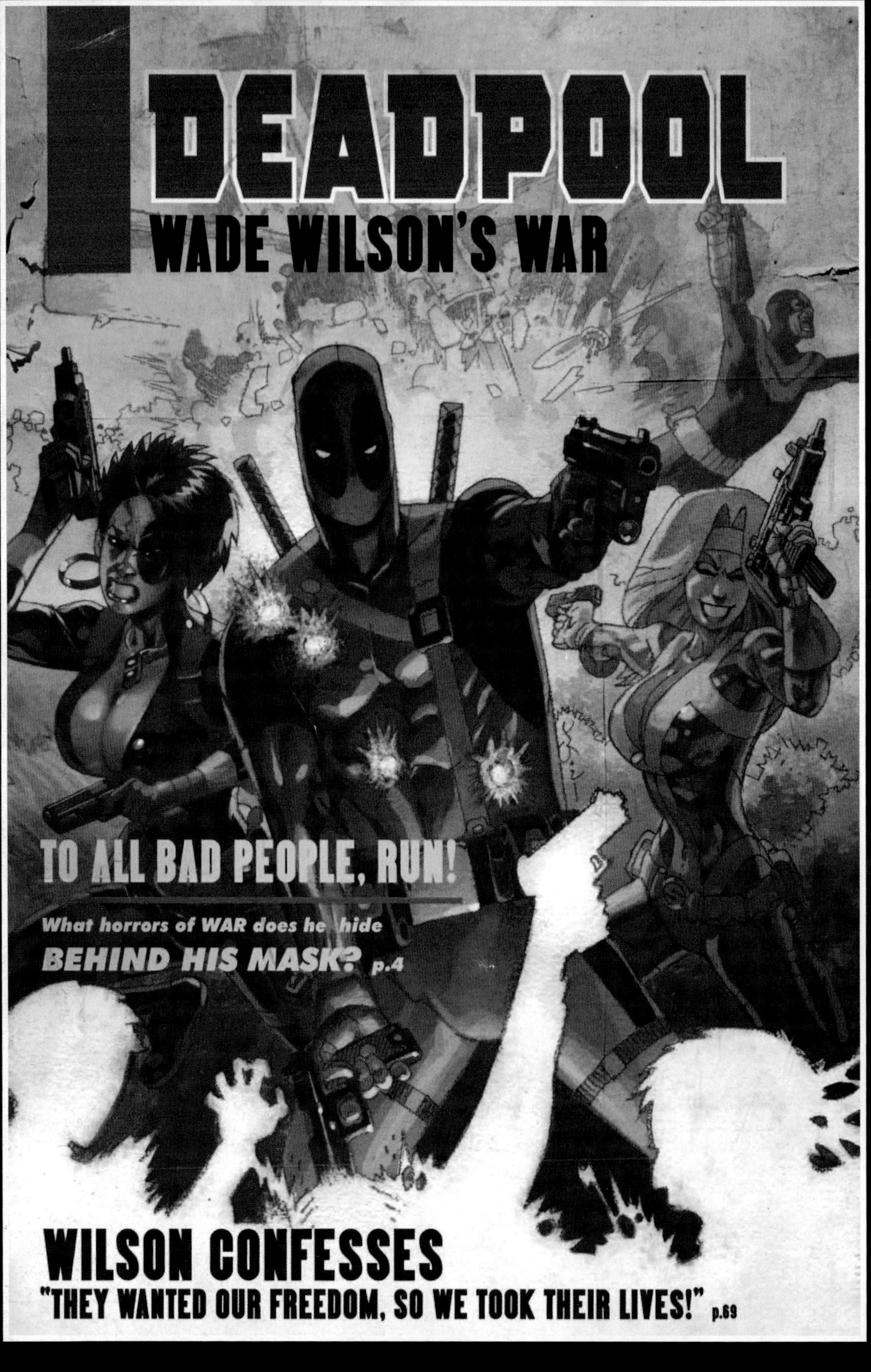
DEADPOOL
WADE WILSON'S WAR
TO ALL BAD PEOPLE, RUN!
What horrors of WAR does he hide
BEHIND HIS MASK? p.4
WILSON CONFESSES
"THEY WANTED OUR FREEDOM, SO WE TOOK THEIR LIVES!" p.69

DEADPOOL: WADE WILSON'S WAR #1

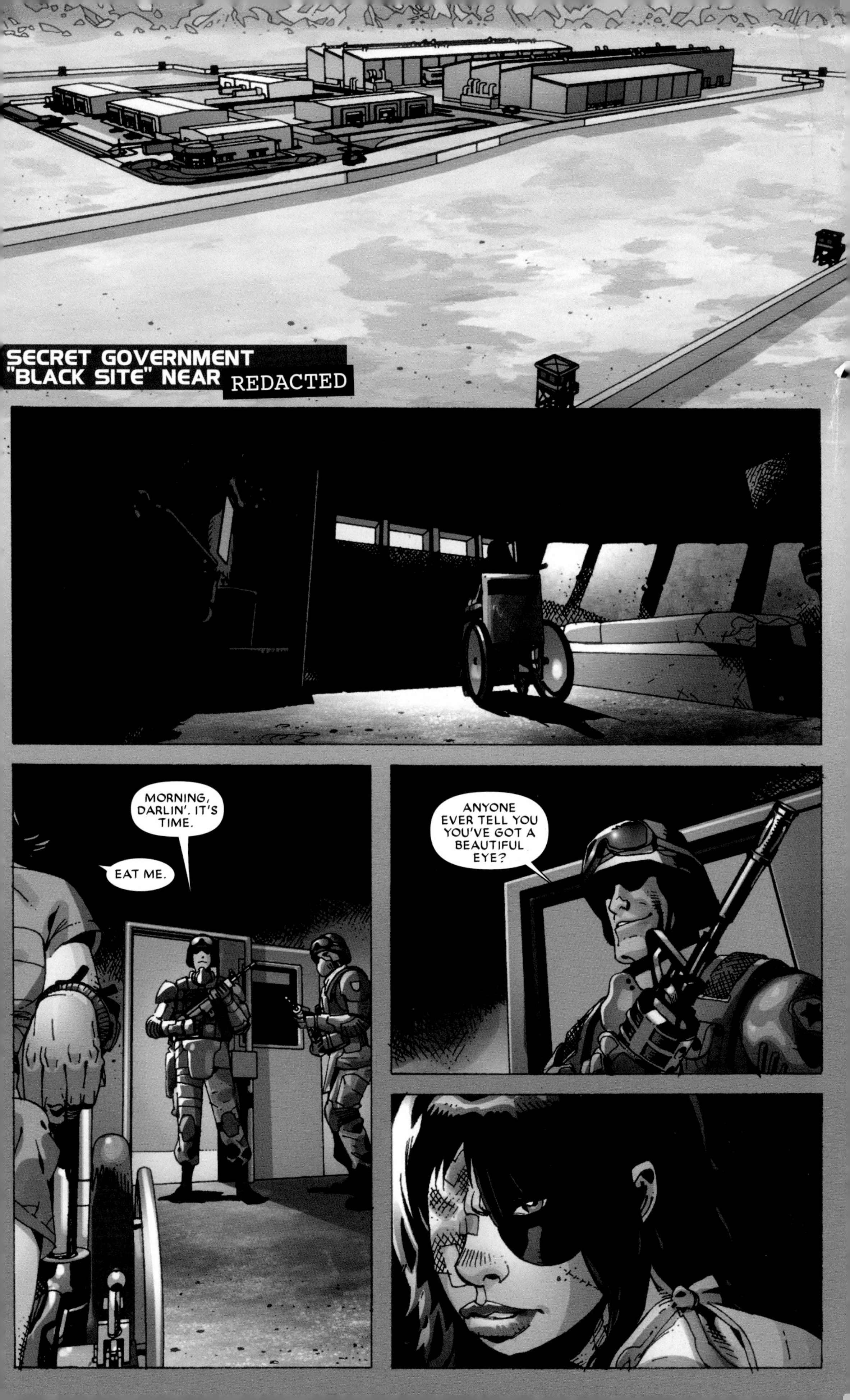
SECRET GOVERNMENT "BLACK SITE" NEAR REDACTED
MORNING, DARLIN'. IT'S TIME.
EAT ME.
ANYONE EVER TELL YOU YOU'VE GOT A BEAUTIFUL EYE?

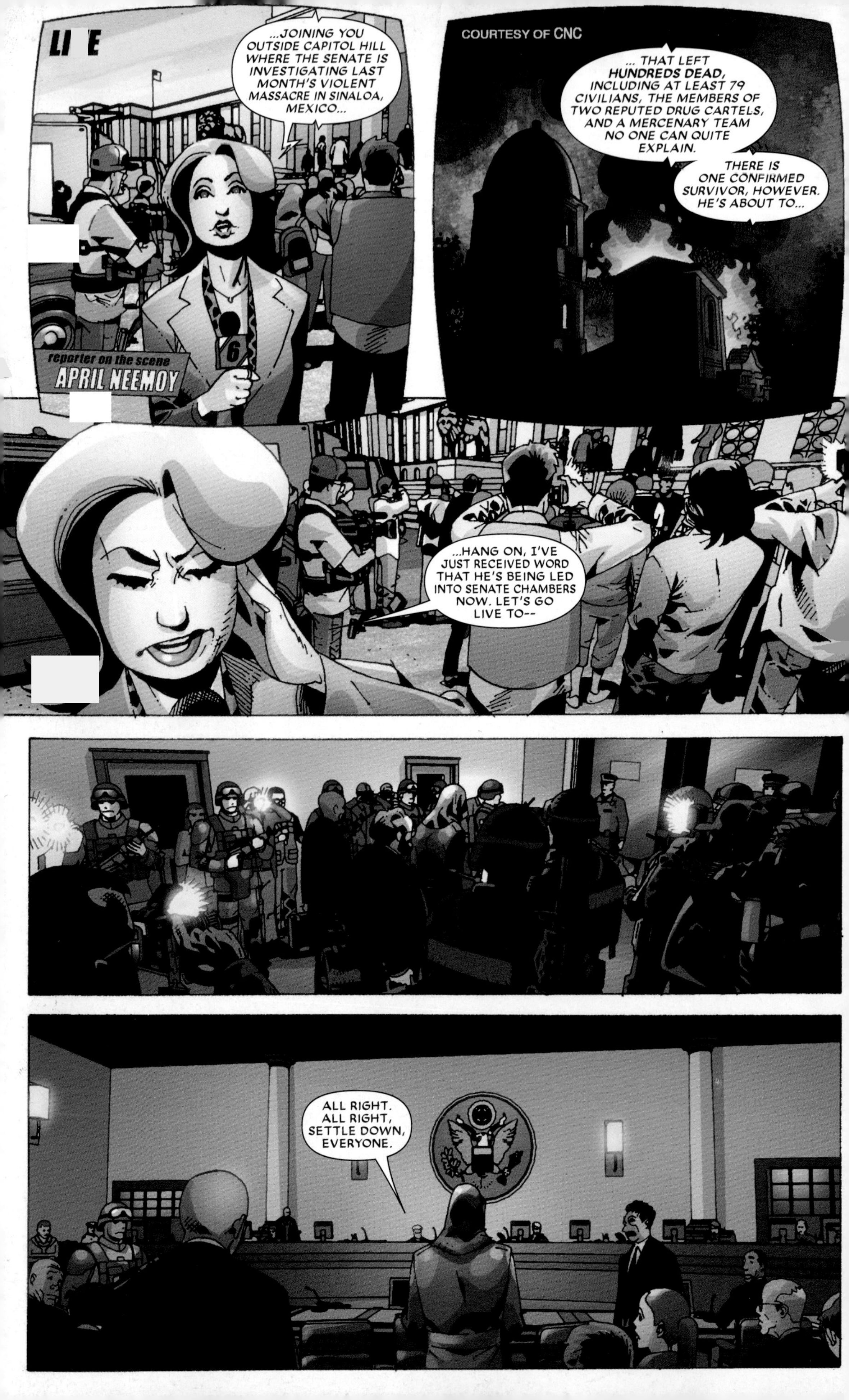
LI E
...JOINING YOU OUTSIDE CAPITOL HILL WHERE THE SENATE IS INVESTIGATING LAST MONTH'S VIOLENT MASSACRE IN SINALOA, MEXICO...
reporter on the scene
APRIL NEEMOY
6
COURTESY OF CNC
... THAT LEFT HUNDREDS DEAD, INCLUDING AT LEAST 79 CIVILIANS, THE MEMBERS OF TWO REPUTED DRUG CARTELS, AND A MERCENARY TEAM NO ONE CAN QUITE EXPLAIN.
THERE IS ONE CONFIRMED SURVIVOR, HOWEVER. HE'S ABOUT TO...
...HANG ON, I'VE JUST RECEIVED WORD THAT HE'S BEING LED INTO SENATE CHAMBERS NOW. LET'S GO LIVE TO--
ALL RIGHT. ALL RIGHT, SETTLE DOWN, EVERYONE.

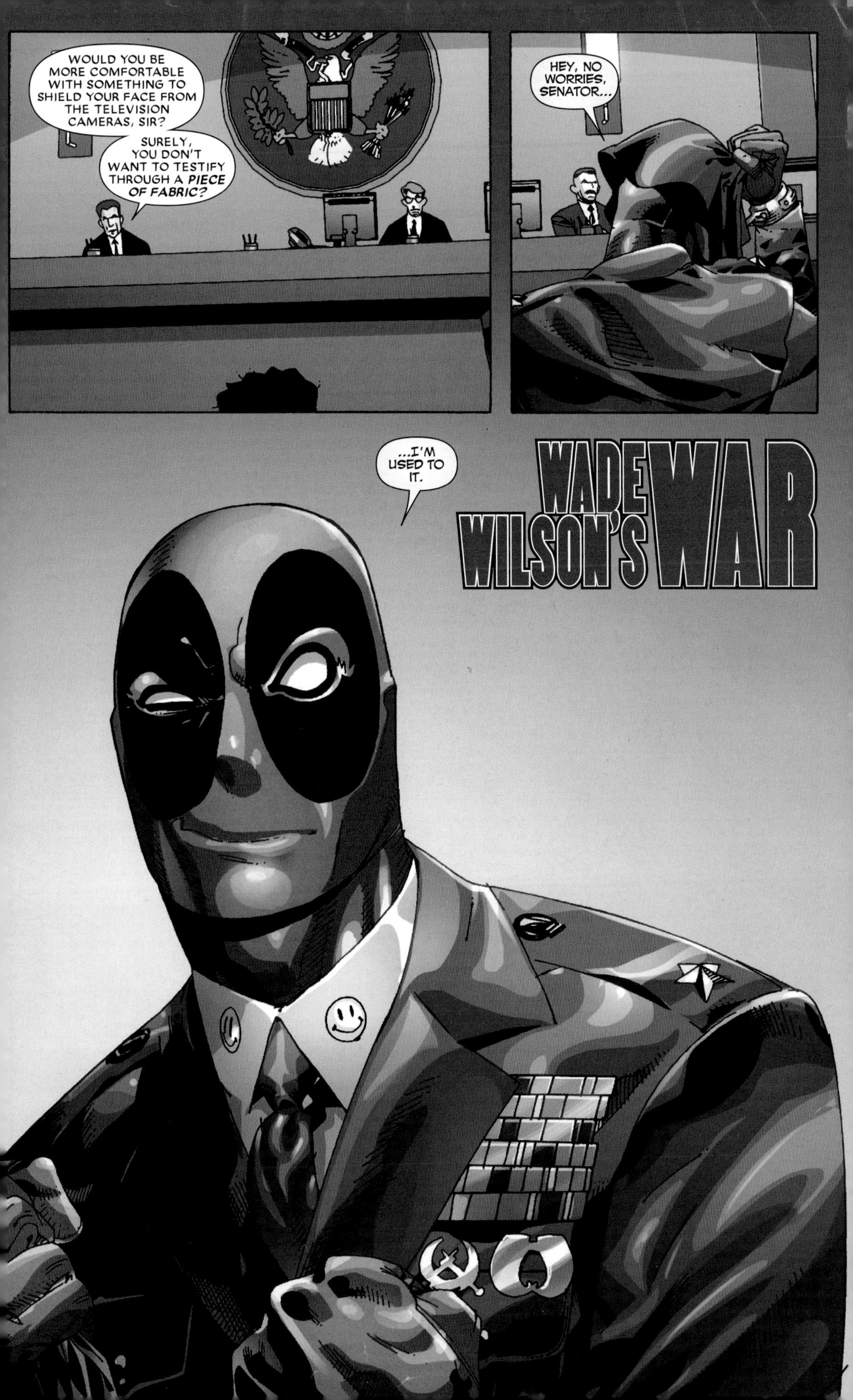

WOULD YOU BE MORE COMFORTABLE WITH SOMETHING TO SHIELD YOUR FACE FROM THE TELEVISION CAMERAS, SIR?
SURELY, YOU DON'T WANT TO TESTIFY THROUGH A *PIECE OF FABRIC?*
HEY, NO WORRIES, SENATOR...
...I'M USED TO IT.
WADE WILSON'S WAR

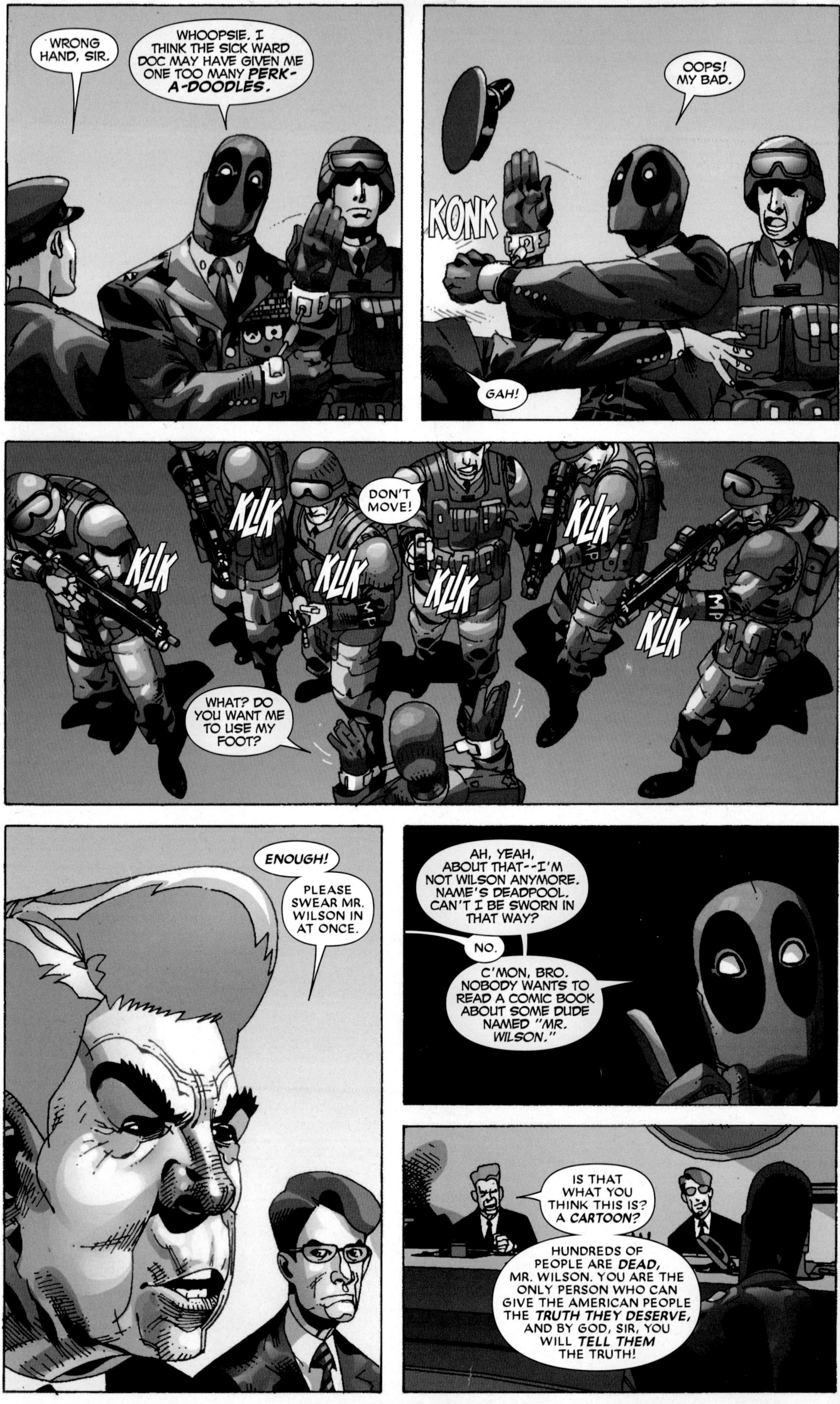
WRONG HAND, SIR.
WHOOPSIE. I THINK THE SICK WARD DOC MAY HAVE GIVEN ME ONE TOO MANY PERK-A-DOODLES.
OOPS! MY BAD.
KONK
GAH!
KLIK
KLIK
DON'T MOVE!
KLIK
KLIK
KLIK
KLIK
WHAT? DO YOU WANT ME TO USE MY FOOT?
ENOUGH!
PLEASE SWEAR MR. WILSON IN AT ONCE.
AH, YEAH, ABOUT THAT--I'M NOT WILSON ANYMORE. NAME'S DEADPOOL. CAN'T I BE SWORN IN THAT WAY?
NO.
C'MON, BRO. NOBODY WANTS TO READ A COMIC BOOK ABOUT SOME DUDE NAMED "MR. WILSON."
IS THAT WHAT YOU THINK THIS IS? A CARTOON?
HUNDREDS OF PEOPLE ARE DEAD, MR. WILSON. YOU ARE THE ONLY PERSON WHO CAN GIVE THE AMERICAN PEOPLE THE TRUTH THEY DESERVE, AND BY GOD, SIR, YOU WILL TELL THEM THE TRUTH!

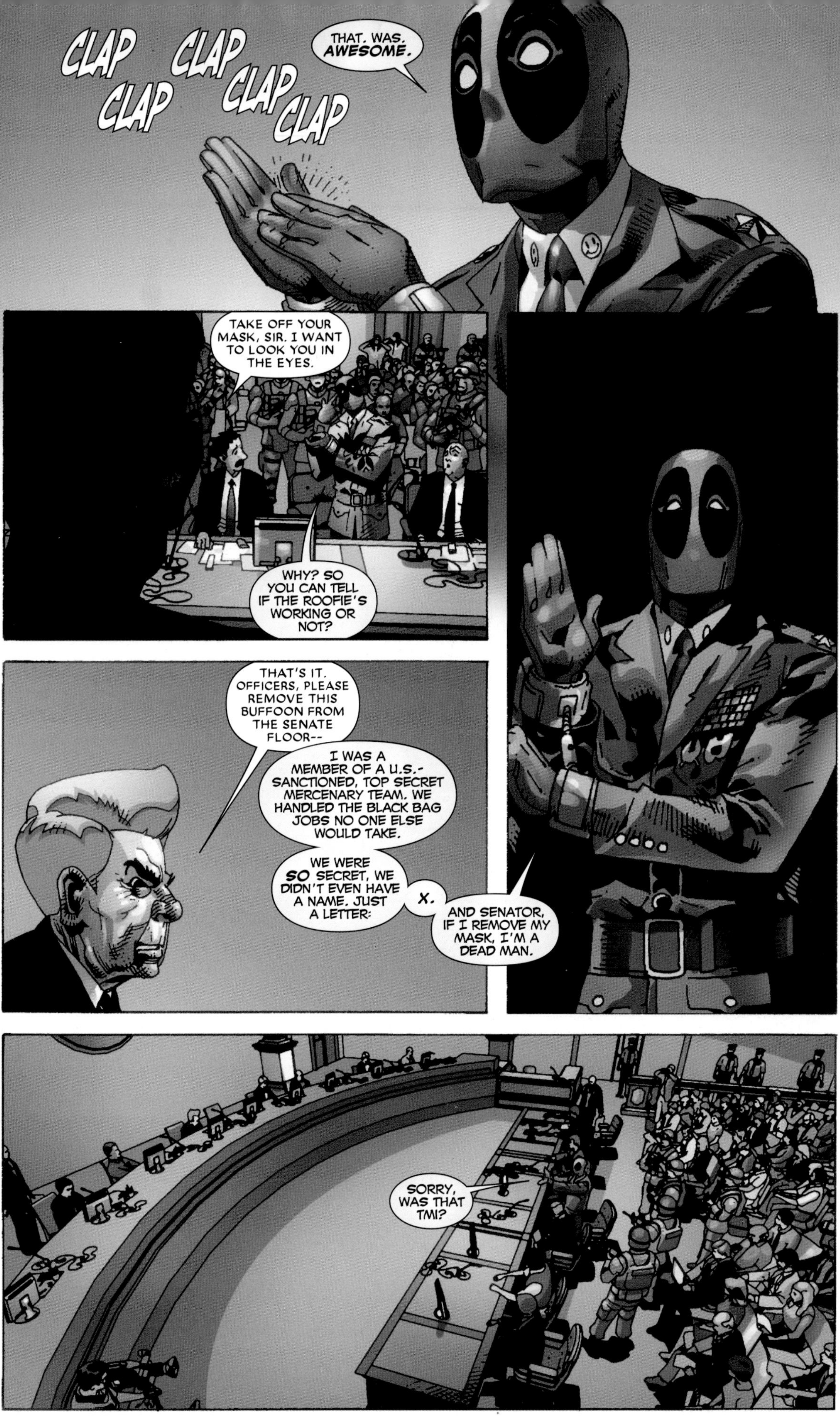
CLAP CLAP CLAP CLAP CLAP
THAT. WAS. AWESOME.
TAKE OFF YOUR MASK, SIR. I WANT TO LOOK YOU IN THE EYES.
WHY? SO YOU CAN TELL IF THE ROOFIE'S WORKING OR NOT?
THAT'S IT. OFFICERS, PLEASE REMOVE THIS BUFFOON FROM THE SENATE FLOOR--
I WAS A MEMBER OF A U.S.-SANCTIONED, TOP SECRET MERCENARY TEAM. WE HANDLED THE BLACK BAG JOBS NO ONE ELSE WOULD TAKE.
WE WERE SO SECRET, WE DIDN'T EVEN HAVE A NAME. JUST A LETTER:
X.
AND SENATOR, IF I REMOVE MY MASK, I'M A DEAD MAN.
SORRY, WAS THAT TMI?

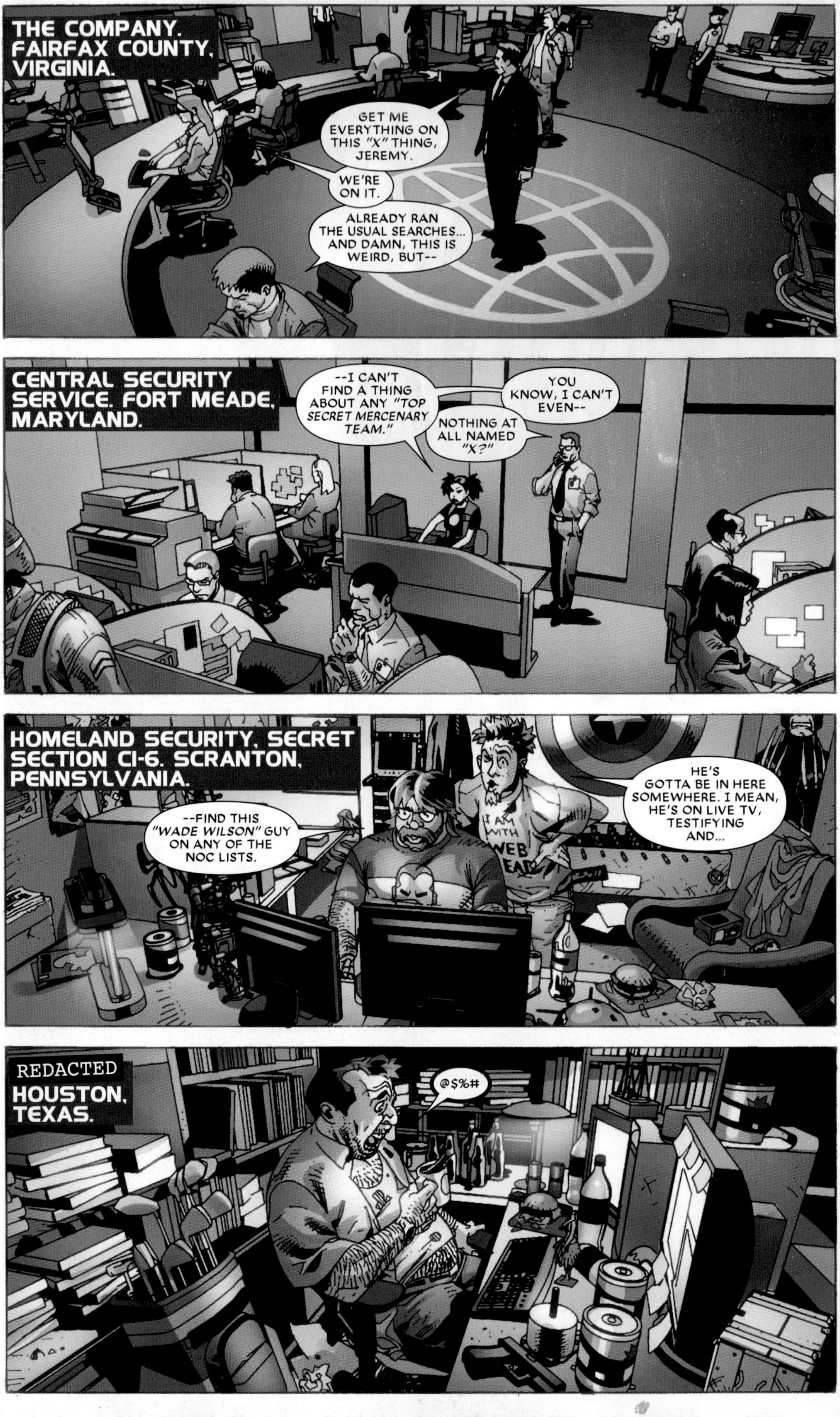
THE COMPANY. FAIRFAX COUNTY, VIRGINIA.
GET ME EVERYTHING ON THIS "X" THING, JEREMY.
WE'RE ON IT.
ALREADY RAN THE USUAL SEARCHES... AND DAMN, THIS IS WEIRD, BUT--
CENTRAL SECURITY SERVICE. FORT MEADE, MARYLAND.
--I CAN'T FIND A THING ABOUT ANY "TOP SECRET MERCENARY TEAM."
NOTHING AT ALL NAMED "X?"
YOU KNOW, I CAN'T EVEN--
HOMELAND SECURITY, SECRET SECTION CI-6. SCRANTON, PENNSYLVANIA.
--FIND THIS "WADE WILSON" GUY ON ANY OF THE NOC LISTS.
HE'S GOTTA BE IN HERE SOMEWHERE. I MEAN, HE'S ON LIVE TV, TESTIFYING AND...
REDACTED
HOUSTON, TEXAS.
@$%#

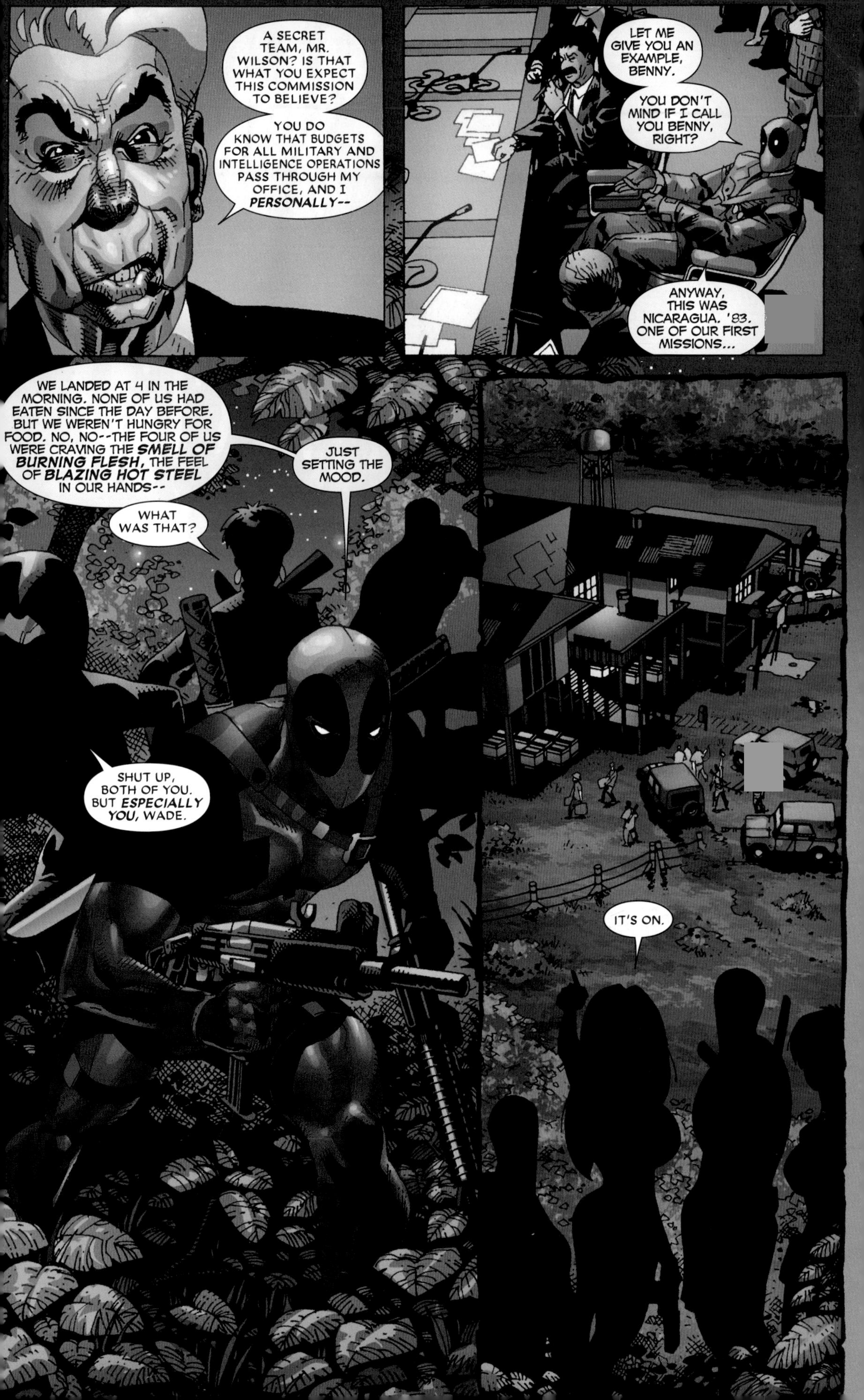
A SECRET TEAM, MR. WILSON? IS THAT WHAT YOU EXPECT THIS COMMISSION TO BELIEVE?
YOU DO KNOW THAT BUDGETS FOR ALL MILITARY AND INTELLIGENCE OPERATIONS PASS THROUGH MY OFFICE, AND I *PERSONALLY*--
LET ME GIVE YOU AN EXAMPLE, BENNY.
YOU DON'T MIND IF I CALL YOU BENNY, RIGHT?
ANYWAY, THIS WAS NICARAGUA. '83. ONE OF OUR FIRST MISSIONS...
WE LANDED AT 4 IN THE MORNING. NONE OF US HAD EATEN SINCE THE DAY BEFORE. BUT WE WEREN'T HUNGRY FOR FOOD. NO, NO--THE FOUR OF US WERE CRAVING THE *SMELL OF BURNING FLESH,* THE FEEL OF *BLAZING HOT STEEL* IN OUR HANDS--
JUST SETTING THE MOOD.
WHAT WAS THAT?
SHUT UP, BOTH OF YOU. BUT *ESPECIALLY YOU,* WADE.
IT'S ON.

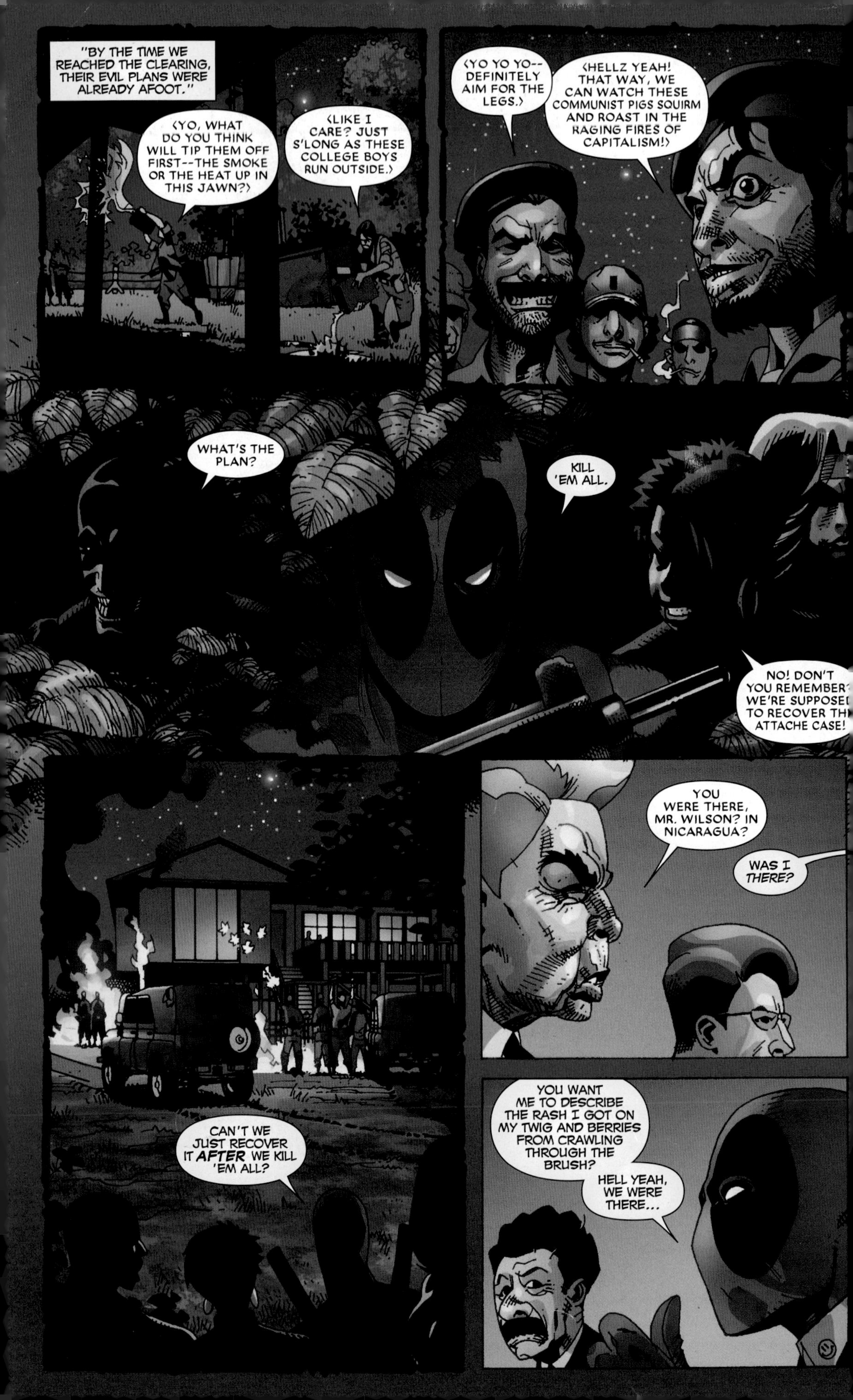
"BY THE TIME WE REACHED THE CLEARING, THEIR EVIL PLANS WERE ALREADY AFOOT."
‹YO, WHAT DO YOU THINK WILL TIP THEM OFF FIRST--THE SMOKE OR THE HEAT UP IN THIS JAWN?›
‹LIKE I CARE? JUST S'LONG AS THESE COLLEGE BOYS RUN OUTSIDE.›
‹YO YO YO--DEFINITELY AIM FOR THE LEGS.›
‹HELLZ YEAH! THAT WAY, WE CAN WATCH THESE COMMUNIST PIGS SQUIRM AND ROAST IN THE RAGING FIRES OF CAPITALISM!›
WHAT'S THE PLAN?
KILL 'EM ALL.
NO! DON'T YOU REMEMBER? WE'RE SUPPOSED TO RECOVER THE ATTACHE CASE!
CAN'T WE JUST RECOVER IT **AFTER** WE KILL 'EM ALL?
YOU WERE THERE, MR. WILSON? IN NICARAGUA?
WAS I THERE?
YOU WANT ME TO DESCRIBE THE RASH I GOT ON MY TWIG AND BERRIES FROM CRAWLING THROUGH THE BRUSH?
HELL YEAH, WE WERE THERE...

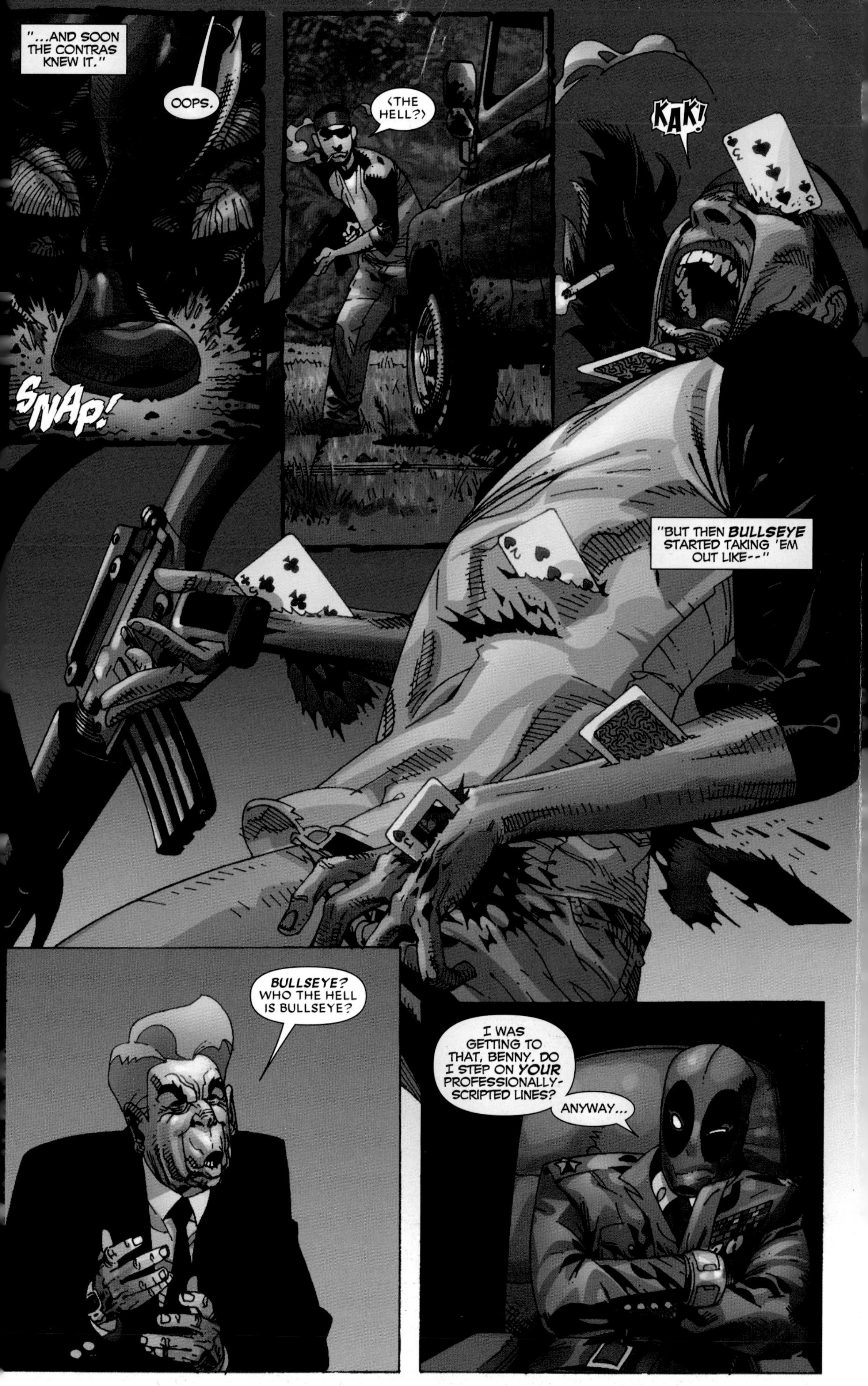
"...AND SOON THE CONTRAS KNEW IT."
OOPS.
SNAP!
‹THE HELL?›
KAK!
"BUT THEN BULLSEYE STARTED TAKING 'EM OUT LIKE--"
BULLSEYE? WHO THE HELL IS BULLSEYE?
I WAS GETTING TO THAT, BENNY. DO I STEP ON YOUR PROFESSIONALLY-SCRIPTED LINES?
ANYWAY...

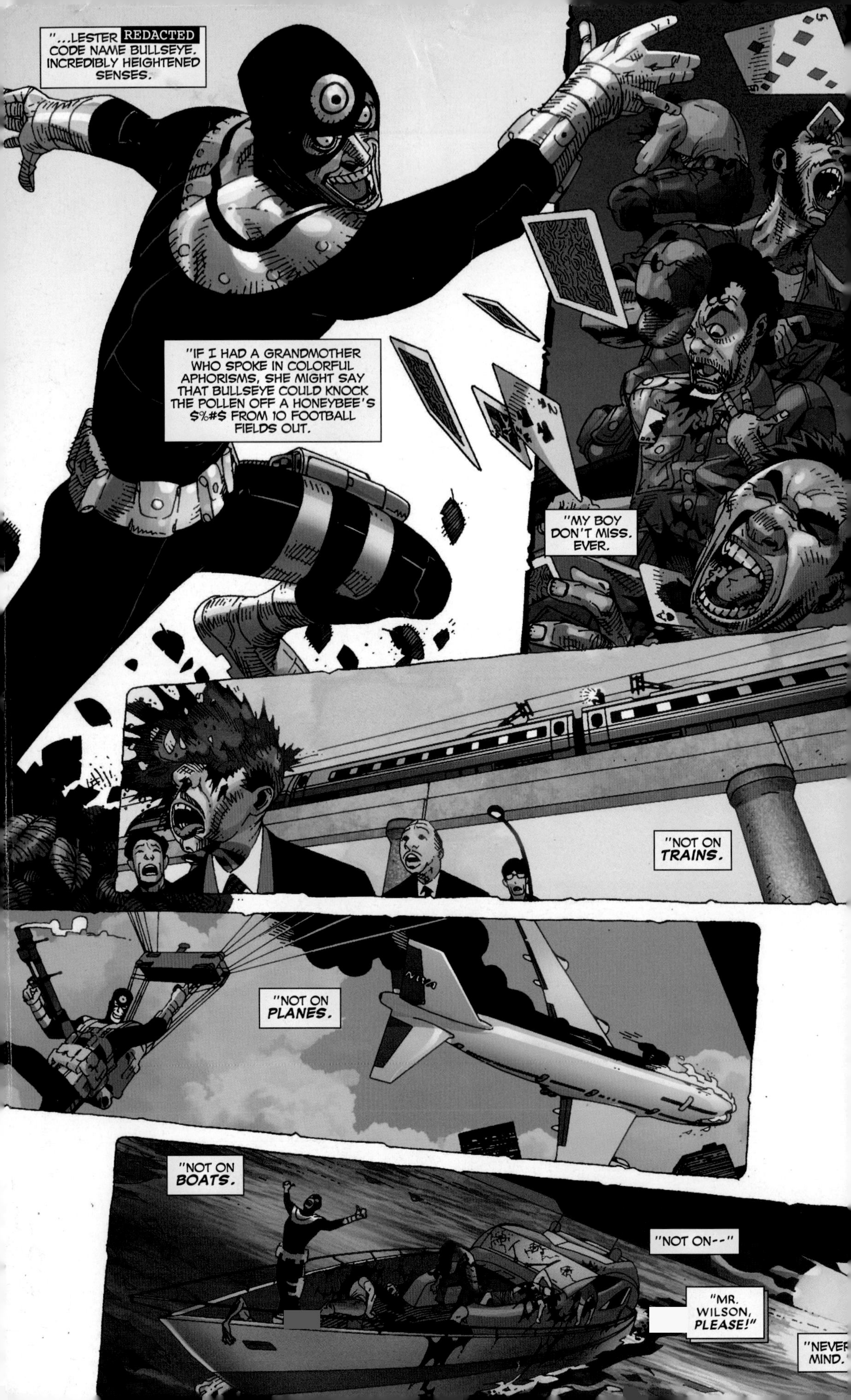
"...LESTER REDACTED CODE NAME BULLSEYE. INCREDIBLY HEIGHTENED SENSES.
"IF I HAD A GRANDMOTHER WHO SPOKE IN COLORFUL APHORISMS, SHE MIGHT SAY THAT BULLSEYE COULD KNOCK THE POLLEN OFF A HONEYBEE'S $%#$ FROM 10 FOOTBALL FIELDS OUT.
"MY BOY DON'T MISS. EVER.
"NOT ON TRAINS.
"NOT ON PLANES.
"NOT ON BOATS.
"NOT ON--"
"MR. WILSON, PLEASE!"
"NEVE MIND.

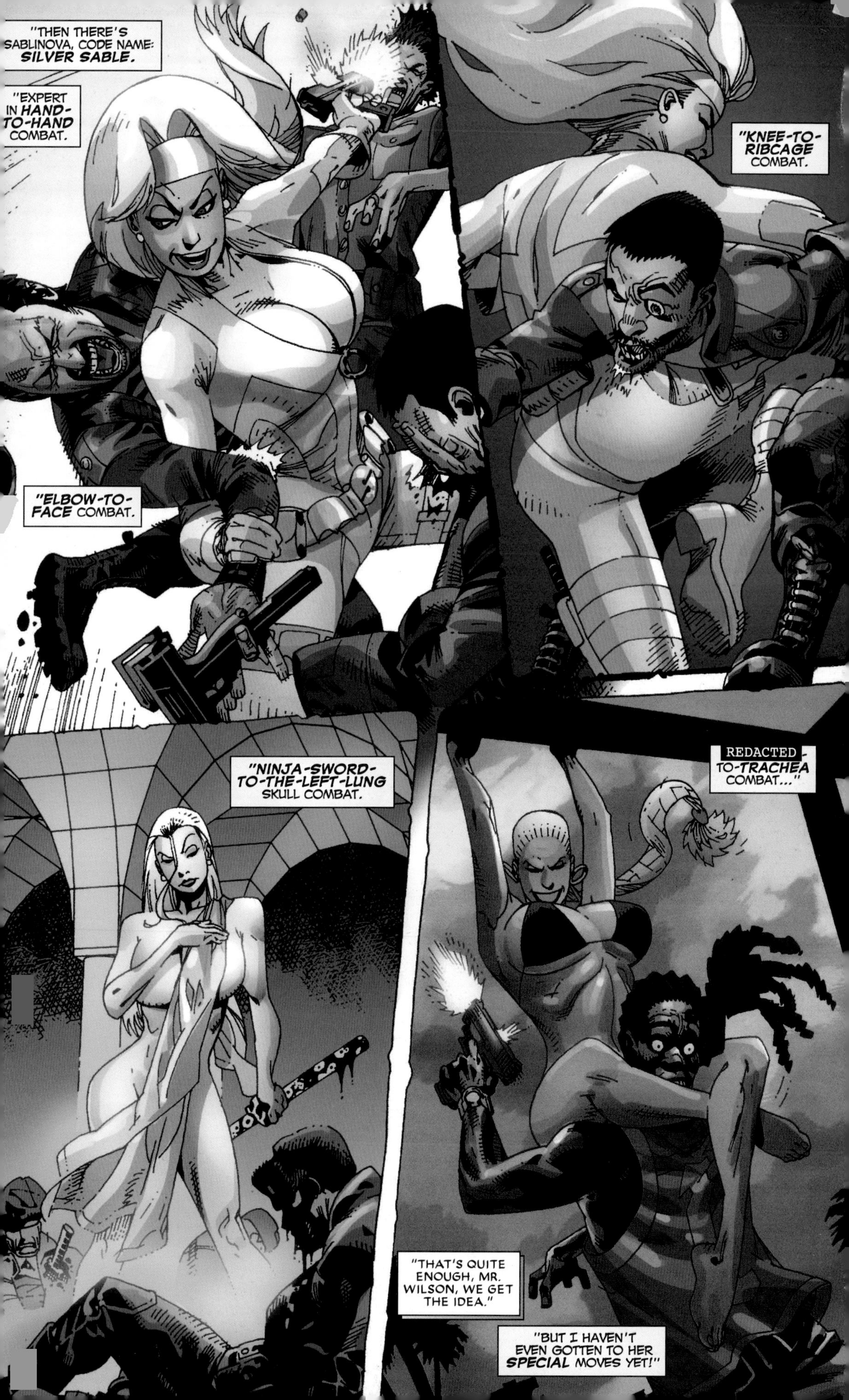
"THEN THERE'S SABLINOVA, CODE NAME: SILVER SABLE.
"EXPERT IN HAND-TO-HAND COMBAT.
"KNEE-TO-RIBCAGE COMBAT.
"ELBOW-TO-FACE COMBAT.
"NINJA-SWORD-TO-THE-LEFT-LUNG SKULL COMBAT.
REDACTED-TO-TRACHEA COMBAT..."
"THAT'S QUITE ENOUGH, MR. WILSON, WE GET THE IDEA."
"BUT I HAVEN'T EVEN GOTTEN TO HER SPECIAL MOVES YET!"

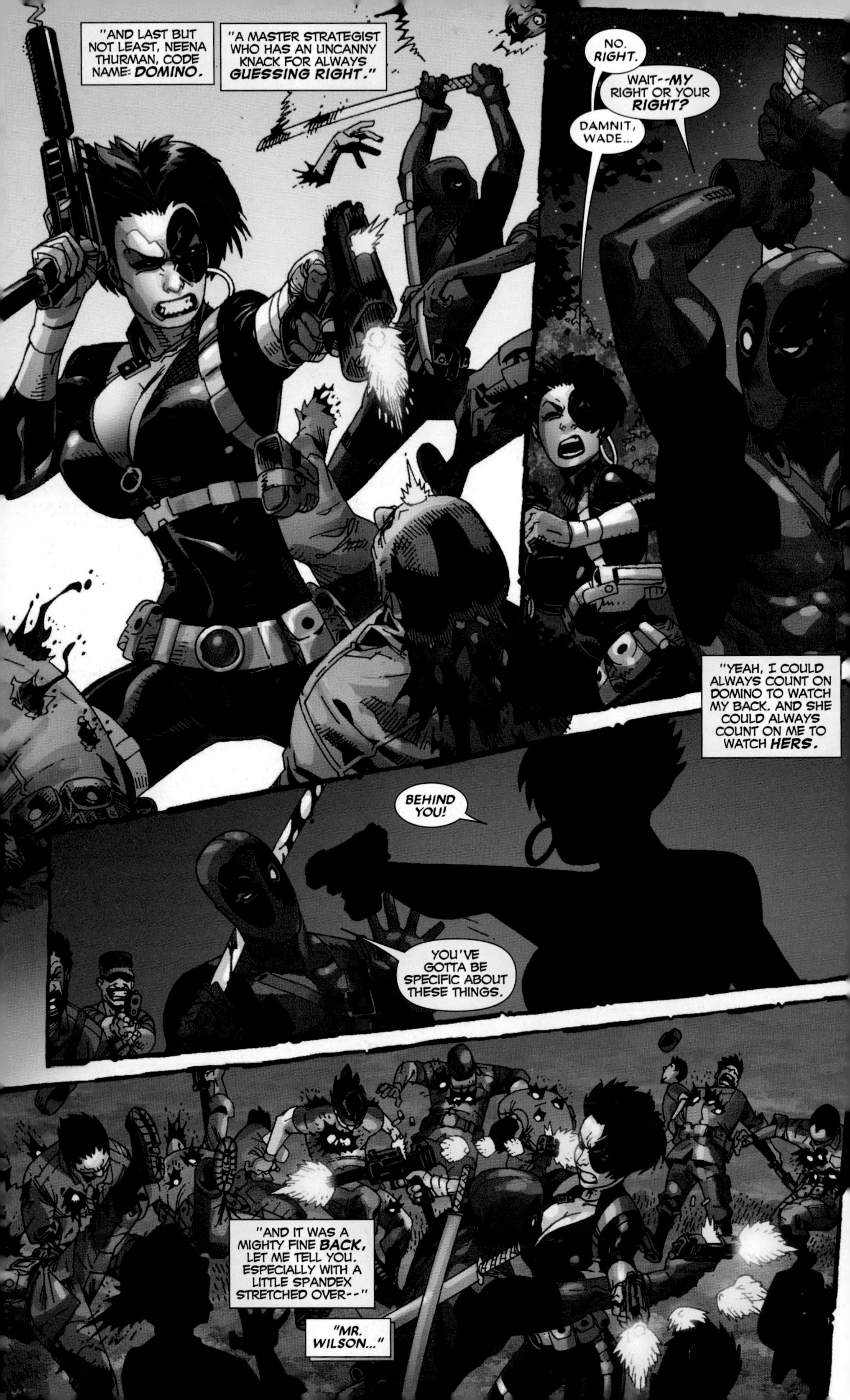
"AND LAST BUT NOT LEAST, NEENA THURMAN, CODE NAME: DOMINO.
"A MASTER STRATEGIST WHO HAS AN UNCANNY KNACK FOR ALWAYS GUESSING RIGHT."
NO. RIGHT.
WAIT--MY RIGHT OR YOUR RIGHT?
DAMNIT, WADE...
"YEAH, I COULD ALWAYS COUNT ON DOMINO TO WATCH MY BACK. AND SHE COULD ALWAYS COUNT ON ME TO WATCH HERS.
BEHIND YOU!
YOU'VE GOTTA BE SPECIFIC ABOUT THESE THINGS.
"AND IT WAS A MIGHTY FINE BACK, LET ME TELL YOU. ESPECIALLY WITH A LITTLE SPANDEX STRETCHED OVER--"
"MR. WILSON..."

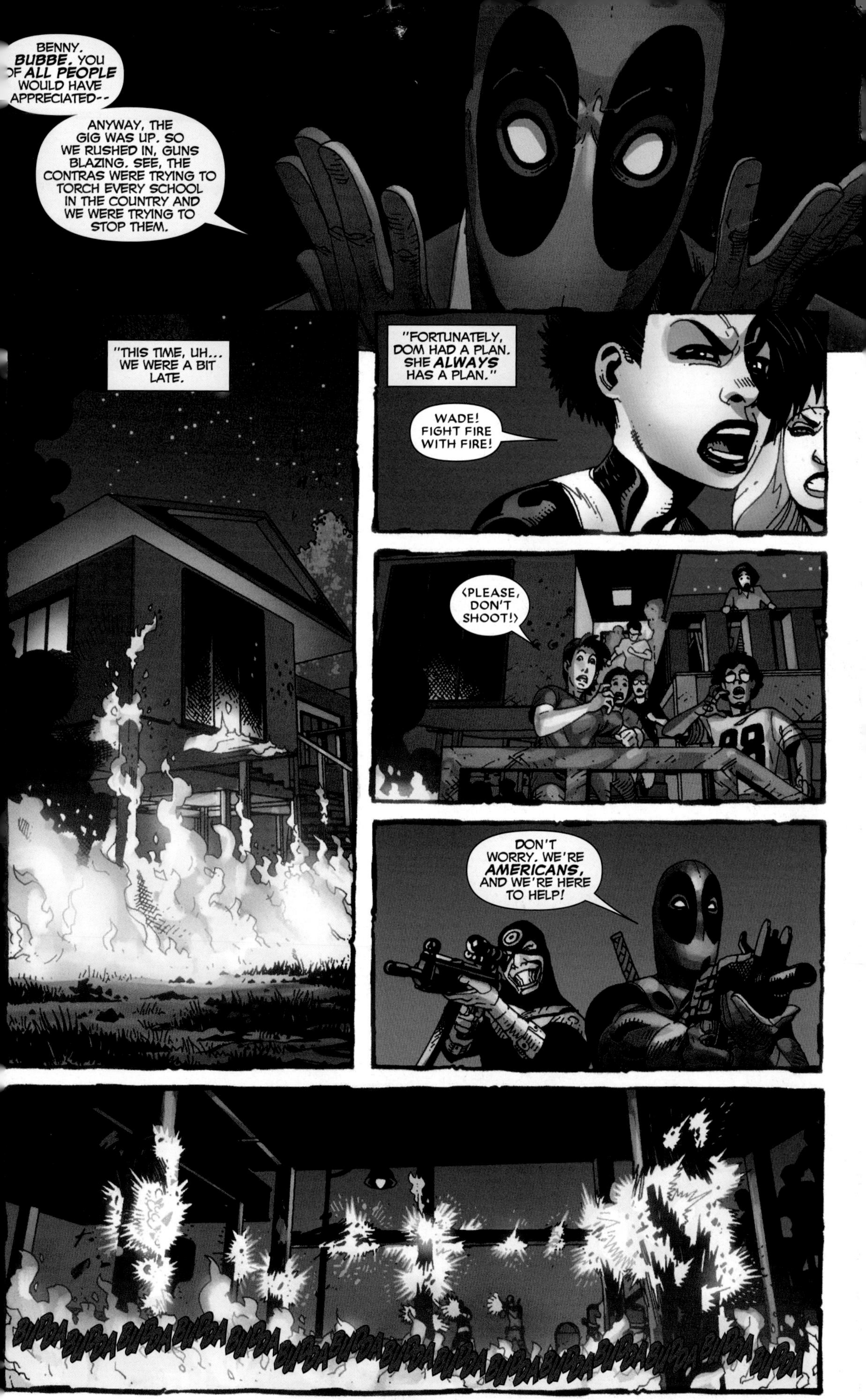
BENNY. BUBBE. YOU OF ALL PEOPLE WOULD HAVE APPRECIATED--
ANYWAY, THE GIG WAS UP. SO WE RUSHED IN, GUNS BLAZING. SEE, THE CONTRAS WERE TRYING TO TORCH EVERY SCHOOL IN THE COUNTRY AND WE WERE TRYING TO STOP THEM.
"THIS TIME, UH... WE WERE A BIT LATE.
"FORTUNATELY, DOM HAD A PLAN. SHE ALWAYS HAS A PLAN."
WADE! FIGHT FIRE WITH FIRE!
<PLEASE, DON'T SHOOT!>
DON'T WORRY. WE'RE AMERICANS, AND WE'RE HERE TO HELP!
BUDDA BUDDA BUDDA BUDDA BUDDA BUDDA BUDDA BUDDA BUDDA BUDDA BUDDA BUDDA BUDDA BUDDA BUDDA

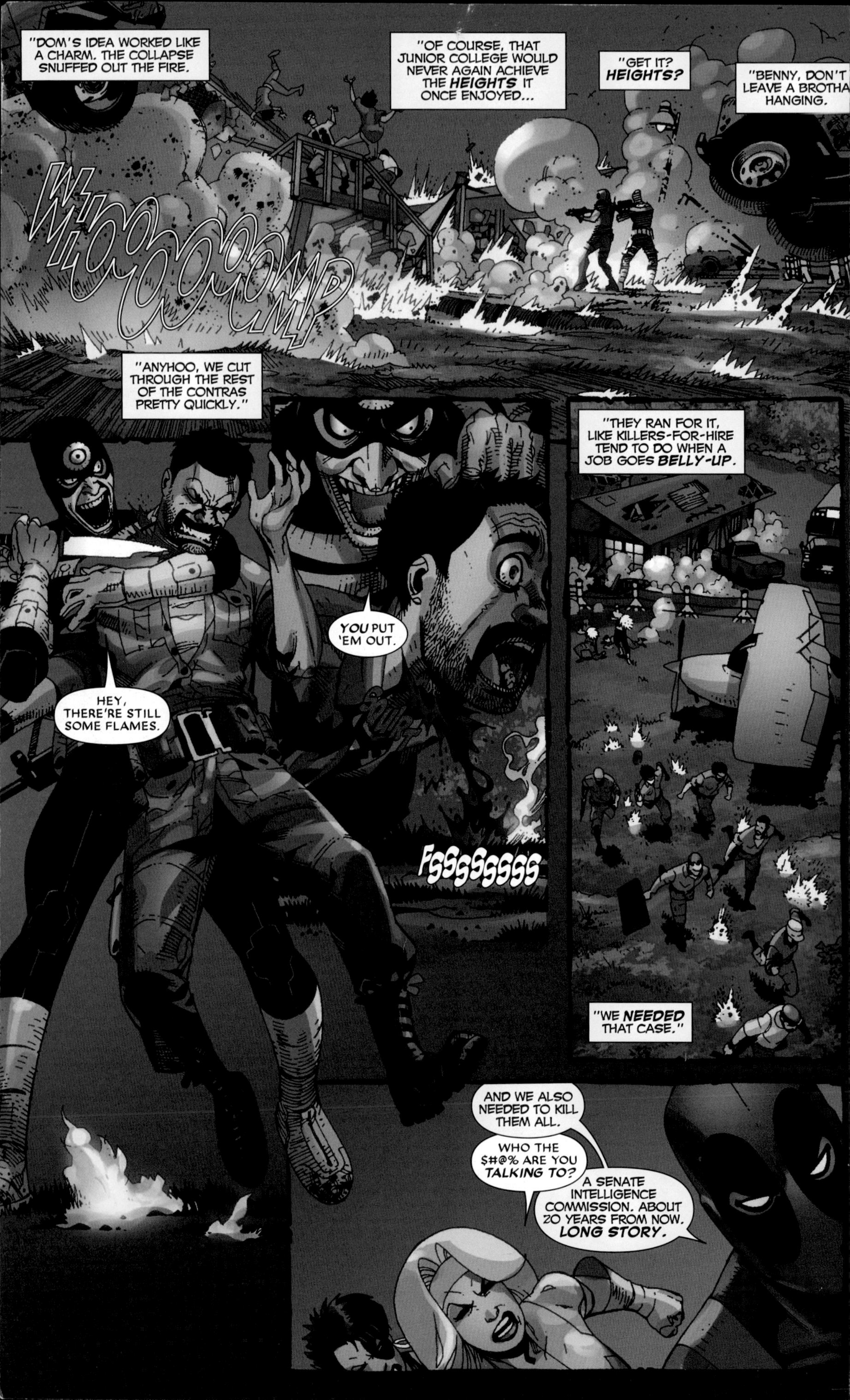
"DOM'S IDEA WORKED LIKE A CHARM. THE COLLAPSE SNUFFED OUT THE FIRE.
"OF COURSE, THAT JUNIOR COLLEGE WOULD NEVER AGAIN ACHIEVE THE HEIGHTS IT ONCE ENJOYED...
"GET IT? HEIGHTS?
"BENNY, DON'T LEAVE A BROTHA HANGING.
WHOOOOOOOOOMP
"ANYHOO, WE CUT THROUGH THE REST OF THE CONTRAS PRETTY QUICKLY."
HEY, THERE'RE STILL SOME FLAMES.
YOU PUT 'EM OUT.
FSSSSSSSS
"THEY RAN FOR IT, LIKE KILLERS-FOR-HIRE TEND TO DO WHEN A JOB GOES BELLY-UP.
"WE NEEDED THAT CASE."
AND WE ALSO NEEDED TO KILL THEM ALL.
WHO THE $#@% ARE YOU TALKING TO?
A SENATE INTELLIGENCE COMMISSION. ABOUT 20 YEARS FROM NOW. LONG STORY.

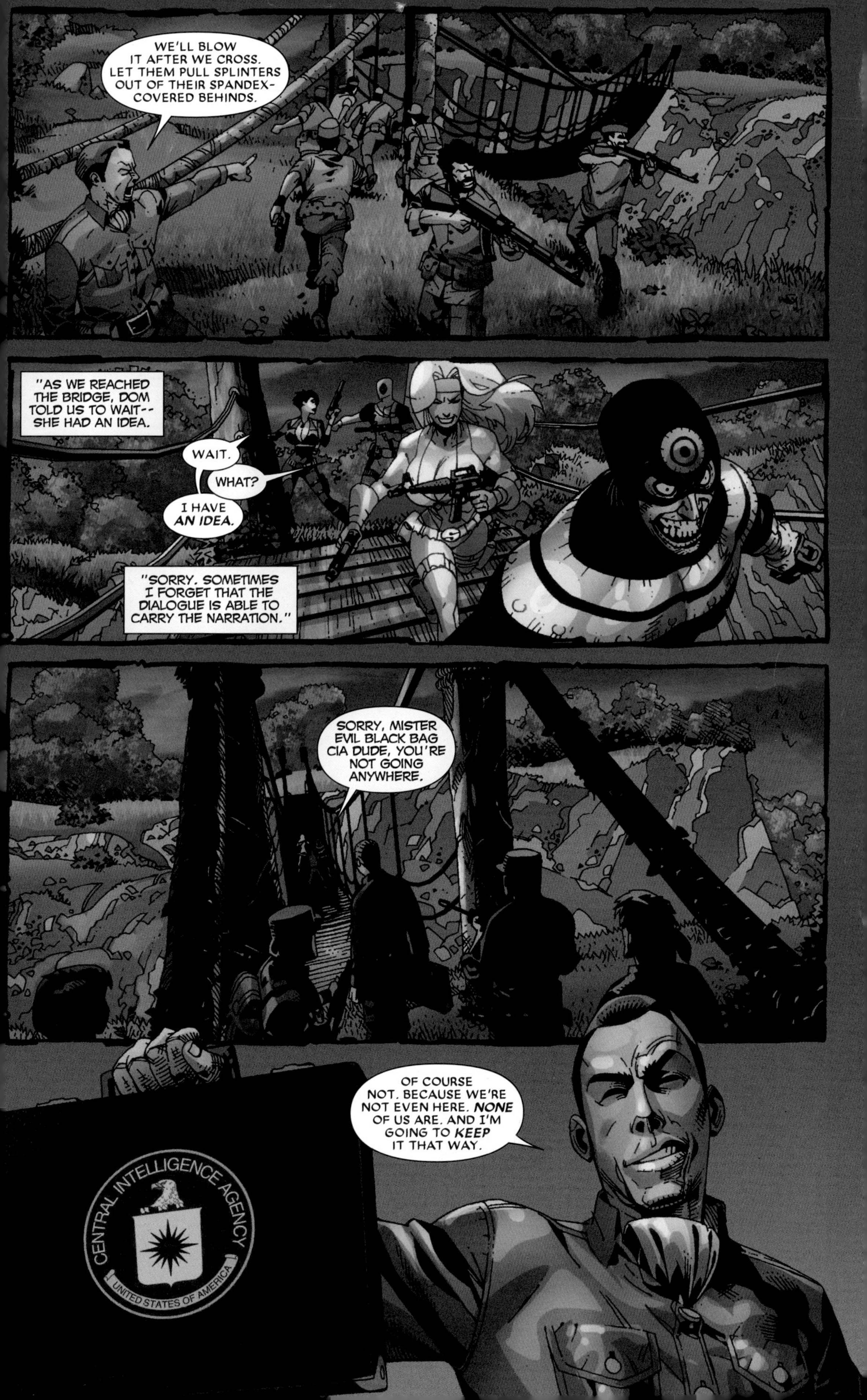
WE'LL BLOW IT AFTER WE CROSS. LET THEM PULL SPLINTERS OUT OF THEIR SPANDEX-COVERED BEHINDS.
"AS WE REACHED THE BRIDGE, DOM TOLD US TO WAIT--SHE HAD AN IDEA.
WAIT.
WHAT?
I HAVE AN IDEA.
"SORRY. SOMETIMES I FORGET THAT THE DIALOGUE IS ABLE TO CARRY THE NARRATION."
SORRY, MISTER EVIL BLACK BAG CIA DUDE, YOU'RE NOT GOING ANYWHERE.
OF COURSE NOT. BECAUSE WE'RE NOT EVEN HERE. NONE OF US ARE. AND I'M GOING TO KEEP IT THAT WAY.
CENTRAL INTELLIGENCE AGENCY
UNITED STATES OF AMERICA

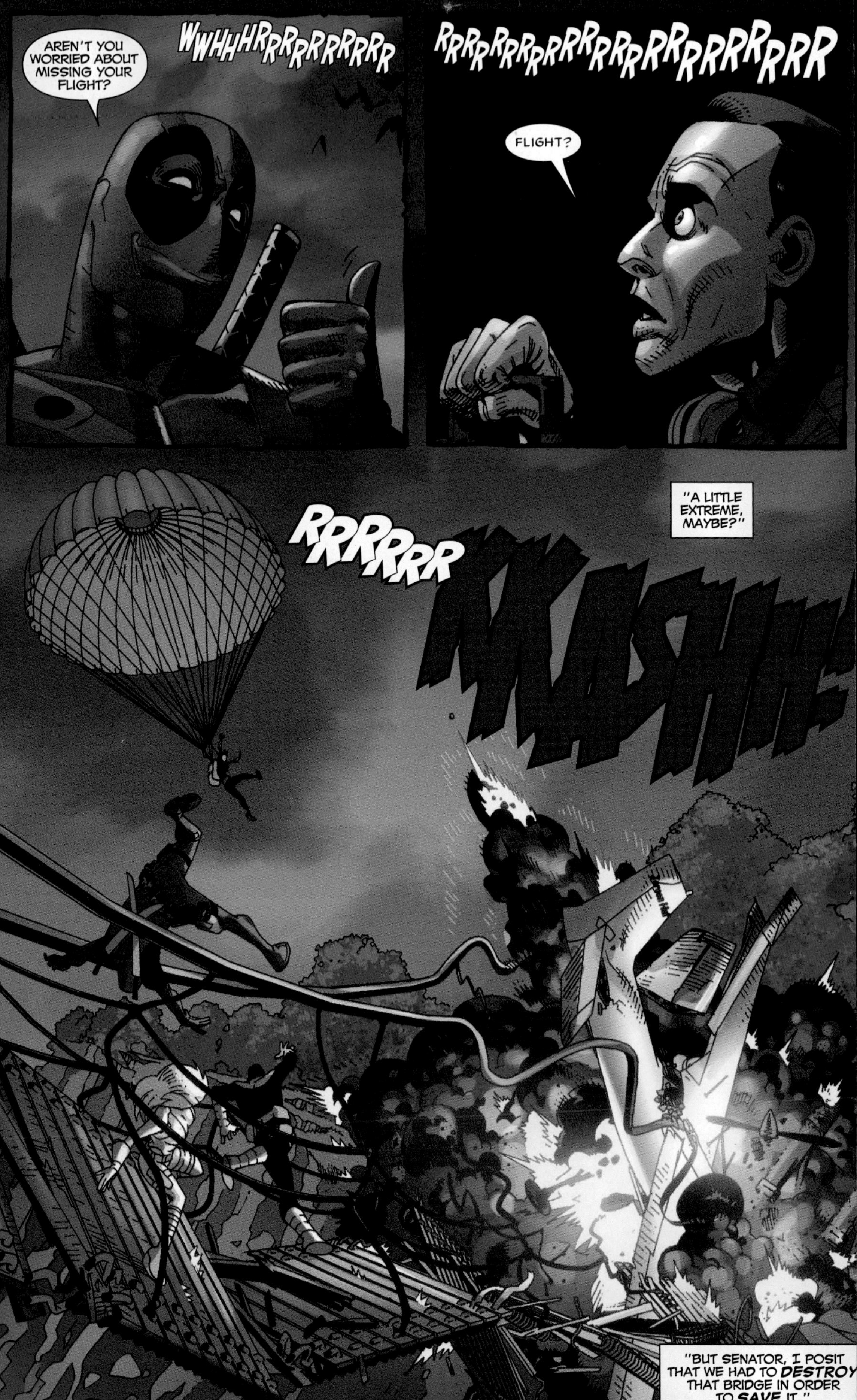

AREN'T YOU WORRIED ABOUT MISSING YOUR FLIGHT?
WWHHHRRRRRRRRRR
RRRRRRRRRRRRRRRRRRRRRRRR
FLIGHT?
"A LITTLE EXTREME, MAYBE?"
RRRRRR
"BUT SENATOR, I POSIT THAT WE HAD TO DESTROY THAT BRIDGE IN ORDER TO SAVE IT."

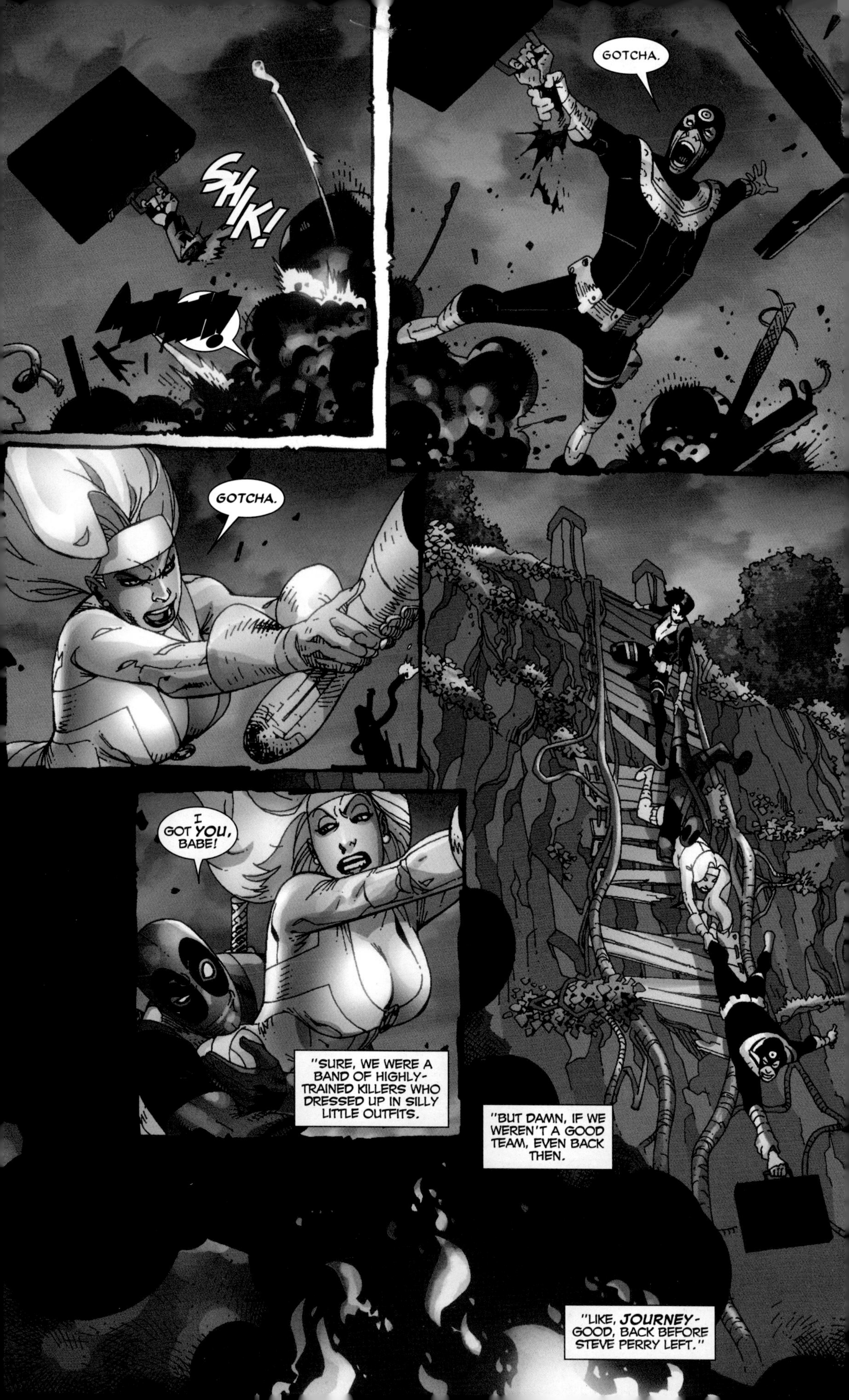
SHIK!
GOTCHA.
GOTCHA.
I GOT YOU, BABE!
"SURE, WE WERE A BAND OF HIGHLY-TRAINED KILLERS WHO DRESSED UP IN SILLY LITTLE OUTFITS.
"BUT DAMN, IF WE WEREN'T A GOOD TEAM, EVEN BACK THEN.
"LIKE, JOURNEY-GOOD, BACK BEFORE STEVE PERRY LEFT."

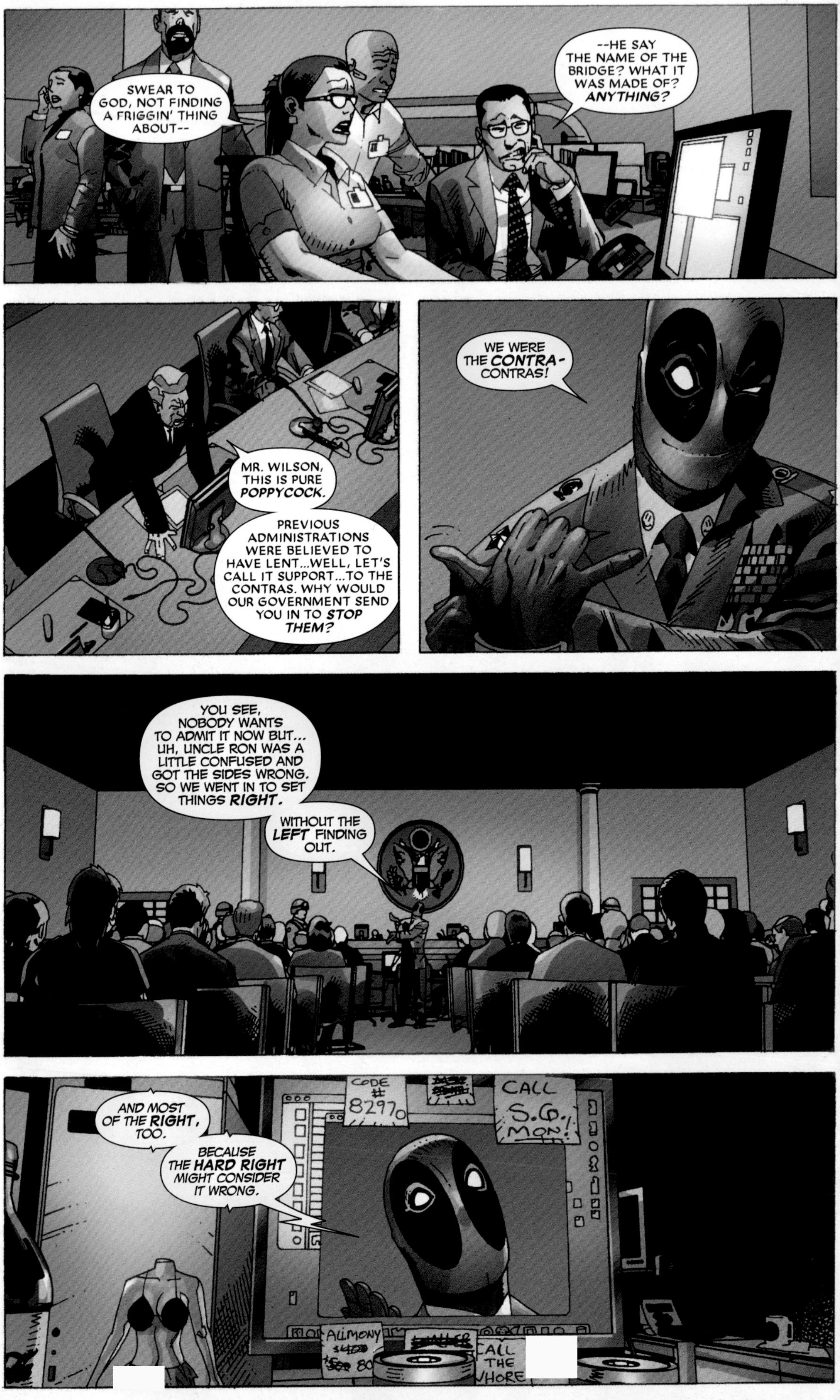
SWEAR TO GOD, NOT FINDING A FRIGGIN' THING ABOUT--
--HE SAY THE NAME OF THE BRIDGE? WHAT IT WAS MADE OF? ANYTHING?
MR. WILSON, THIS IS PURE POPPYCOCK.
PREVIOUS ADMINISTRATIONS WERE BELIEVED TO HAVE LENT...WELL, LET'S CALL IT SUPPORT...TO THE CONTRAS. WHY WOULD OUR GOVERNMENT SEND YOU IN TO STOP THEM?
WE WERE THE CONTRA-CONTRAS!
YOU SEE, NOBODY WANTS TO ADMIT IT NOW BUT... UH, UNCLE RON WAS A LITTLE CONFUSED AND GOT THE SIDES WRONG. SO WE WENT IN TO SET THINGS RIGHT.
WITHOUT THE LEFT FINDING OUT.
AND MOST OF THE RIGHT, TOO.
BECAUSE THE HARD RIGHT MIGHT CONSIDER IT WRONG.
CODE #
CALL S.G. MON!
ALIMONY

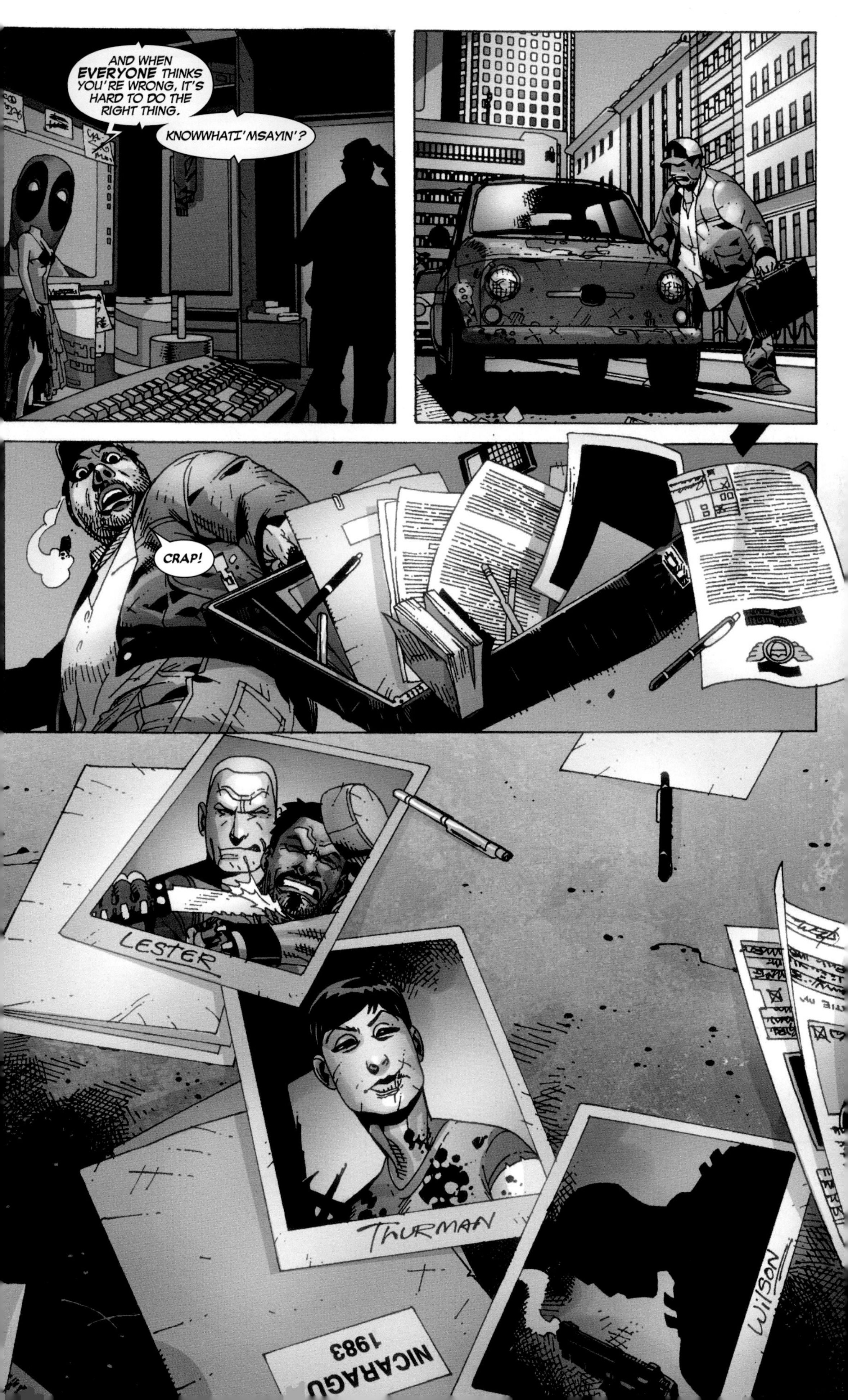
AND WHEN EVERYONE THINKS YOU'RE WRONG, IT'S HARD TO DO THE RIGHT THING.
KNOWWHATI'MSAYIN'?
CRAP!
LESTER
THURMAN
WILSON
NICARAGUA 1983

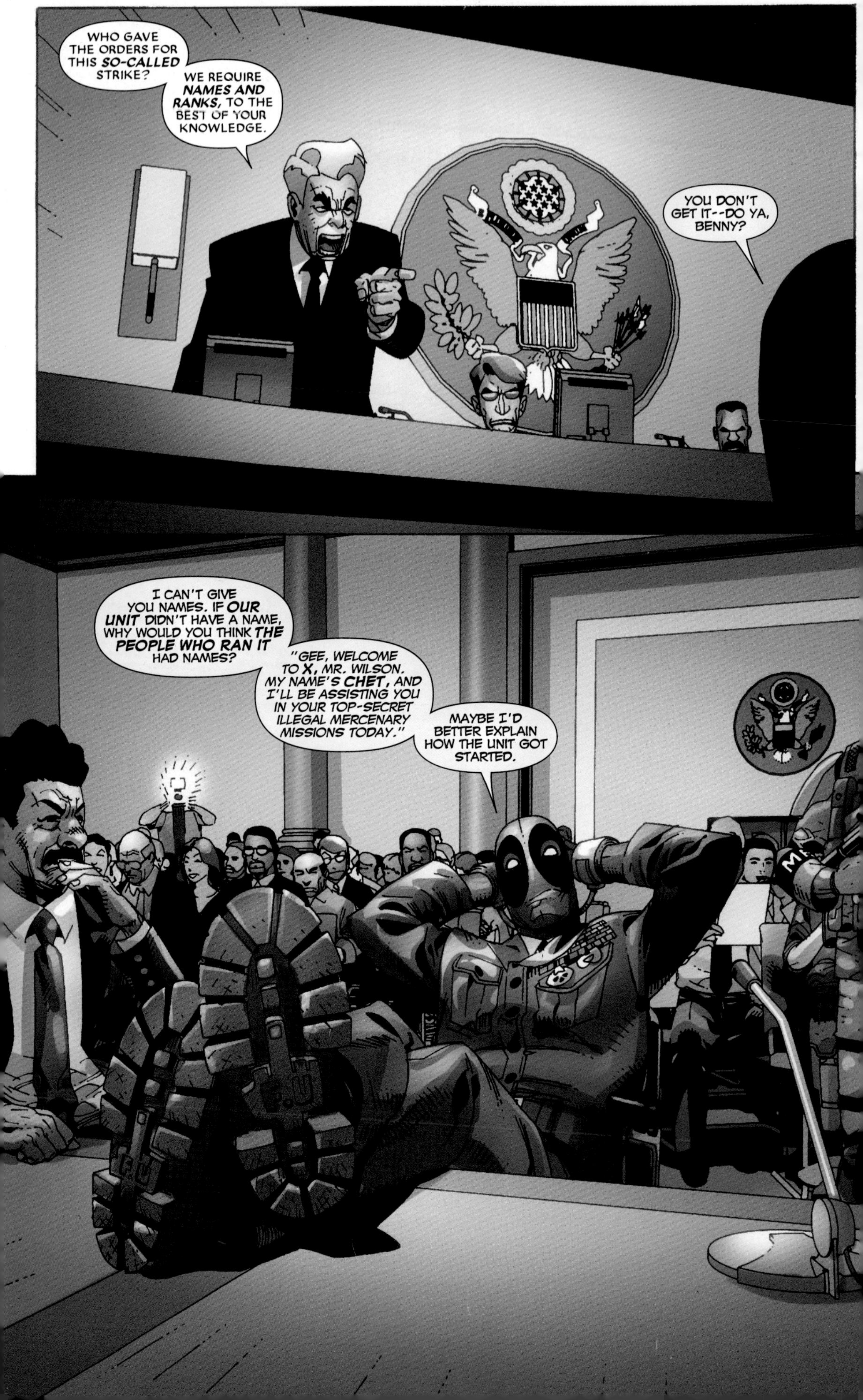
WHO GAVE THE ORDERS FOR THIS SO-CALLED STRIKE?
WE REQUIRE NAMES AND RANKS, TO THE BEST OF YOUR KNOWLEDGE.
YOU DON'T GET IT--DO YA, BENNY?
I CAN'T GIVE YOU NAMES. IF OUR UNIT DIDN'T HAVE A NAME, WHY WOULD YOU THINK THE PEOPLE WHO RAN IT HAD NAMES?
"GEE, WELCOME TO X, MR. WILSON. MY NAME'S CHET, AND I'LL BE ASSISTING YOU IN YOUR TOP-SECRET ILLEGAL MERCENARY MISSIONS TODAY."
MAYBE I'D BETTER EXPLAIN HOW THE UNIT GOT STARTED.

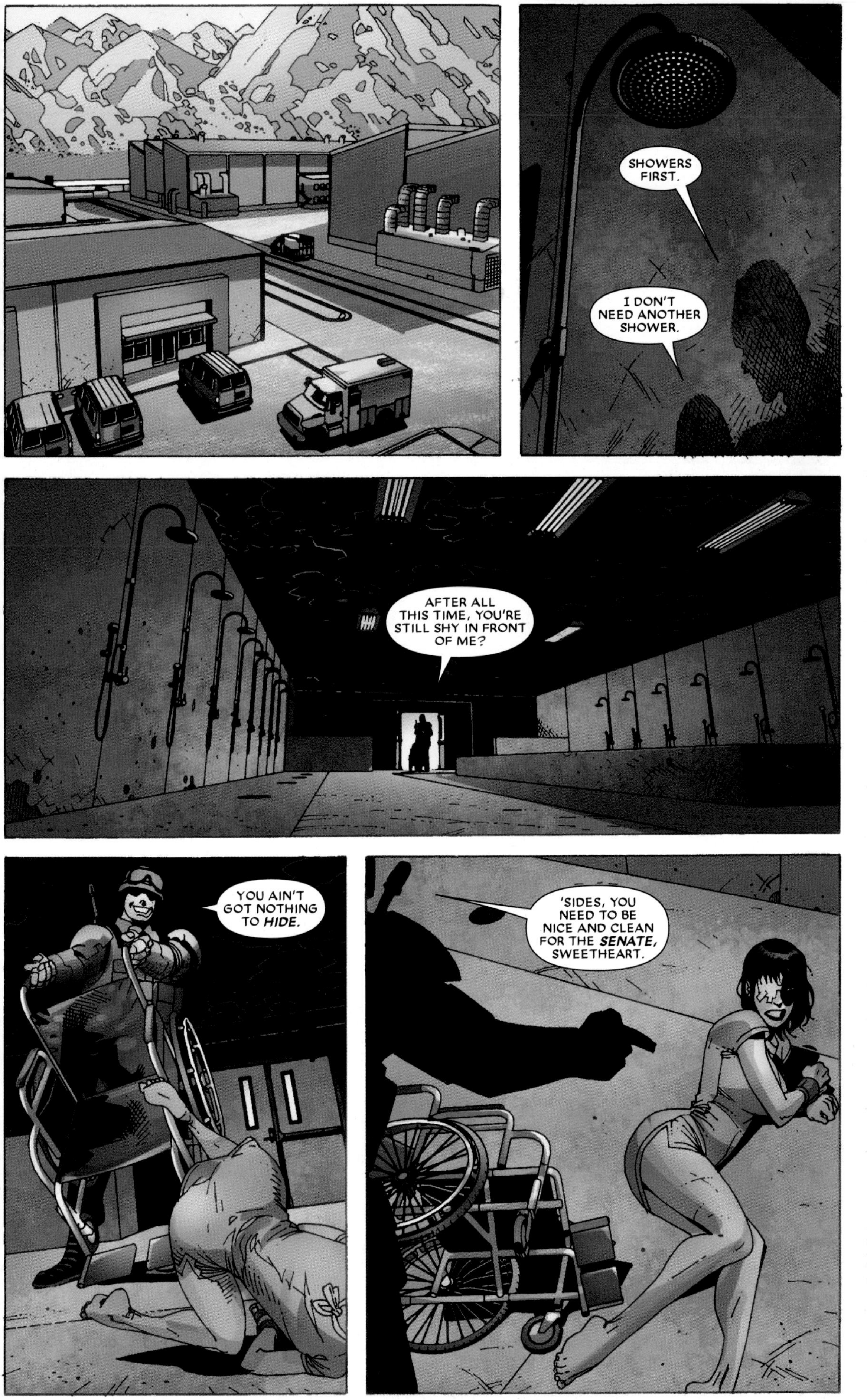
SHOWERS FIRST.
I DON'T NEED ANOTHER SHOWER.
AFTER ALL THIS TIME, YOU'RE STILL SHY IN FRONT OF ME?
YOU AIN'T GOT NOTHING TO *HIDE.*
'SIDES, YOU NEED TO BE NICE AND CLEAN FOR THE *SENATE,* SWEETHEART.

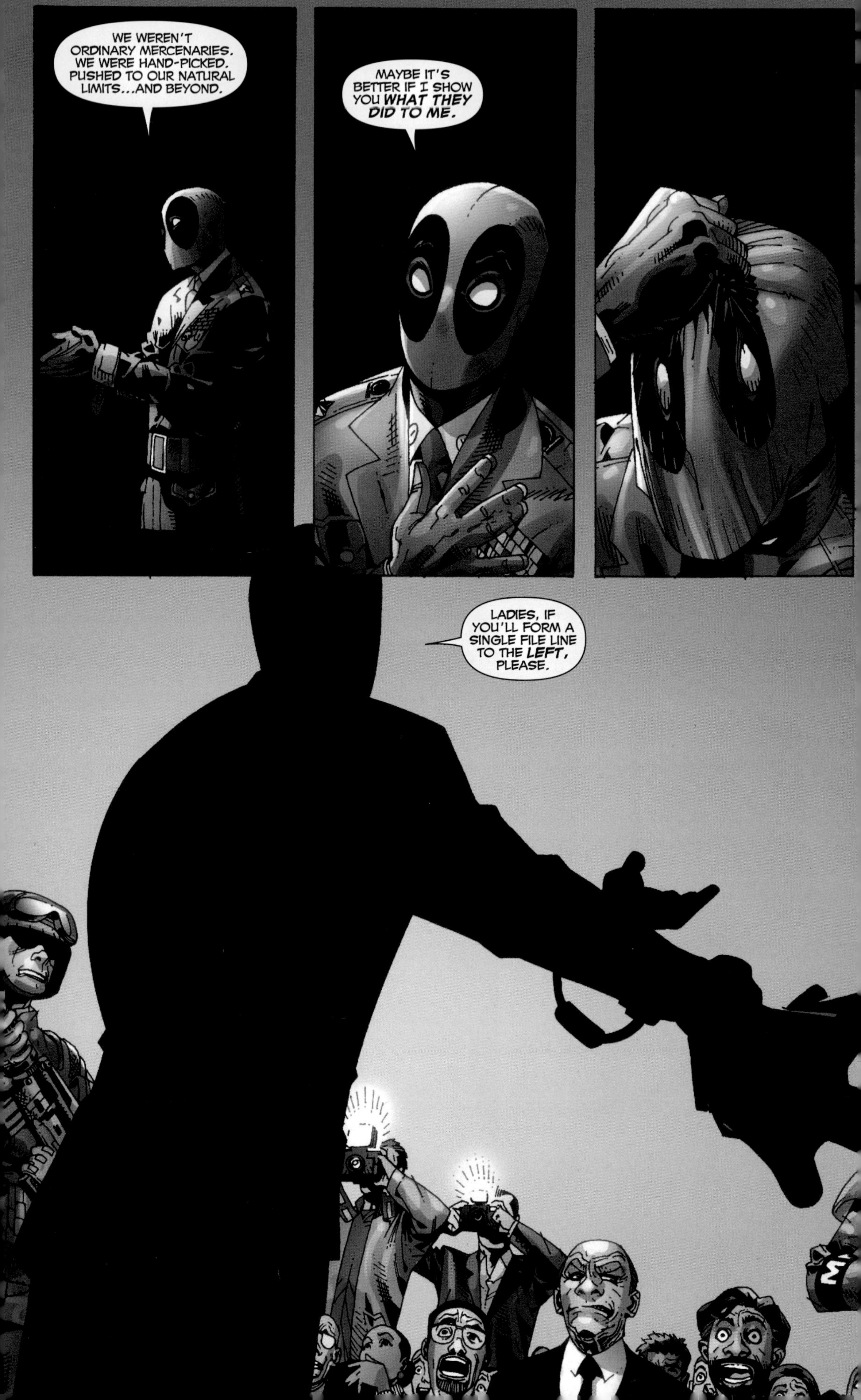
WE WEREN'T ORDINARY MERCENARIES. WE WERE HAND-PICKED. PUSHED TO OUR NATURAL LIMITS...AND BEYOND.
MAYBE IT'S BETTER IF I SHOW YOU WHAT THEY DID TO ME.
LADIES, IF YOU'LL FORM A SINGLE FILE LINE TO THE LEFT, PLEASE.

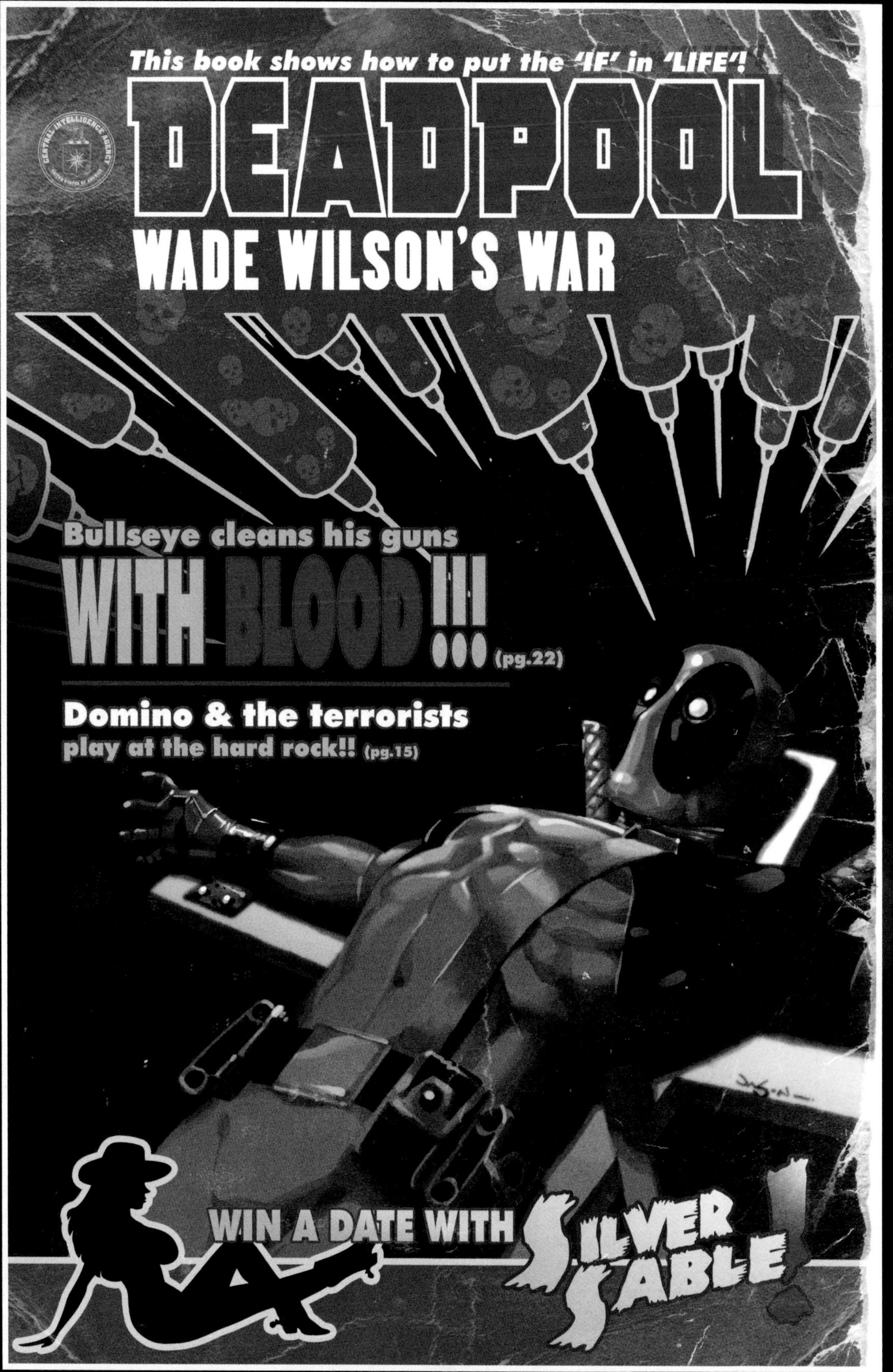
This book shows how to put the 'IF' in 'LIFE'!
DEADPOOL
WADE WILSON'S WAR
Bullseye cleans his guns
WITH BLOOD!!! (pg.22)
Domino & the terrorists
play at the hard rock!! (pg.15)
WIN A DATE WITH SILVER SABLE!

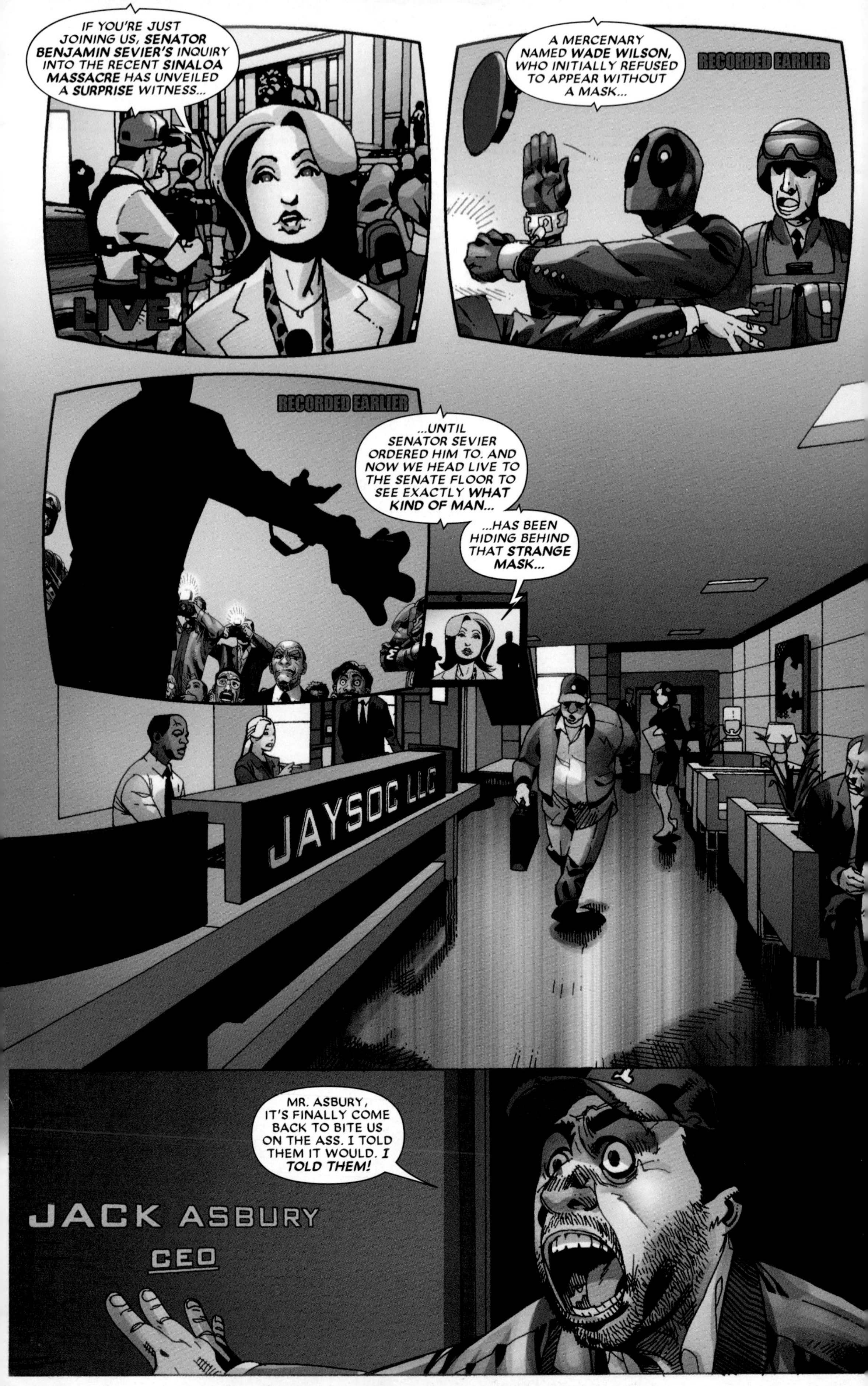

IF YOU'RE JUST JOINING US, SENATOR BENJAMIN SEVIER'S INQUIRY INTO THE RECENT SINALOA MASSACRE HAS UNVEILED A SURPRISE WITNESS...
LIVE
A MERCENARY NAMED WADE WILSON, WHO INITIALLY REFUSED TO APPEAR WITHOUT A MASK...
RECORDED EARLIER
RECORDED EARLIER
...UNTIL SENATOR SEVIER ORDERED HIM TO. AND NOW WE HEAD LIVE TO THE SENATE FLOOR TO SEE EXACTLY WHAT KIND OF MAN...
...HAS BEEN HIDING BEHIND THAT STRANGE MASK...
JAYSOC LLC
MR. ASBURY, IT'S FINALLY COME BACK TO BITE US ON THE ASS. I TOLD THEM IT WOULD. I TOLD THEM!
JACK ASBURY
CEO

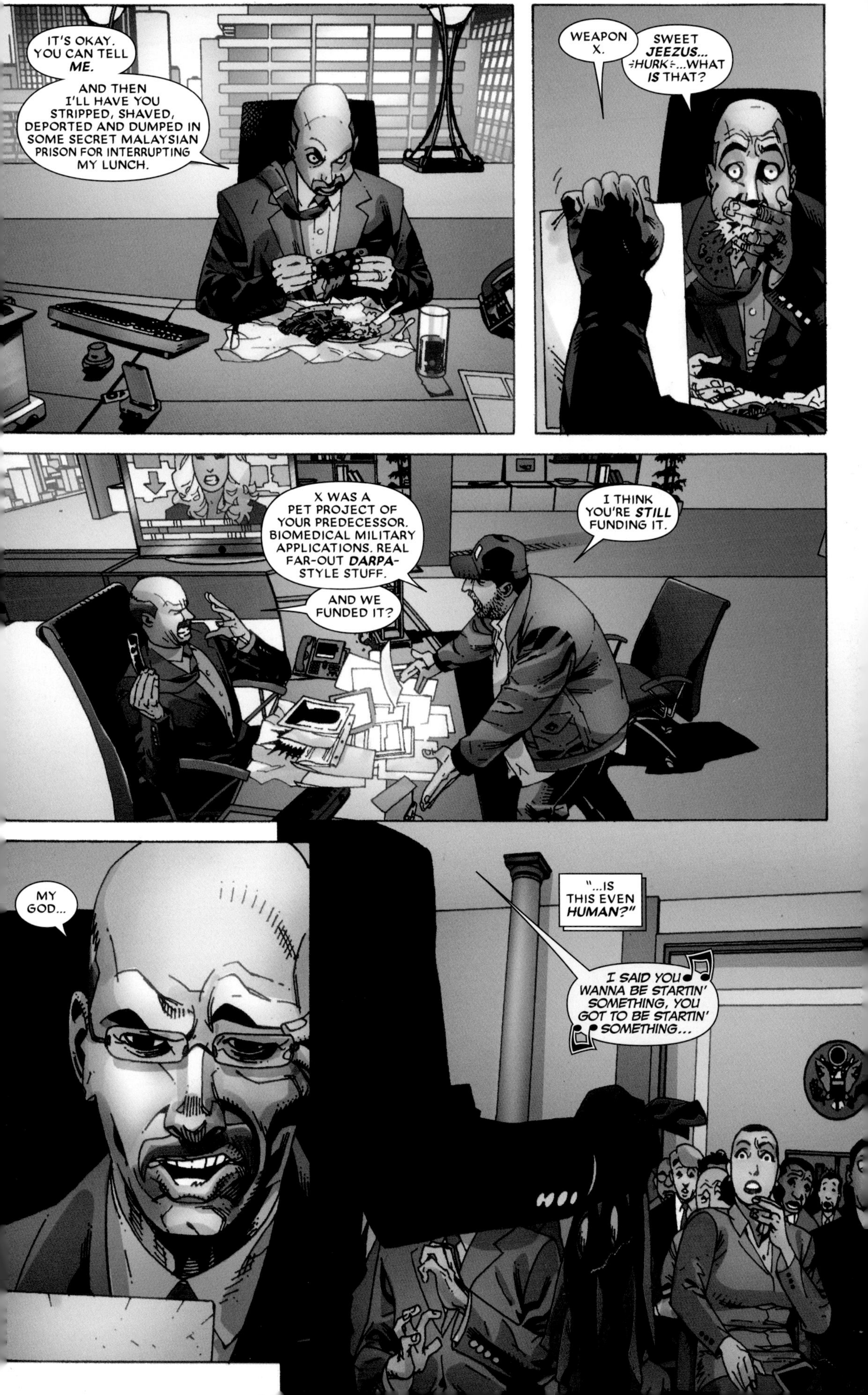
IT'S OKAY. YOU CAN TELL ME.
AND THEN I'LL HAVE YOU STRIPPED, SHAVED, DEPORTED AND DUMPED IN SOME SECRET MALAYSIAN PRISON FOR INTERRUPTING MY LUNCH.
WEAPON X.
SWEET JEEZUS... ÷HURK÷...WHAT IS THAT?
X WAS A PET PROJECT OF YOUR PREDECESSOR. BIOMEDICAL MILITARY APPLICATIONS. REAL FAR-OUT DARPA-STYLE STUFF.
AND WE FUNDED IT?
I THINK YOU'RE STILL FUNDING IT.
MY GOD...
"...IS THIS EVEN HUMAN?"
I SAID YOU WANNA BE STARTIN' SOMETHING, YOU GOT TO BE STARTIN' SOMETHING...

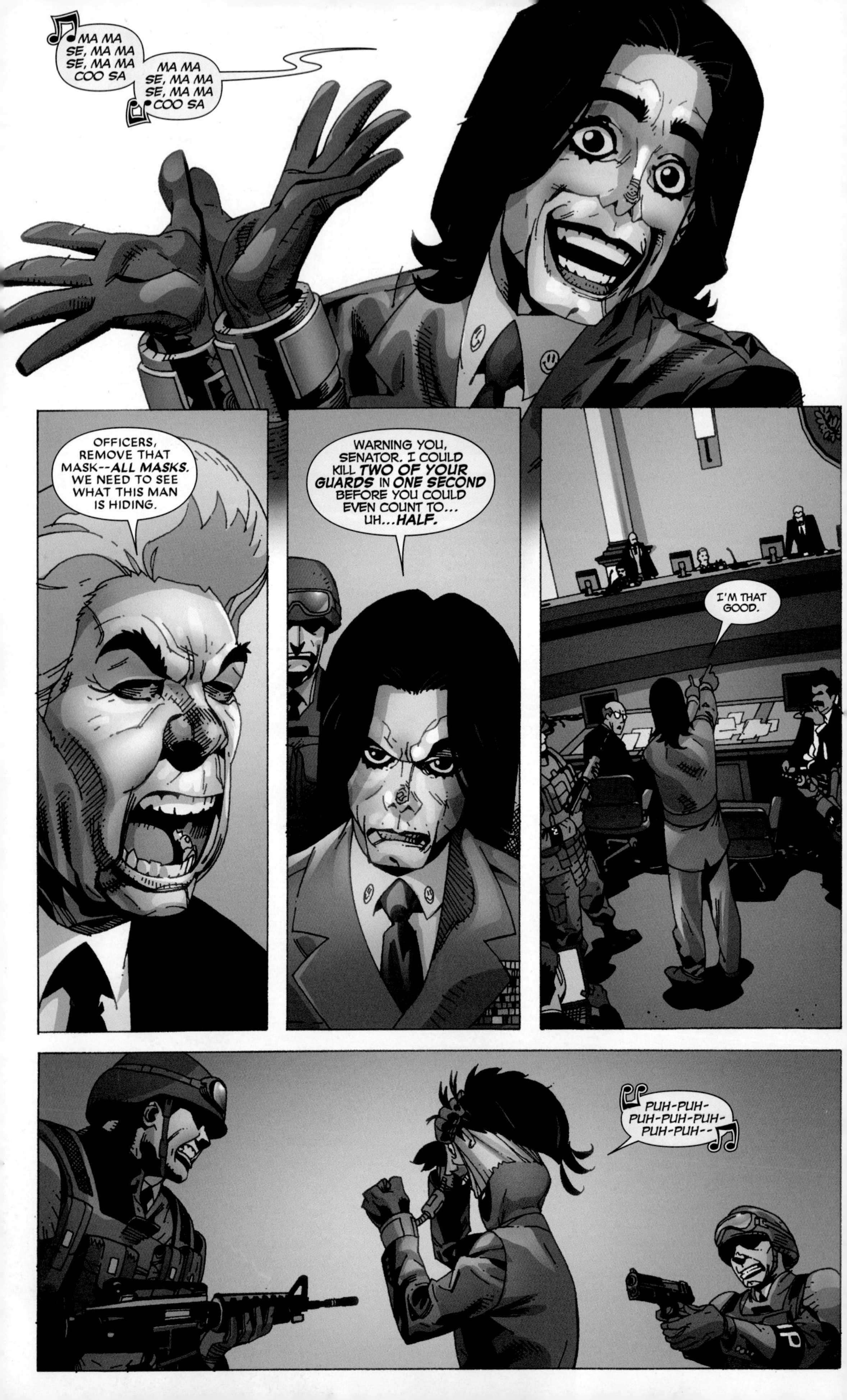
MA MA SE, MA MA SE, MA MA COO SA
MA MA SE, MA MA SE, MA MA COO SA
OFFICERS, REMOVE THAT MASK--ALL MASKS. WE NEED TO SEE WHAT THIS MAN IS HIDING.
WARNING YOU, SENATOR. I COULD KILL TWO OF YOUR GUARDS IN ONE SECOND BEFORE YOU COULD EVEN COUNT TO... UH...HALF.
I'M THAT GOOD.
PUH-PUH-PUH-PUH-PUH-PUH-PUH--

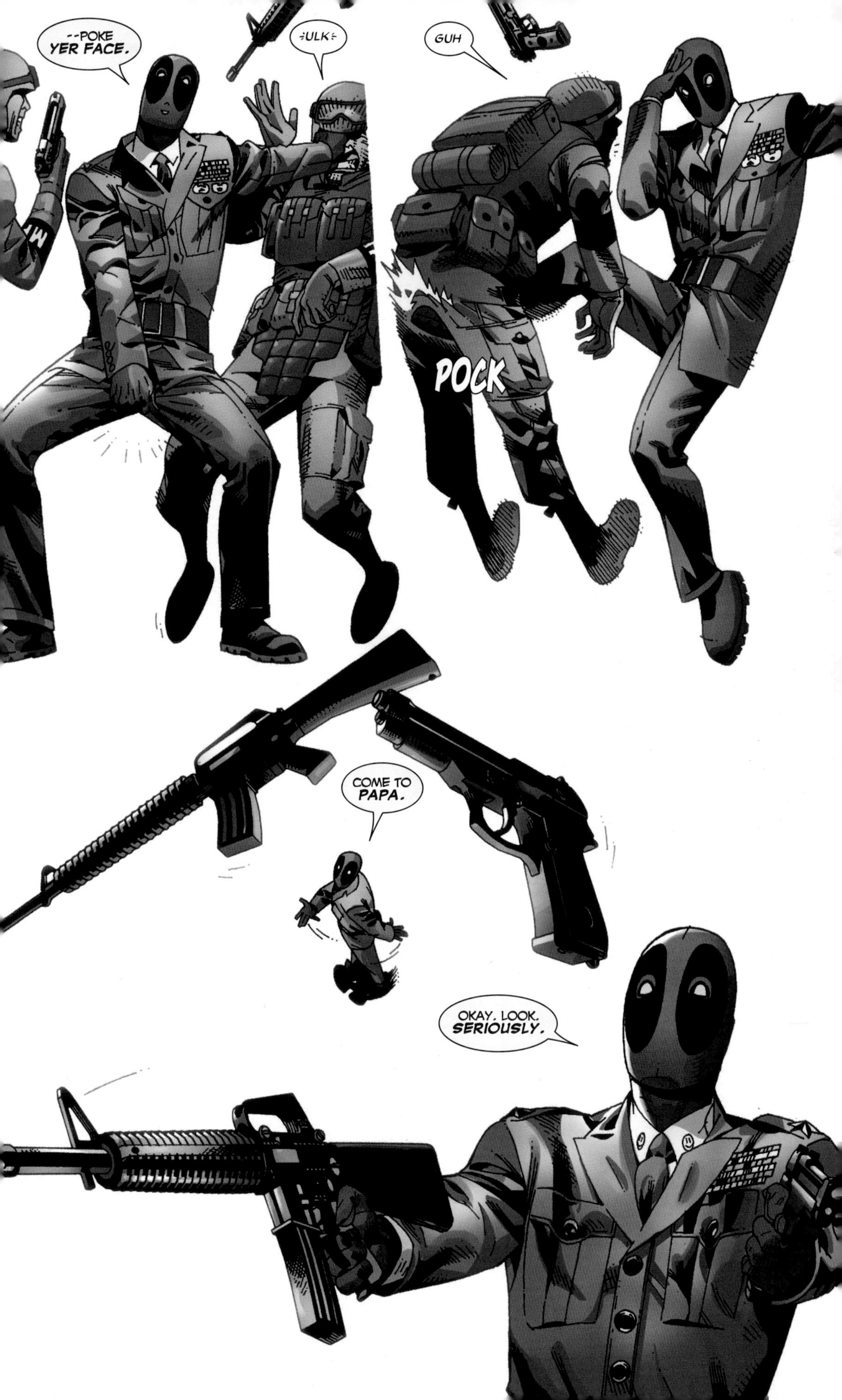
--POKE YER FACE.
ULK
GUH
POCK
COME TO PAPA.
OKAY. LOOK. SERIOUSLY.

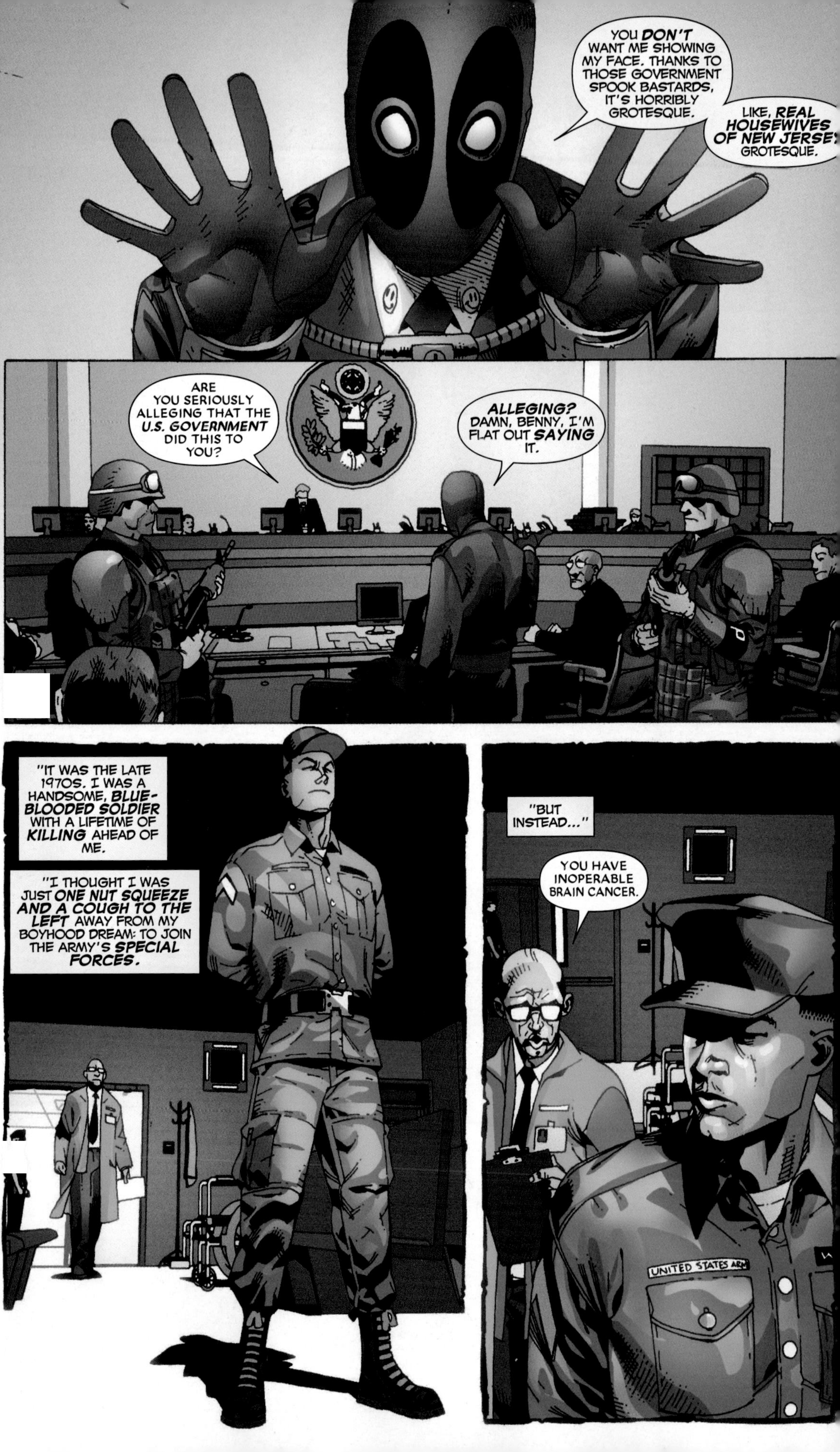
YOU DON'T WANT ME SHOWING MY FACE. THANKS TO THOSE GOVERNMENT SPOOK BASTARDS, IT'S HORRIBLY GROTESQUE.
LIKE, REAL HOUSEWIVES OF NEW JERSEY GROTESQUE.
ARE YOU SERIOUSLY ALLEGING THAT THE U.S. GOVERNMENT DID THIS TO YOU?
ALLEGING? DAMN, BENNY, I'M FLAT OUT SAYING IT.
"IT WAS THE LATE 1970S. I WAS A HANDSOME, BLUE-BLOODED SOLDIER WITH A LIFETIME OF KILLING AHEAD OF ME.
"I THOUGHT I WAS JUST ONE NUT SQUEEZE AND A COUGH TO THE LEFT AWAY FROM MY BOYHOOD DREAM: TO JOIN THE ARMY'S SPECIAL FORCES.
"BUT INSTEAD..."
YOU HAVE INOPERABLE BRAIN CANCER.

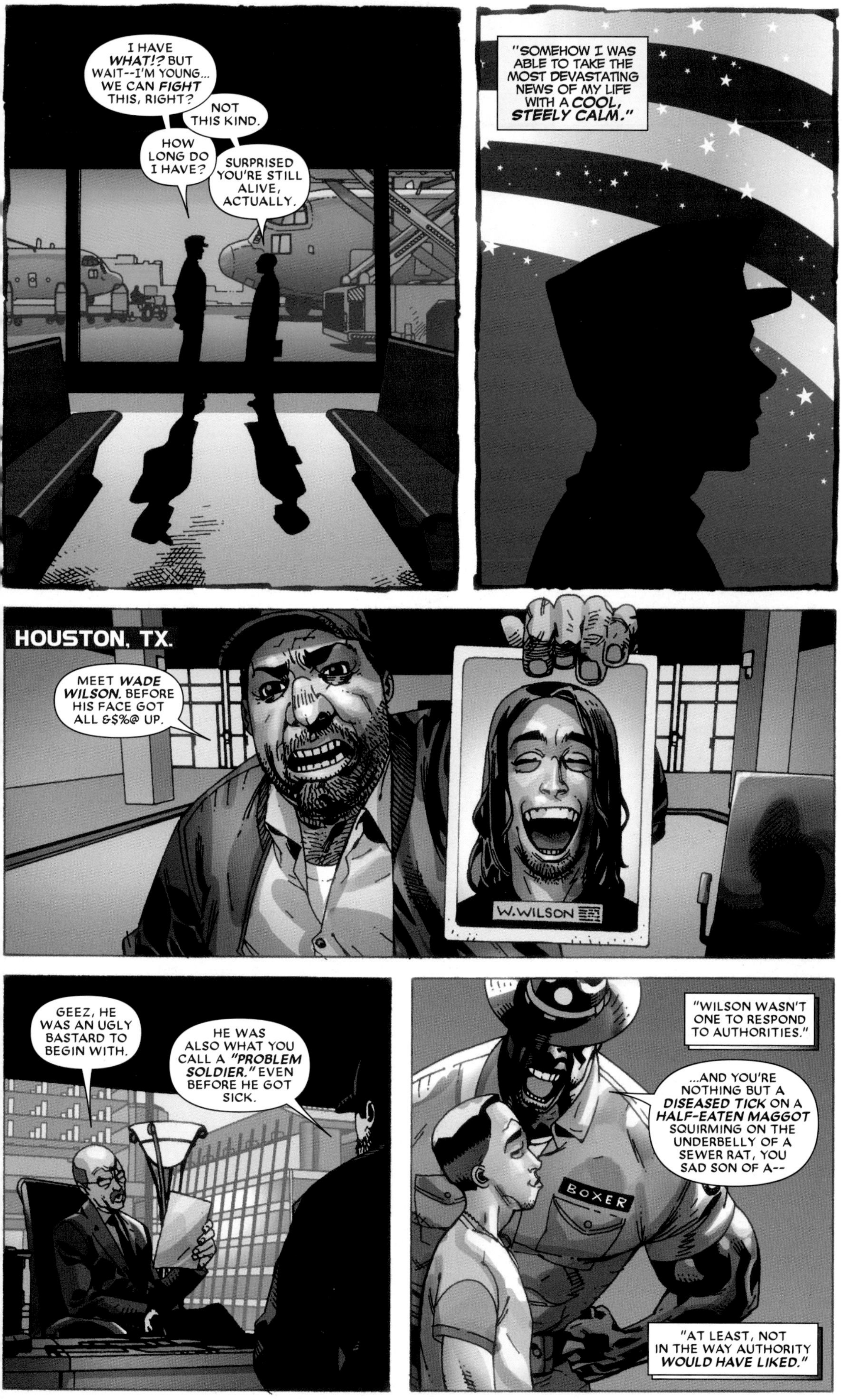
I HAVE *WHAT!?* BUT WAIT--I'M YOUNG... WE CAN *FIGHT* THIS, RIGHT?
NOT THIS KIND.
HOW LONG DO I HAVE?
SURPRISED YOU'RE STILL ALIVE, ACTUALLY.
"SOMEHOW I WAS ABLE TO TAKE THE MOST DEVASTATING NEWS OF MY LIFE WITH A *COOL, STEELY CALM.*"
HOUSTON, TX.
MEET *WADE WILSON.* BEFORE HIS FACE GOT ALL &$%@ UP.
W. WILSON
GEEZ, HE WAS AN UGLY BASTARD TO BEGIN WITH.
HE WAS ALSO WHAT YOU CALL A *"PROBLEM SOLDIER."* EVEN BEFORE HE GOT SICK.
"WILSON WASN'T ONE TO RESPOND TO AUTHORITIES."
...AND YOU'RE NOTHING BUT A *DISEASED TICK* ON A *HALF-EATEN MAGGOT* SQUIRMING ON THE UNDERBELLY OF A SEWER RAT, YOU SAD SON OF A--
BOXER
"AT LEAST, NOT IN THE WAY AUTHORITY *WOULD HAVE LIKED.*"

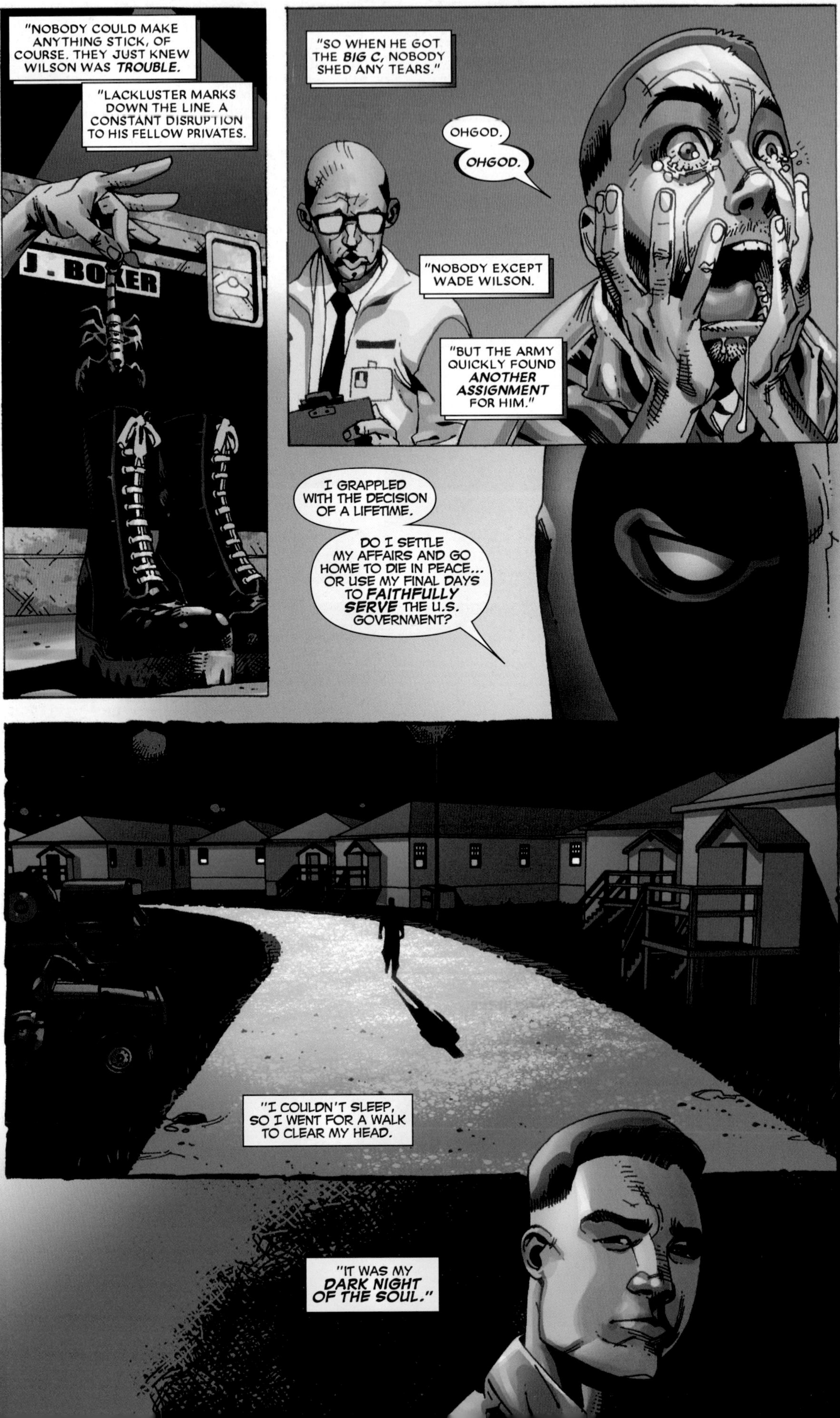
"NOBODY COULD MAKE ANYTHING STICK, OF COURSE. THEY JUST KNEW WILSON WAS TROUBLE.
"LACKLUSTER MARKS DOWN THE LINE. A CONSTANT DISRUPTION TO HIS FELLOW PRIVATES.
J. BOKER
"SO WHEN HE GOT THE BIG C, NOBODY SHED ANY TEARS."
OHGOD.
OHGOD.
"NOBODY EXCEPT WADE WILSON.
"BUT THE ARMY QUICKLY FOUND ANOTHER ASSIGNMENT FOR HIM."
I GRAPPLED WITH THE DECISION OF A LIFETIME.
DO I SETTLE MY AFFAIRS AND GO HOME TO DIE IN PEACE... OR USE MY FINAL DAYS TO FAITHFULLY SERVE THE U.S. GOVERNMENT?
"I COULDN'T SLEEP, SO I WENT FOR A WALK TO CLEAR MY HEAD.
"IT WAS MY DARK NIGHT OF THE SOUL."

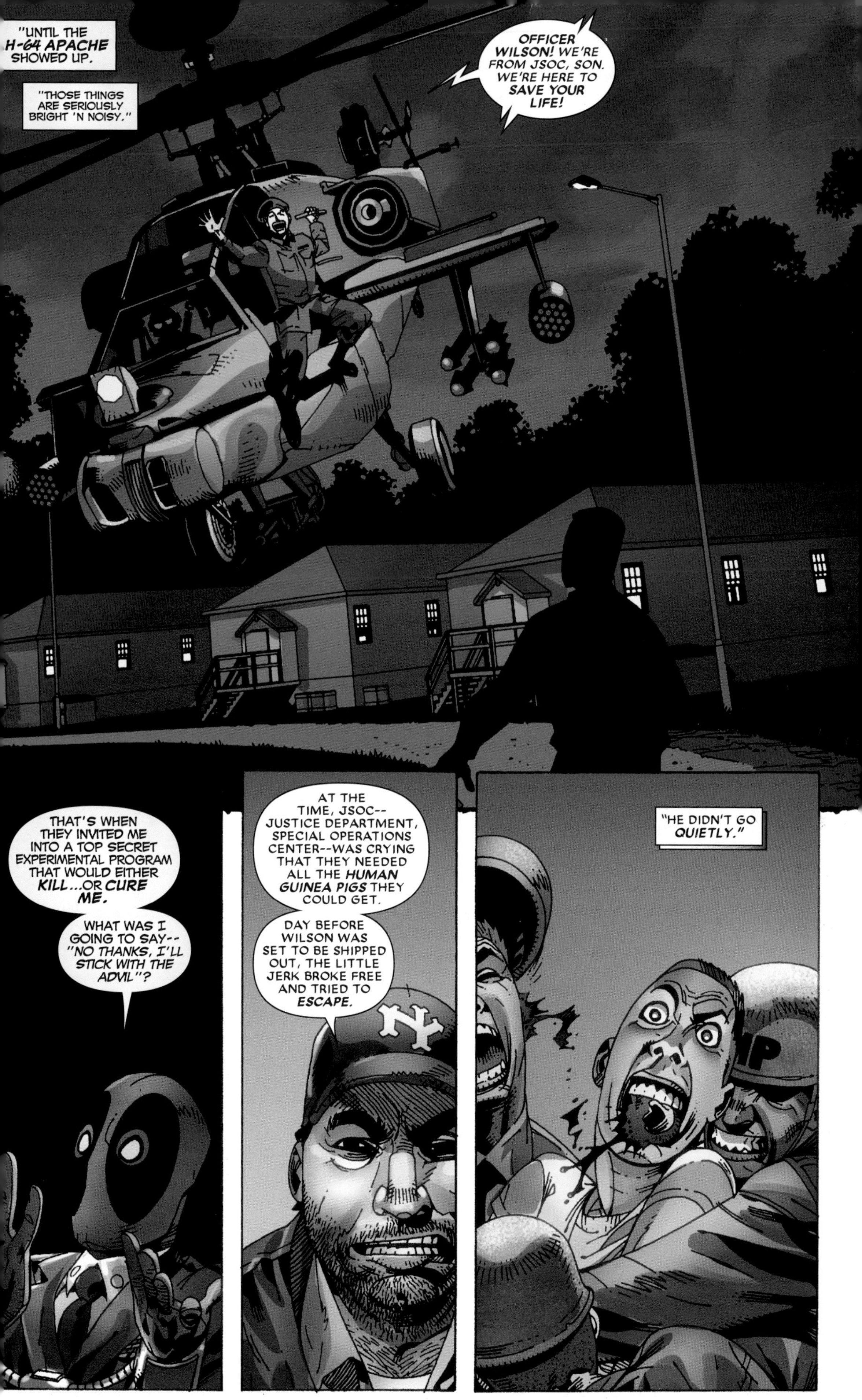
"UNTIL THE H-64 APACHE SHOWED UP.
"THOSE THINGS ARE SERIOUSLY BRIGHT 'N NOISY."
OFFICER WILSON! WE'RE FROM JSOC, SON. WE'RE HERE TO SAVE YOUR LIFE!
THAT'S WHEN THEY INVITED ME INTO A TOP SECRET EXPERIMENTAL PROGRAM THAT WOULD EITHER KILL...OR CURE ME.
WHAT WAS I GOING TO SAY-- "NO THANKS, I'LL STICK WITH THE ADVIL"?
AT THE TIME, JSOC-- JUSTICE DEPARTMENT, SPECIAL OPERATIONS CENTER--WAS CRYING THAT THEY NEEDED ALL THE HUMAN GUINEA PIGS THEY COULD GET.
DAY BEFORE WILSON WAS SET TO BE SHIPPED OUT, THE LITTLE JERK BROKE FREE AND TRIED TO ESCAPE.
"HE DIDN'T GO QUIETLY."

"SO I VOLUNTEERED FOR THE MISSION THAT WOULD CHANGE MY LIFE-- *AND THE HISTORY BOOKS,* IF I DO SAY SO MYSELF.

"THE SECRET PROCEDURE INVOLVED MORE NEEDLES THAN AN *ACUPUNCTURE FETISH CONVENTION.*

"BUT I DIDN'T FLINCH.

"I WAS TOLD THE PAIN WOULD BE *BEYOND HUMAN COMPREHENSION--* THE WHITE-HOT RELENTLESS BURNING OF *EVERY NERVE ENDING* THROUGHOUT MY BODY.

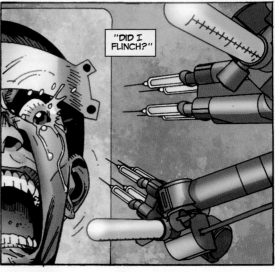

"DID I FLINCH?"

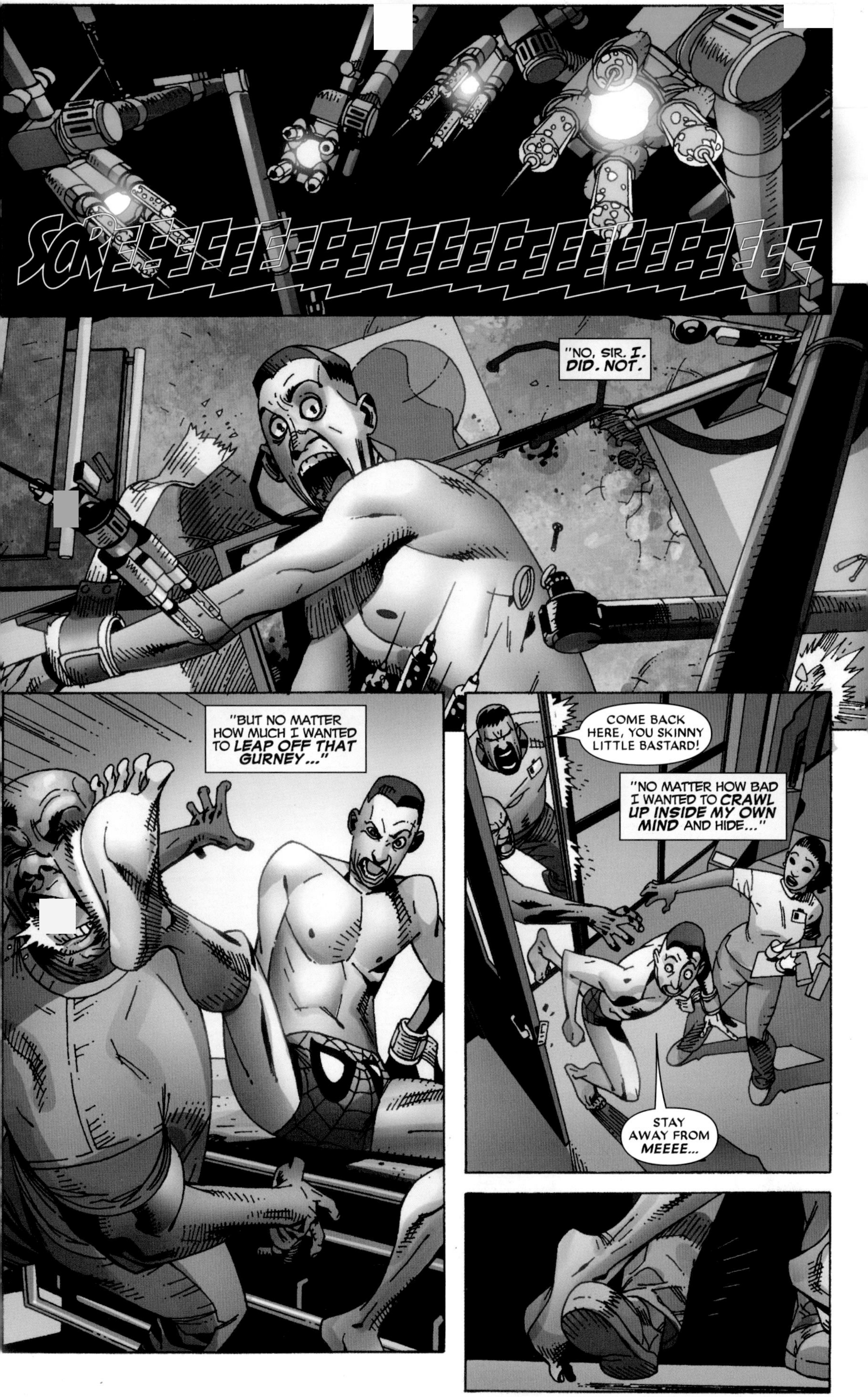
SCREEEEEEEEEEEEEEEEEEEEEEE
"NO, SIR. I. DID. NOT.
"BUT NO MATTER HOW MUCH I WANTED TO LEAP OFF THAT GURNEY..."
COME BACK HERE, YOU SKINNY LITTLE BASTARD!
"NO MATTER HOW BAD I WANTED TO CRAWL UP INSIDE MY OWN MIND AND HIDE..."
STAY AWAY FROM MEEEE...

UFF

NO... YOU CAN'T DO THIS... I'M SICK... I'M AN *AMERICAN CITIZEN*... MOMMY...

OH, SHUT THE #$@% UP, WILSON.

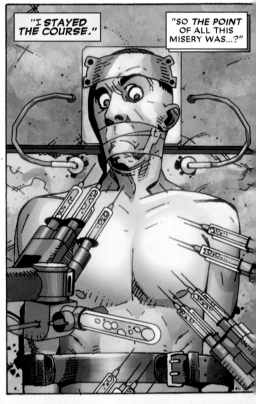

"I *STAYED THE COURSE.*"

"SO *THE POINT* OF ALL THIS MISERY WAS...?"

WEAPON X WAS A *"BOOST"* SYSTEM. TAKE THE SUBJECT'S NATURAL ABILITIES AND *AMPLIFY THEM.* IMMUNE SYSTEMS, STRENGTH, REACTION TIME...EVERYTHING.

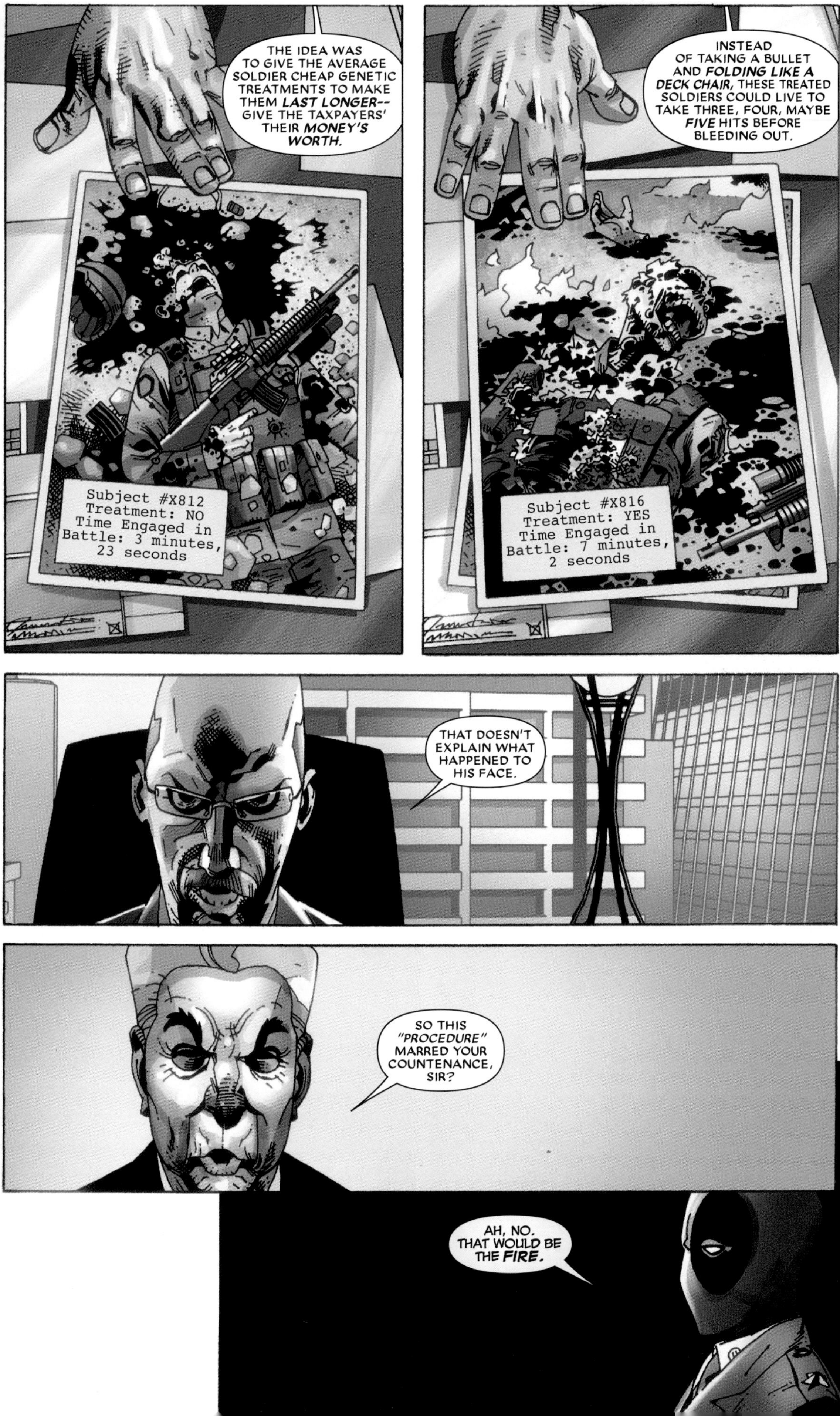
THE IDEA WAS TO GIVE THE AVERAGE SOLDIER CHEAP GENETIC TREATMENTS TO MAKE THEM LAST LONGER-- GIVE THE TAXPAYERS' THEIR MONEY'S WORTH.
Subject #X812 Treatment: NO Time Engaged in Battle: 3 minutes, 23 seconds
INSTEAD OF TAKING A BULLET AND FOLDING LIKE A DECK CHAIR, THESE TREATED SOLDIERS COULD LIVE TO TAKE THREE, FOUR, MAYBE FIVE HITS BEFORE BLEEDING OUT.
Subject #X816 Treatment: YES Time Engaged in Battle: 7 minutes, 2 seconds
THAT DOESN'T EXPLAIN WHAT HAPPENED TO HIS FACE.
SO THIS "PROCEDURE" MARRED YOUR COUNTENANCE, SIR?
AH, NO. THAT WOULD BE THE FIRE.

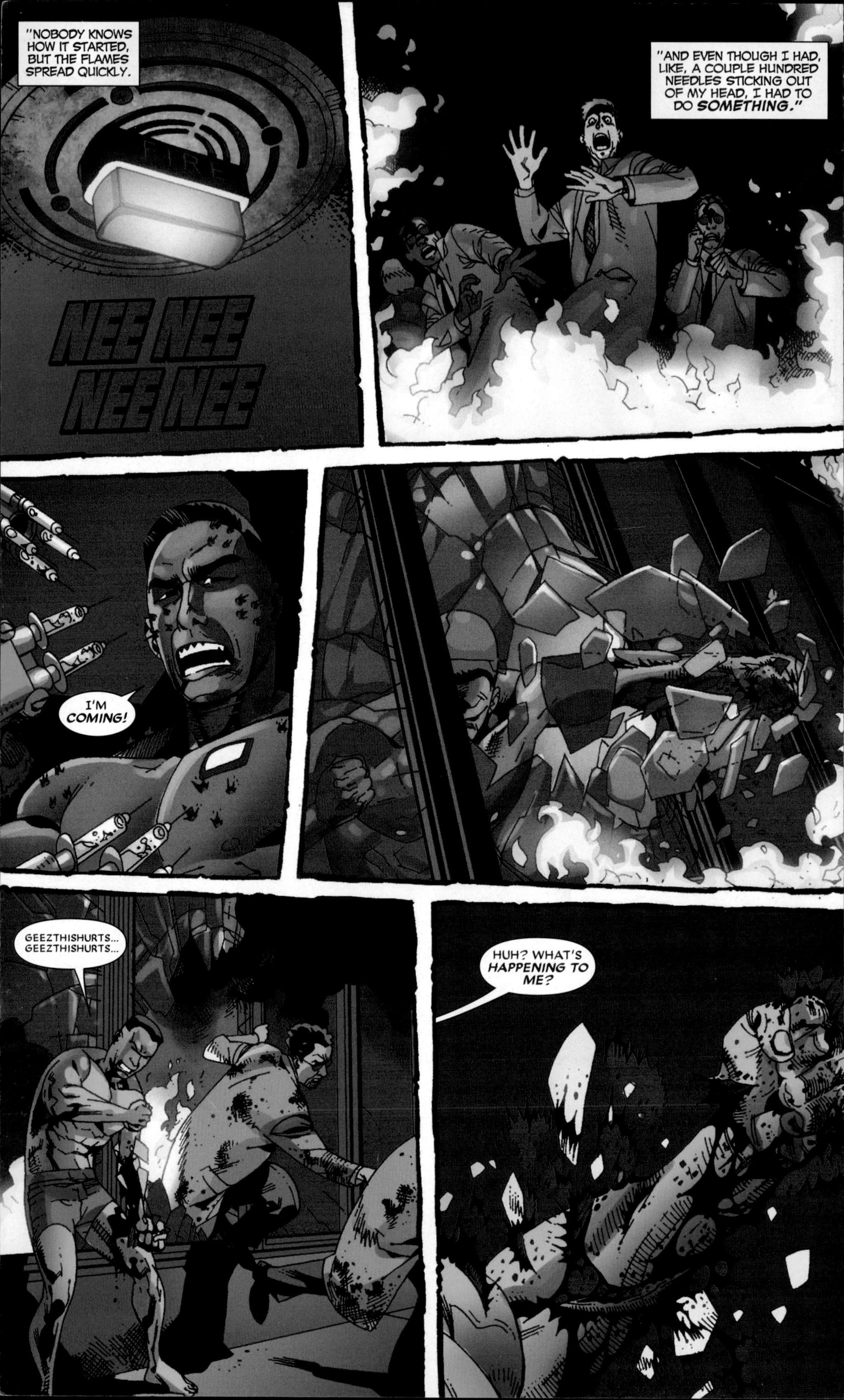
"NOBODY KNOWS HOW IT STARTED, BUT THE FLAMES SPREAD QUICKLY.
NEE NEE NEE NEE
"AND EVEN THOUGH I HAD, LIKE, A COUPLE HUNDRED NEEDLES STICKING OUT OF MY HEAD, I HAD TO DO SOMETHING."
I'M COMING!
GEEZTHISHURTS... GEEZTHISHURTS...
HUH? WHAT'S HAPPENING TO ME?

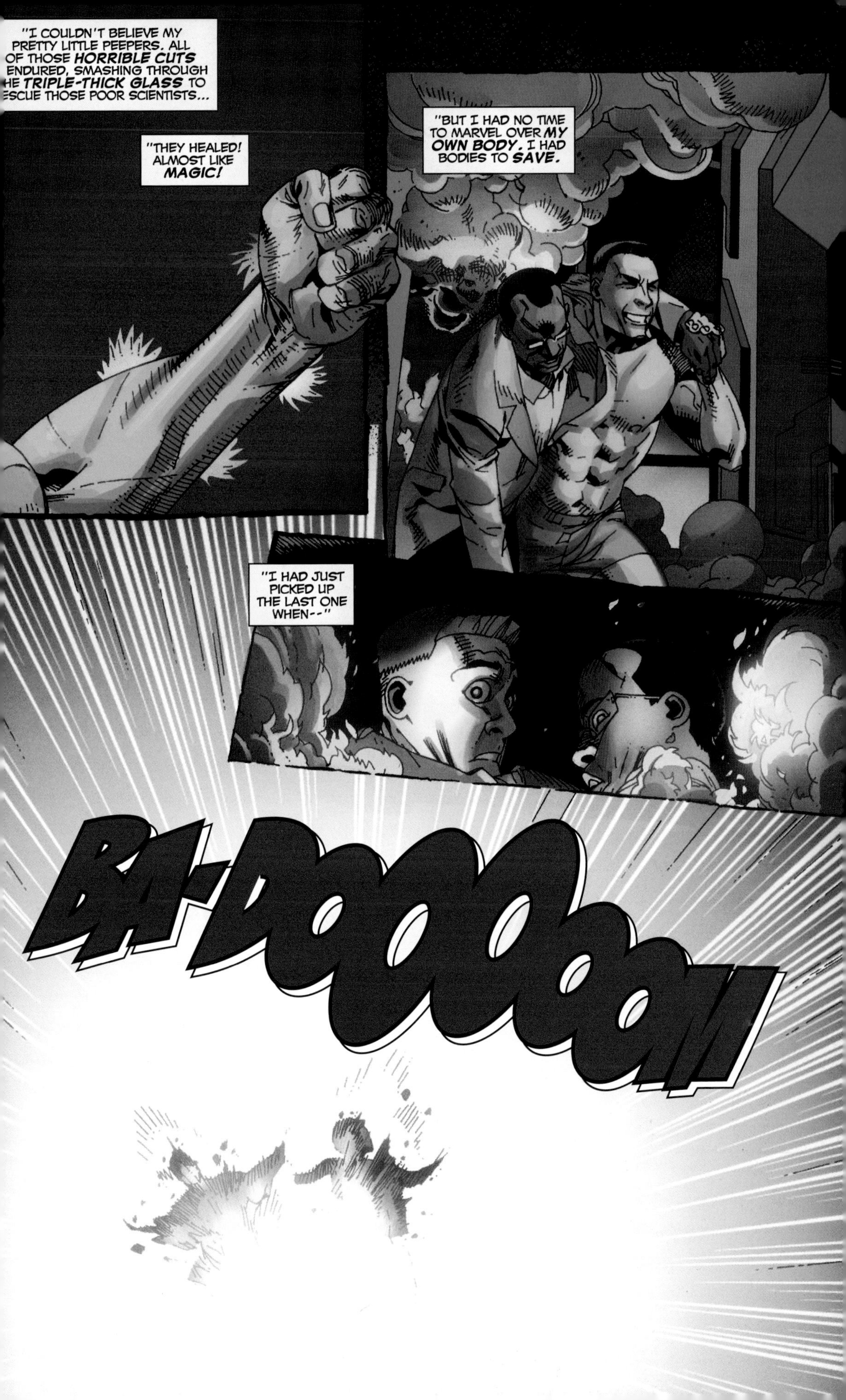
"I COULDN'T BELIEVE MY PRETTY LITTLE PEEPERS. ALL OF THOSE HORRIBLE CUTS ENDURED, SMASHING THROUGH HE TRIPLE-THICK GLASS TO ESCUE THOSE POOR SCIENTISTS...
"THEY HEALED! ALMOST LIKE MAGIC!
"BUT I HAD NO TIME TO MARVEL OVER MY OWN BODY. I HAD BODIES TO SAVE.
"I HAD JUST PICKED UP THE LAST ONE WHEN--"
BA-DOOOOOM!

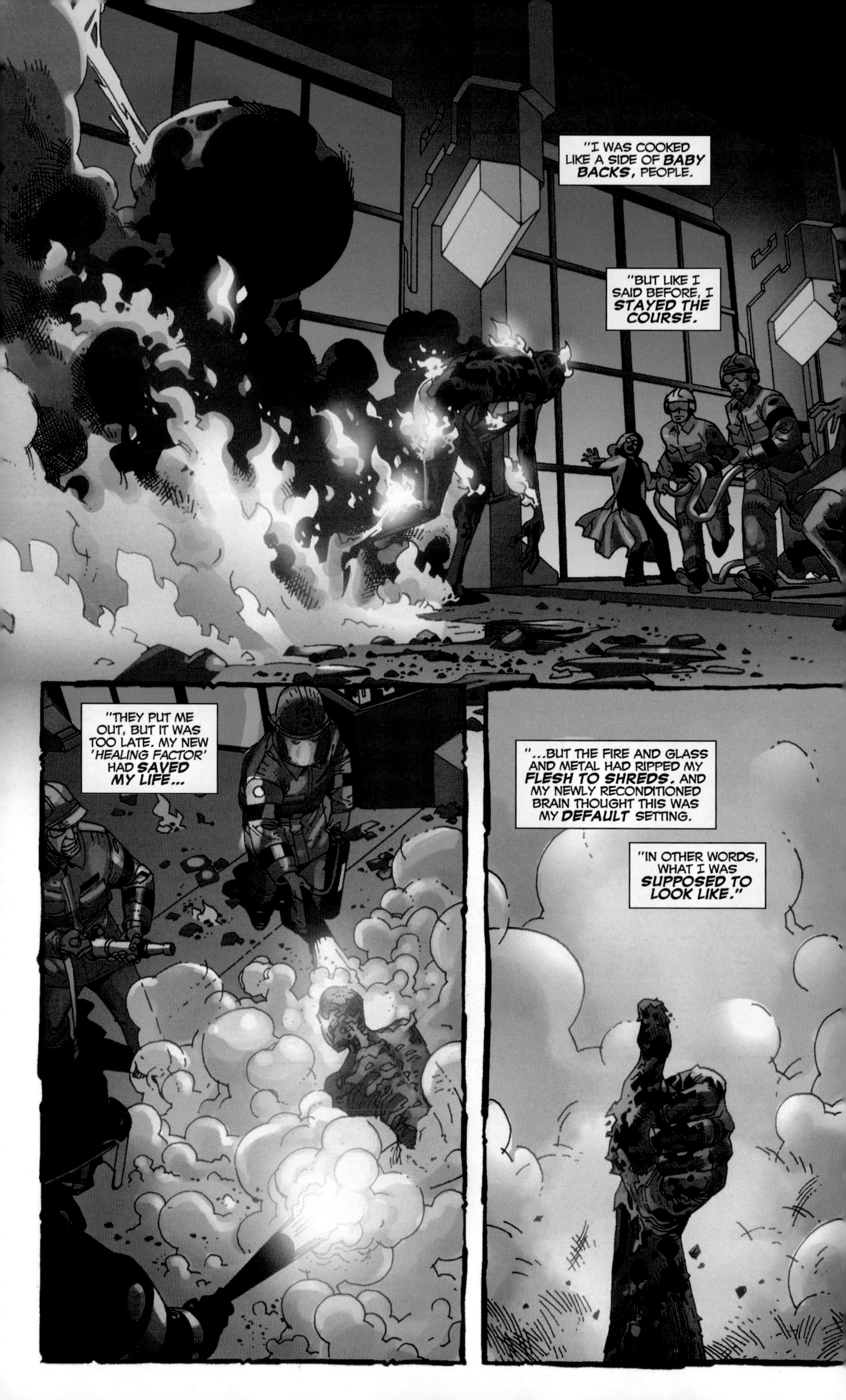
"I WAS COOKED LIKE A SIDE OF BABY BACKS, PEOPLE.
"BUT LIKE I SAID BEFORE, I STAYED THE COURSE.
"THEY PUT ME OUT, BUT IT WAS TOO LATE. MY NEW 'HEALING FACTOR' HAD SAVED MY LIFE...
"...BUT THE FIRE AND GLASS AND METAL HAD RIPPED MY FLESH TO SHREDS. AND MY NEWLY RECONDITIONED BRAIN THOUGHT THIS WAS MY DEFAULT SETTING.
"IN OTHER WORDS, WHAT I WAS SUPPOSED TO LOOK LIKE."

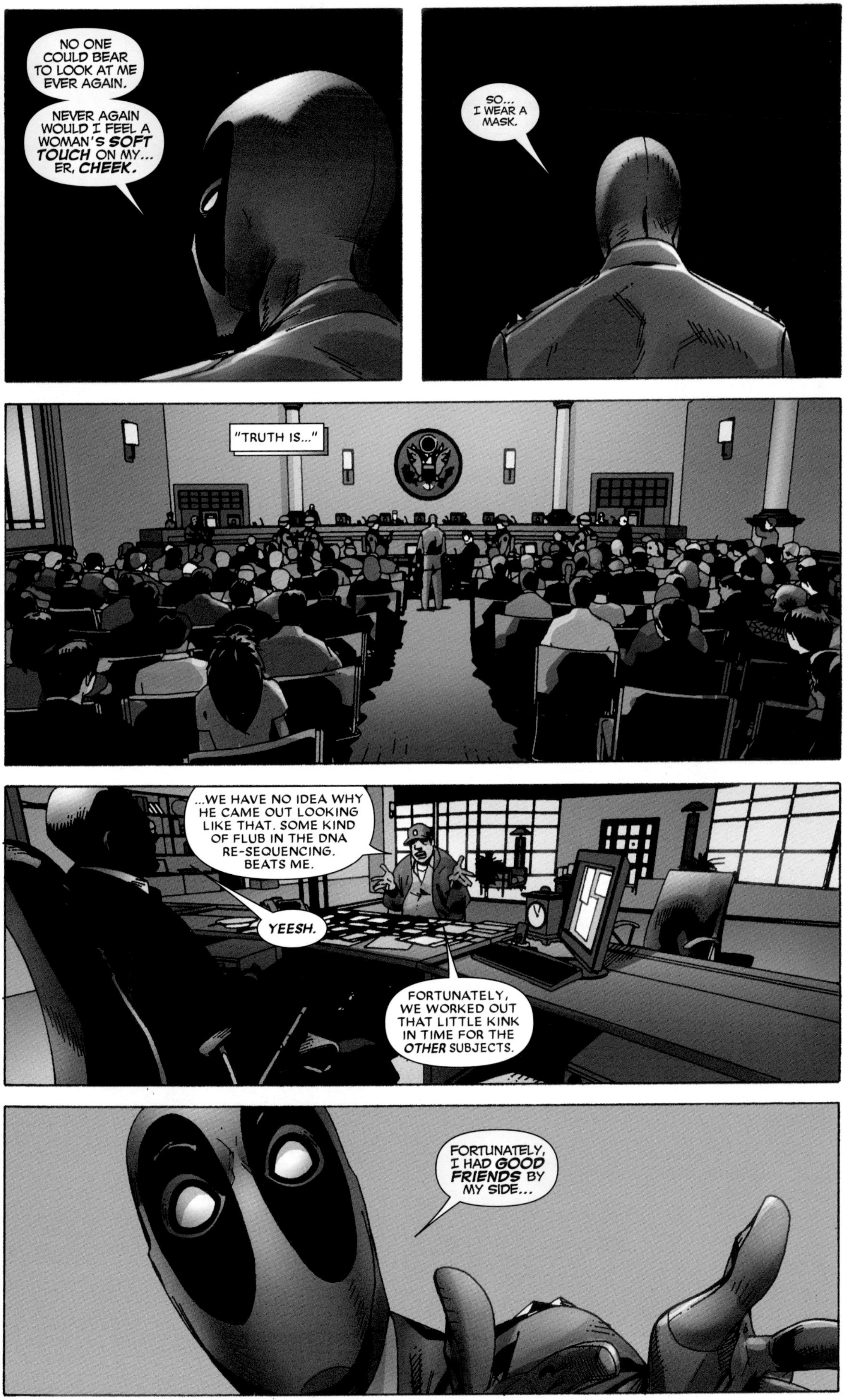
NO ONE COULD BEAR TO LOOK AT ME EVER AGAIN.
NEVER AGAIN WOULD I FEEL A WOMAN'S SOFT TOUCH ON MY... ER, CHEEK.
SO... I WEAR A MASK.
"TRUTH IS..."
...WE HAVE NO IDEA WHY HE CAME OUT LOOKING LIKE THAT. SOME KIND OF FLUB IN THE DNA RE-SEQUENCING. BEATS ME.
YEESH.
FORTUNATELY, WE WORKED OUT THAT LITTLE KINK IN TIME FOR THE OTHER SUBJECTS.
FORTUNATELY, I HAD GOOD FRIENDS BY MY SIDE...

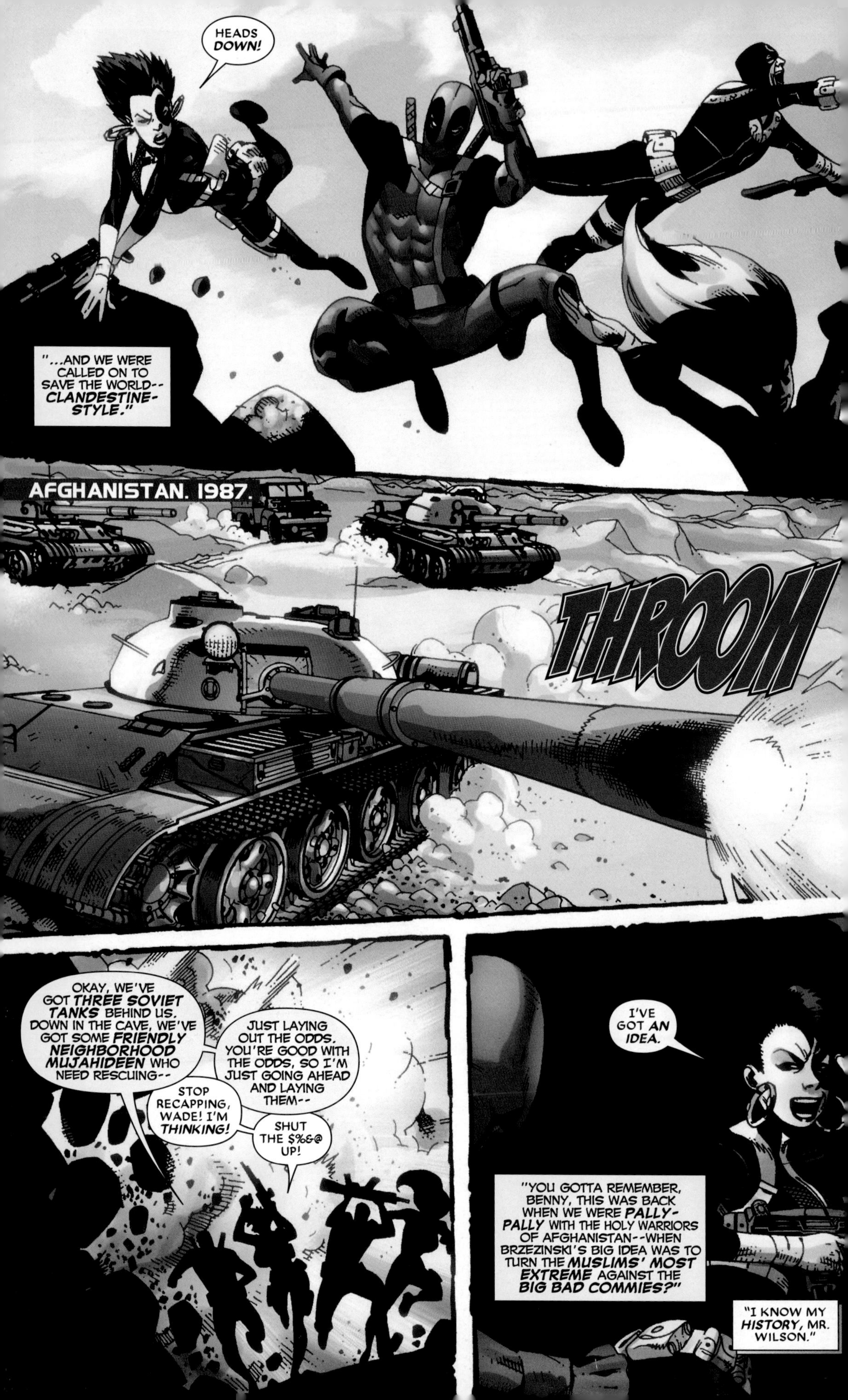

HEADS DOWN!
"...AND WE WERE CALLED ON TO SAVE THE WORLD--CLANDESTINE-STYLE."
AFGHANISTAN. 1987.
THROOM
OKAY, WE'VE GOT THREE SOVIET TANKS BEHIND US. DOWN IN THE CAVE, WE'VE GOT SOME FRIENDLY NEIGHBORHOOD MUJAHIDEEN WHO NEED RESCUING--
STOP RECAPPING, WADE! I'M THINKING!
JUST LAYING OUT THE ODDS. YOU'RE GOOD WITH THE ODDS, SO I'M JUST GOING AHEAD AND LAYING THEM--
SHUT THE $%&@ UP!
I'VE GOT AN IDEA.
"YOU GOTTA REMEMBER, BENNY, THIS WAS BACK WHEN WE WERE PALLY-PALLY WITH THE HOLY WARRIORS OF AFGHANISTAN--WHEN BRZEZINSKI'S BIG IDEA WAS TO TURN THE MUSLIMS' MOST EXTREME AGAINST THE BIG BAD COMMIES?"
"I KNOW MY HISTORY, MR. WILSON."

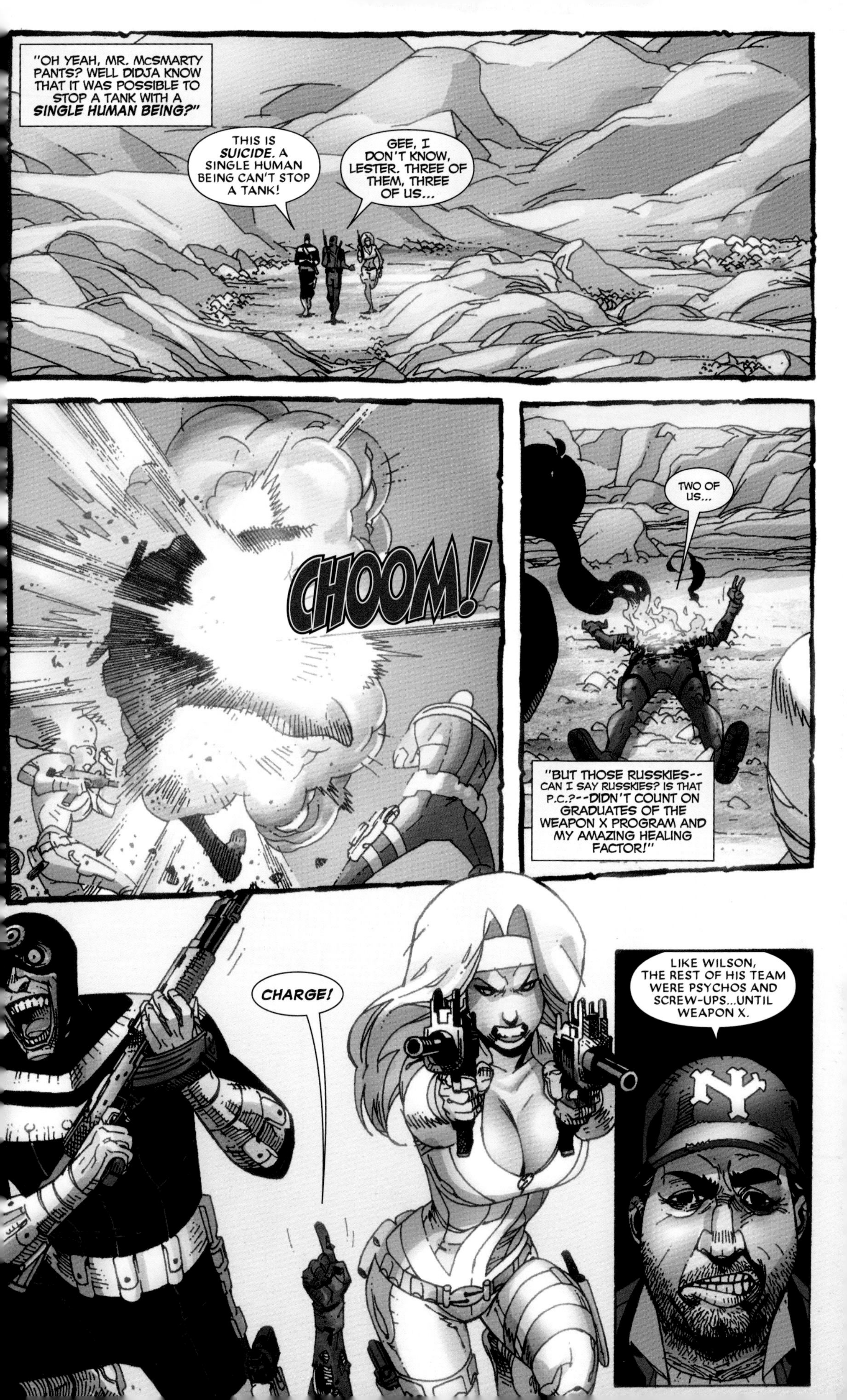
"OH YEAH, MR. McSMARTY PANTS? WELL DIDJA KNOW THAT IT WAS POSSIBLE TO STOP A TANK WITH A SINGLE HUMAN BEING?"
THIS IS SUICIDE. A SINGLE HUMAN BEING CAN'T STOP A TANK!
GEE, I DON'T KNOW, LESTER. THREE OF THEM, THREE OF US...
CHOOM!
TWO OF US...
"BUT THOSE RUSSKIES--CAN I SAY RUSSKIES? IS THAT P.C.?--DIDN'T COUNT ON GRADUATES OF THE WEAPON X PROGRAM AND MY AMAZING HEALING FACTOR!"
CHARGE!
LIKE WILSON, THE REST OF HIS TEAM WERE PSYCHOS AND SCREW-UPS...UNTIL WEAPON X.

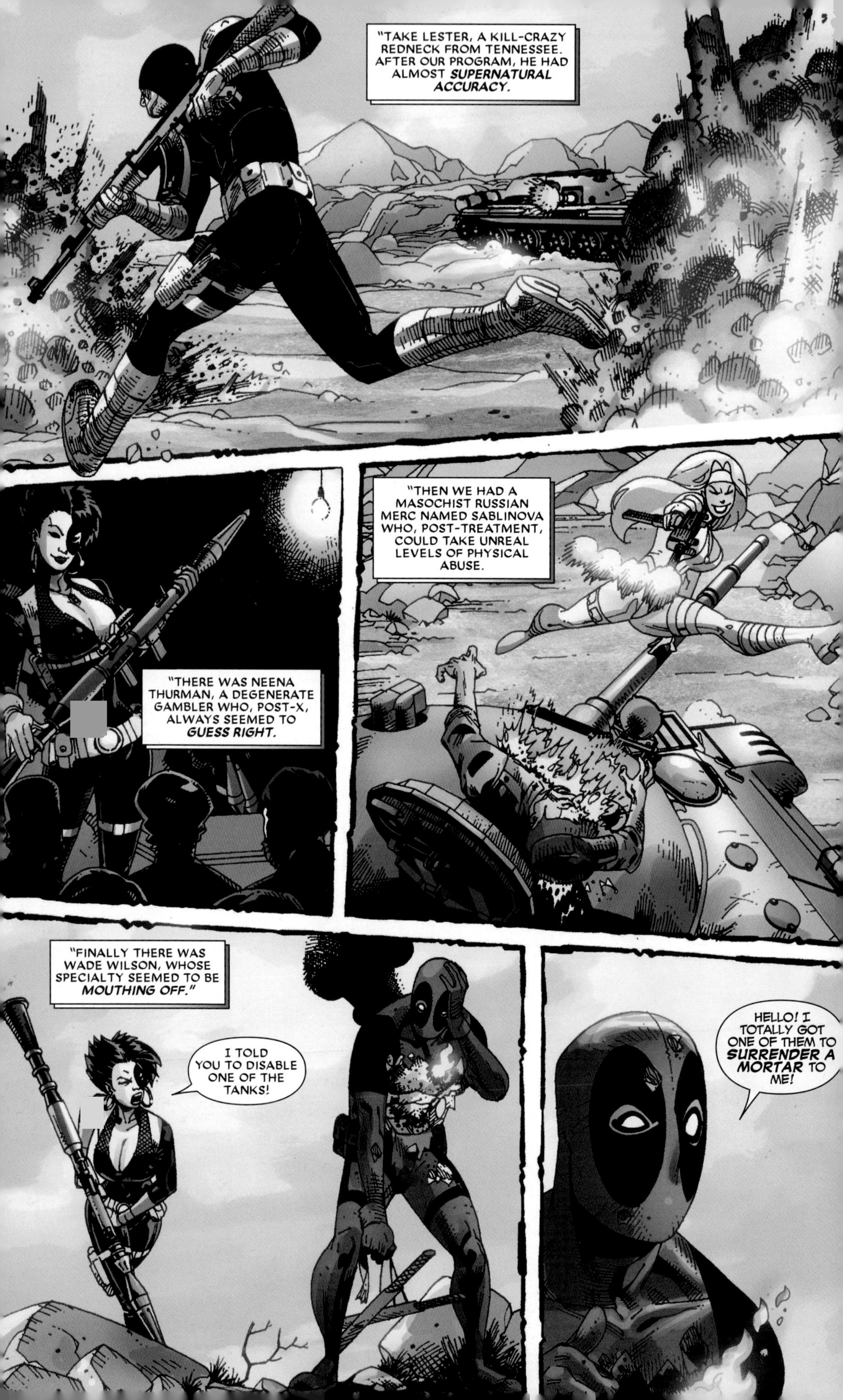
"TAKE LESTER, A KILL-CRAZY REDNECK FROM TENNESSEE. AFTER OUR PROGRAM, HE HAD ALMOST SUPERNATURAL ACCURACY.
"THERE WAS NEENA THURMAN, A DEGENERATE GAMBLER WHO, POST-X, ALWAYS SEEMED TO GUESS RIGHT.
"THEN WE HAD A MASOCHIST RUSSIAN MERC NAMED SABLINOVA WHO, POST-TREATMENT, COULD TAKE UNREAL LEVELS OF PHYSICAL ABUSE.
"FINALLY THERE WAS WADE WILSON, WHOSE SPECIALTY SEEMED TO BE MOUTHING OFF."
I TOLD YOU TO DISABLE ONE OF THE TANKS!
HELLO! I TOTALLY GOT ONE OF THEM TO SURRENDER A MORTAR TO ME!

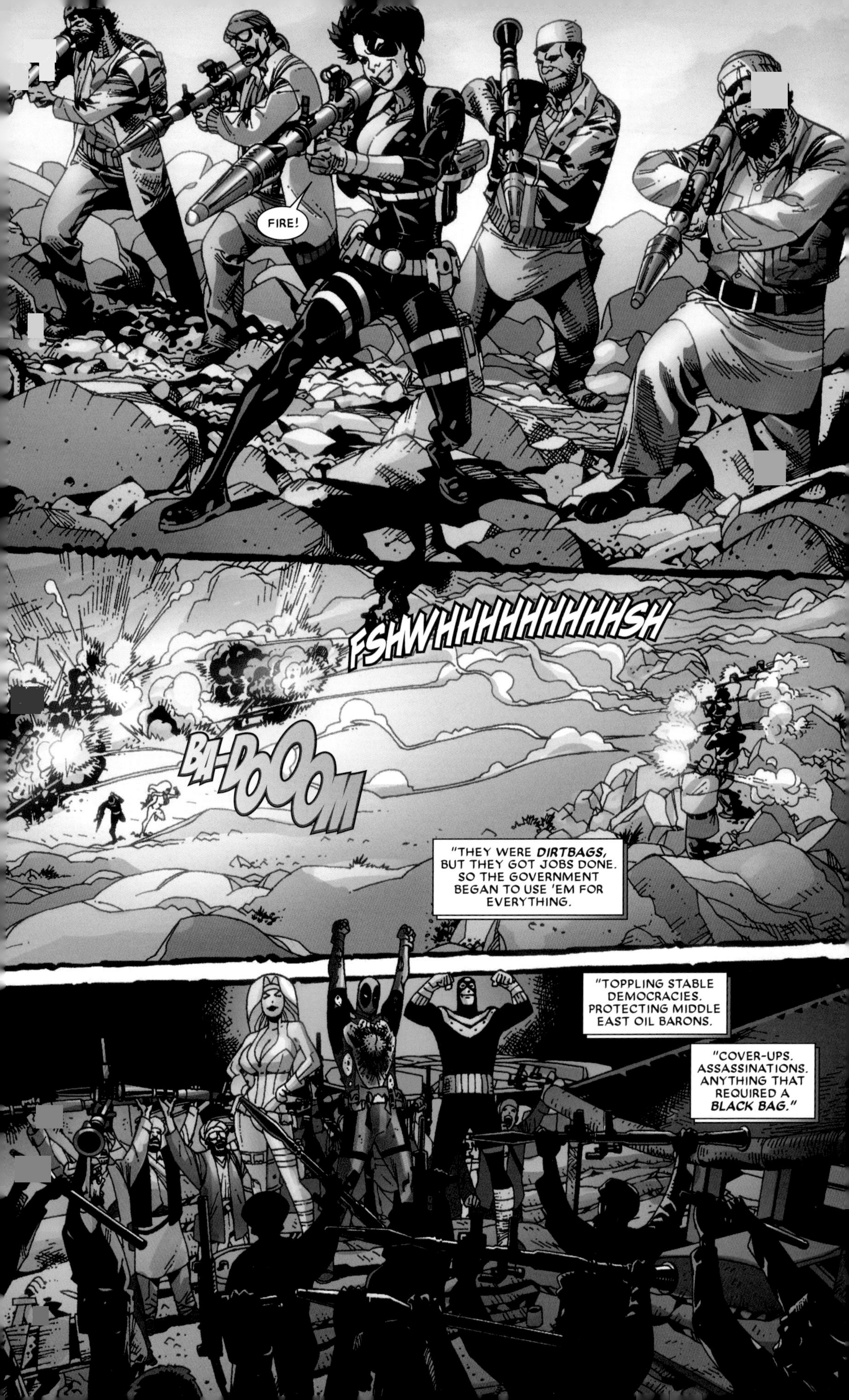
FIRE!
FSHWHHHHHHHHHSH
BA-DOOOOM
"THEY WERE *DIRTBAGS,* BUT THEY GOT JOBS DONE. SO THE GOVERNMENT BEGAN TO USE 'EM FOR EVERYTHING.
"TOPPLING STABLE DEMOCRACIES. PROTECTING MIDDLE EAST OIL BARONS.
"COVER-UPS. ASSASSINATIONS. ANYTHING THAT REQUIRED A *BLACK BAG.*"

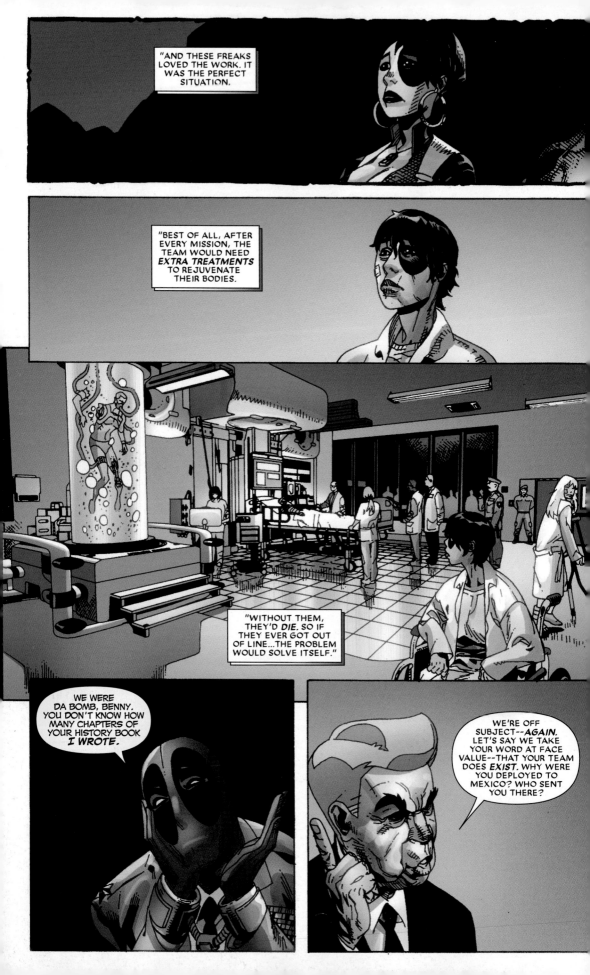

"AND THESE FREAKS LOVED THE WORK. IT WAS THE PERFECT SITUATION.

"BEST OF ALL, AFTER EVERY MISSION, THE TEAM WOULD NEED *EXTRA TREATMENTS* TO REJUVENATE THEIR BODIES.

"WITHOUT THEM, THEY'D *DIE*. SO IF THEY EVER GOT OUT OF LINE...THE PROBLEM WOULD SOLVE ITSELF."

WE WERE DA BOMB, BENNY. YOU DON'T KNOW HOW MANY CHAPTERS OF YOUR HISTORY BOOK *I WROTE.*

WE'RE OFF SUBJECT--*AGAIN.* LET'S SAY WE TAKE YOUR WORD AT FACE VALUE--THAT YOUR TEAM DOES *EXIST.* WHY WERE YOU DEPLOYED TO MEXICO? WHO SENT YOU THERE?

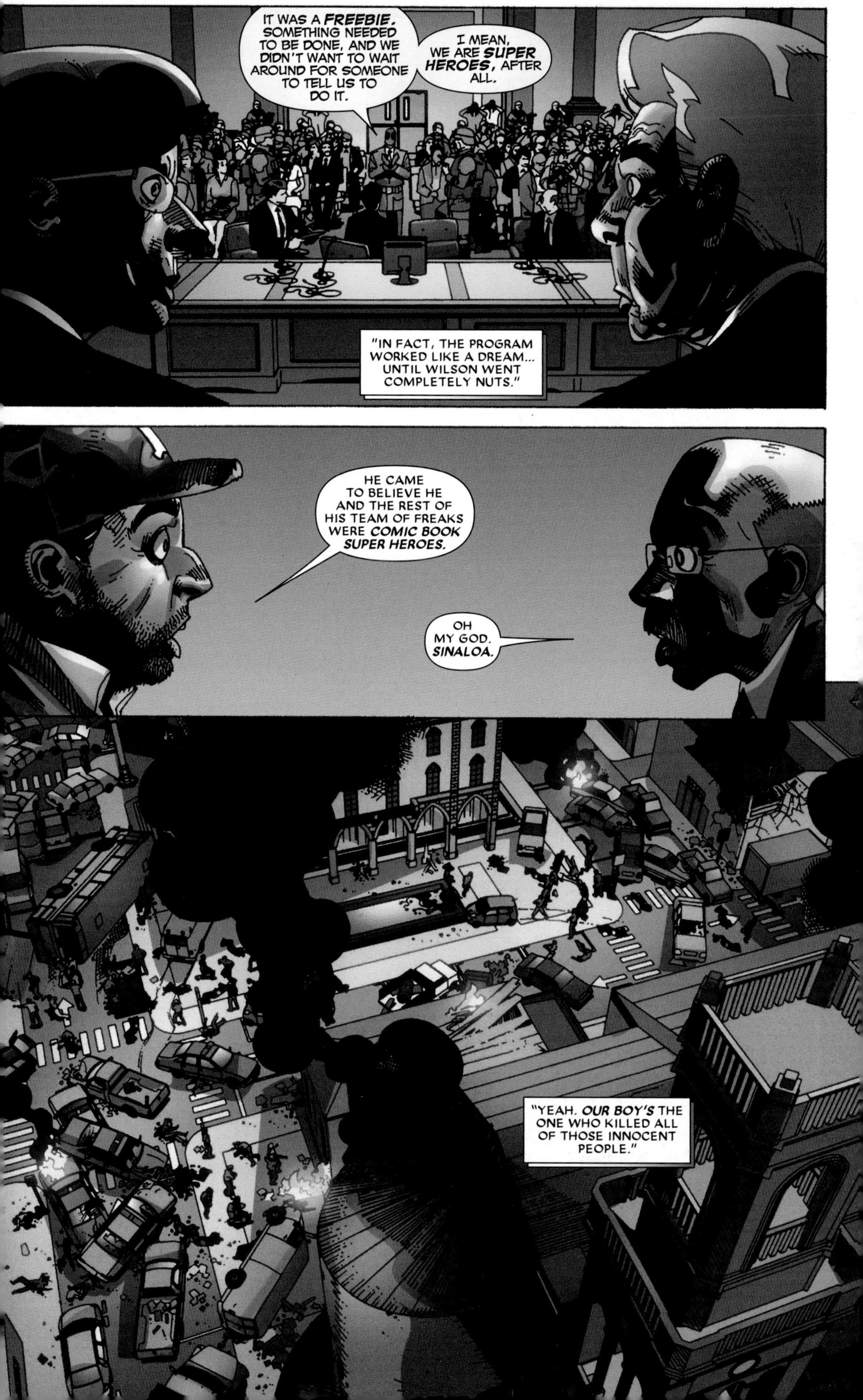
IT WAS A FREEBIE. SOMETHING NEEDED TO BE DONE, AND WE DIDN'T WANT TO WAIT AROUND FOR SOMEONE TO TELL US TO DO IT.
I MEAN, WE ARE SUPER HEROES, AFTER ALL.
"IN FACT, THE PROGRAM WORKED LIKE A DREAM... UNTIL WILSON WENT COMPLETELY NUTS."
HE CAME TO BELIEVE HE AND THE REST OF HIS TEAM OF FREAKS WERE COMIC BOOK SUPER HEROES.
OH MY GOD. SINALOA.
"YEAH. OUR BOY'S THE ONE WHO KILLED ALL OF THOSE INNOCENT PEOPLE."

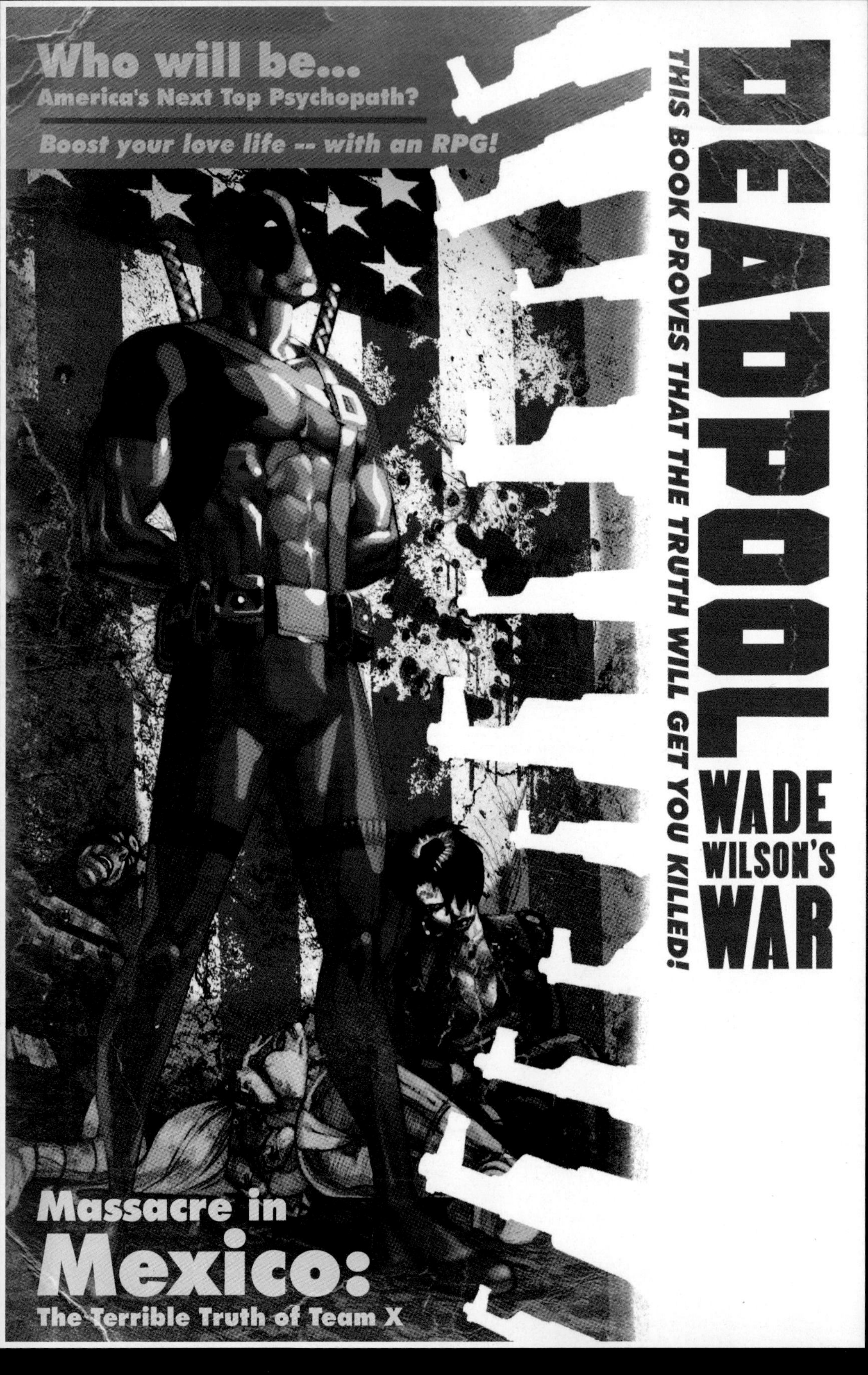
Who will be...
America's Next Top Psychopath?
Boost your love life -- with an RPG!
DEADPOOL
THIS BOOK PROVES THAT THE TRUTH WILL GET YOU KILLED!
WADE WILSON'S WAR
Massacre in Mexico:
The Terrible Truth of Team X

DEADPOOL: WADE WILSON'S WAR #3

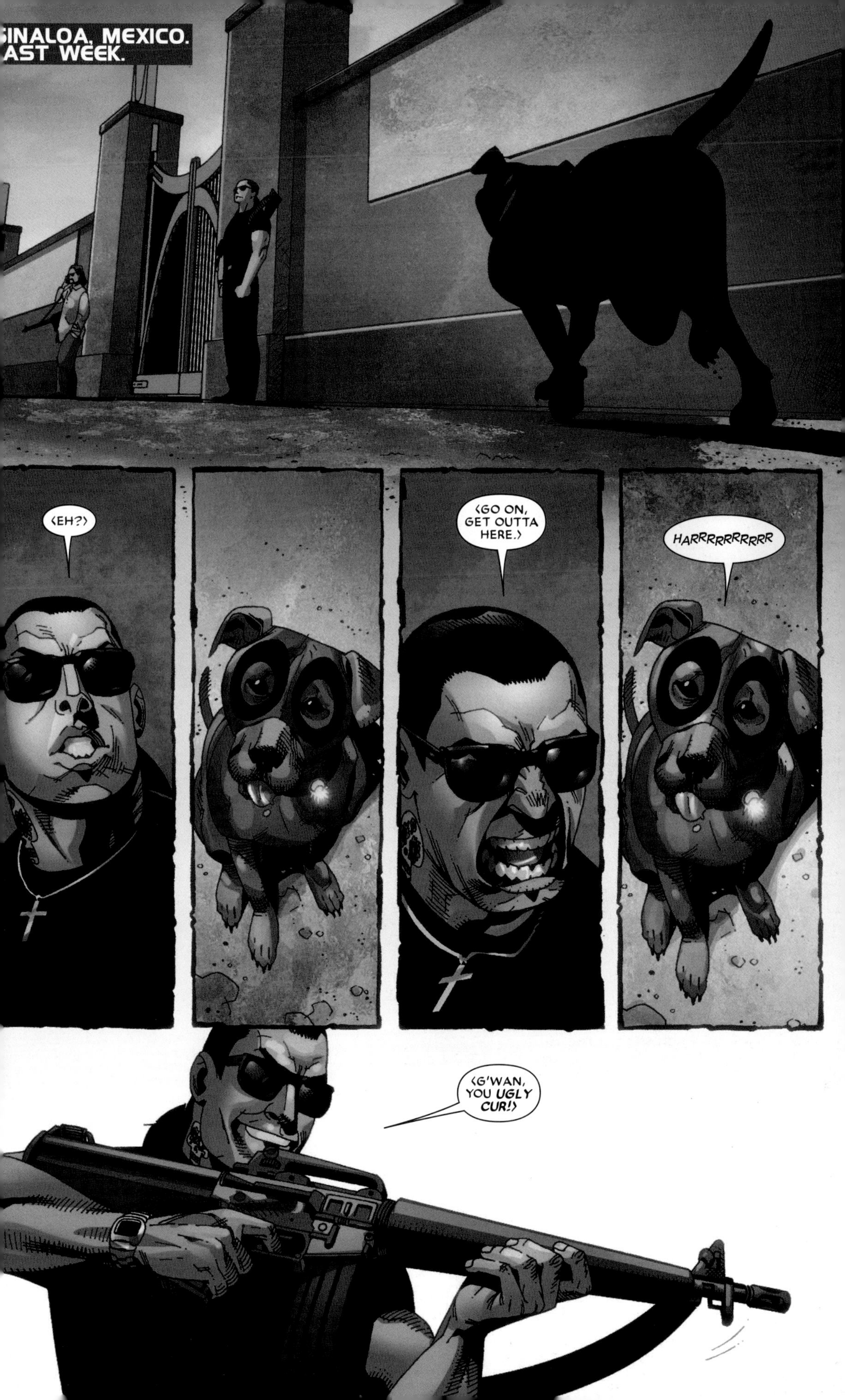

SINALOA, MEXICO. LAST WEEK.
‹EH?›
‹GO ON, GET OUTTA HERE.›
HARRRRRRRRRR
‹G'WAN, YOU UGLY CUR!›

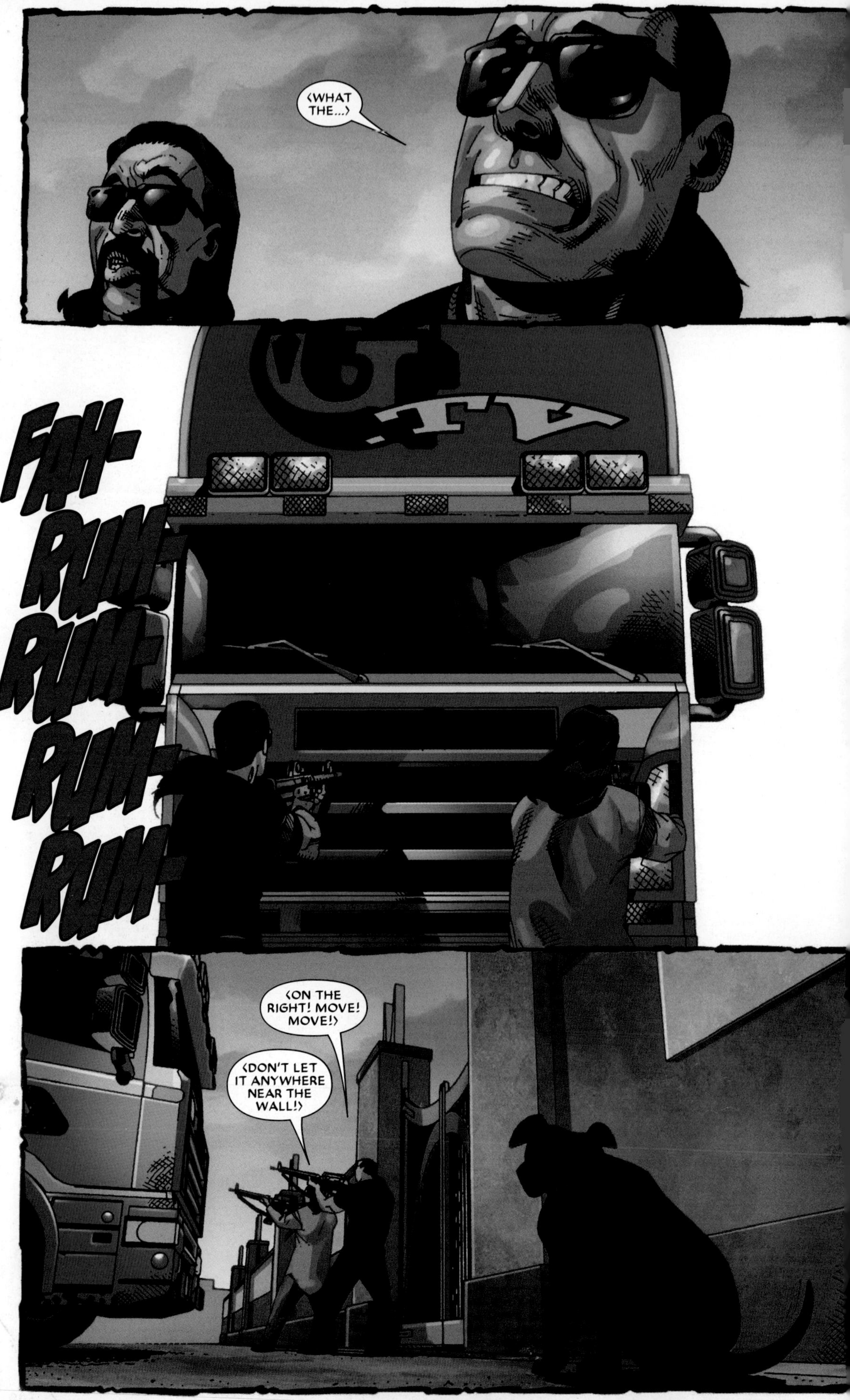
‹WHAT THE...›
FAH-RUM-RUM-RUM-RUM-
‹ON THE RIGHT! MOVE! MOVE!›
‹DON'T LET IT ANYWHERE NEAR THE WALL!›

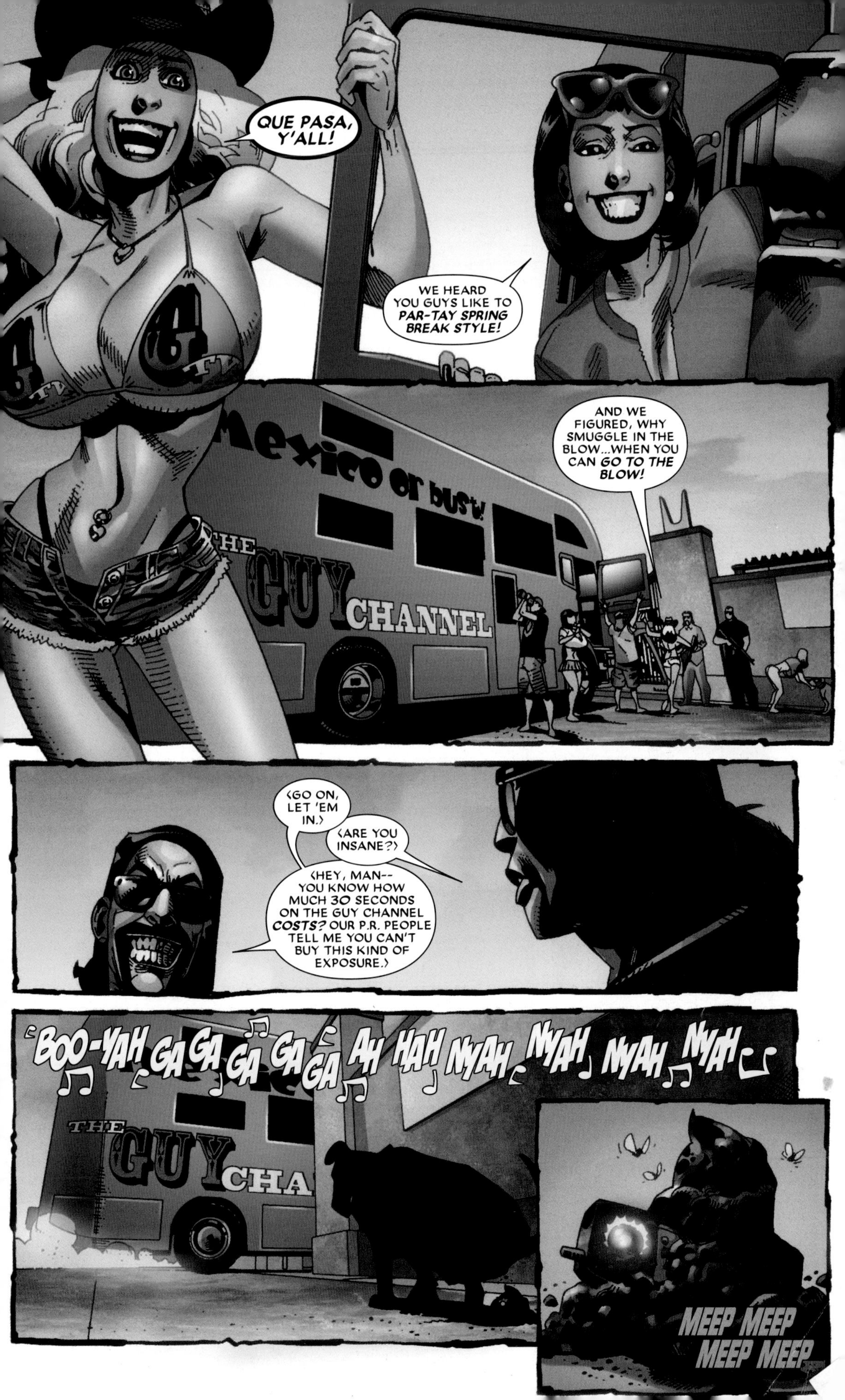

QUE PASA, Y'ALL!
WE HEARD YOU GUYS LIKE TO *PAR-TAY SPRING BREAK STYLE!*
mexico or bust!
THE GUY CHANNEL
AND WE FIGURED, WHY SMUGGLE IN THE BLOW...WHEN YOU CAN *GO TO THE BLOW!*
‹GO ON, LET 'EM IN.›
‹ARE YOU INSANE?›
‹HEY, MAN-- YOU KNOW HOW MUCH 30 SECONDS ON THE GUY CHANNEL *COSTS?* OUR P.R. PEOPLE TELL ME YOU CAN'T BUY THIS KIND OF EXPOSURE.›
BOO-YAH GA GA GA GA GA AH HAH NYAH NYAH NYAH NYAH
THE GUY CHA
MEEP MEEP MEEP MEEP

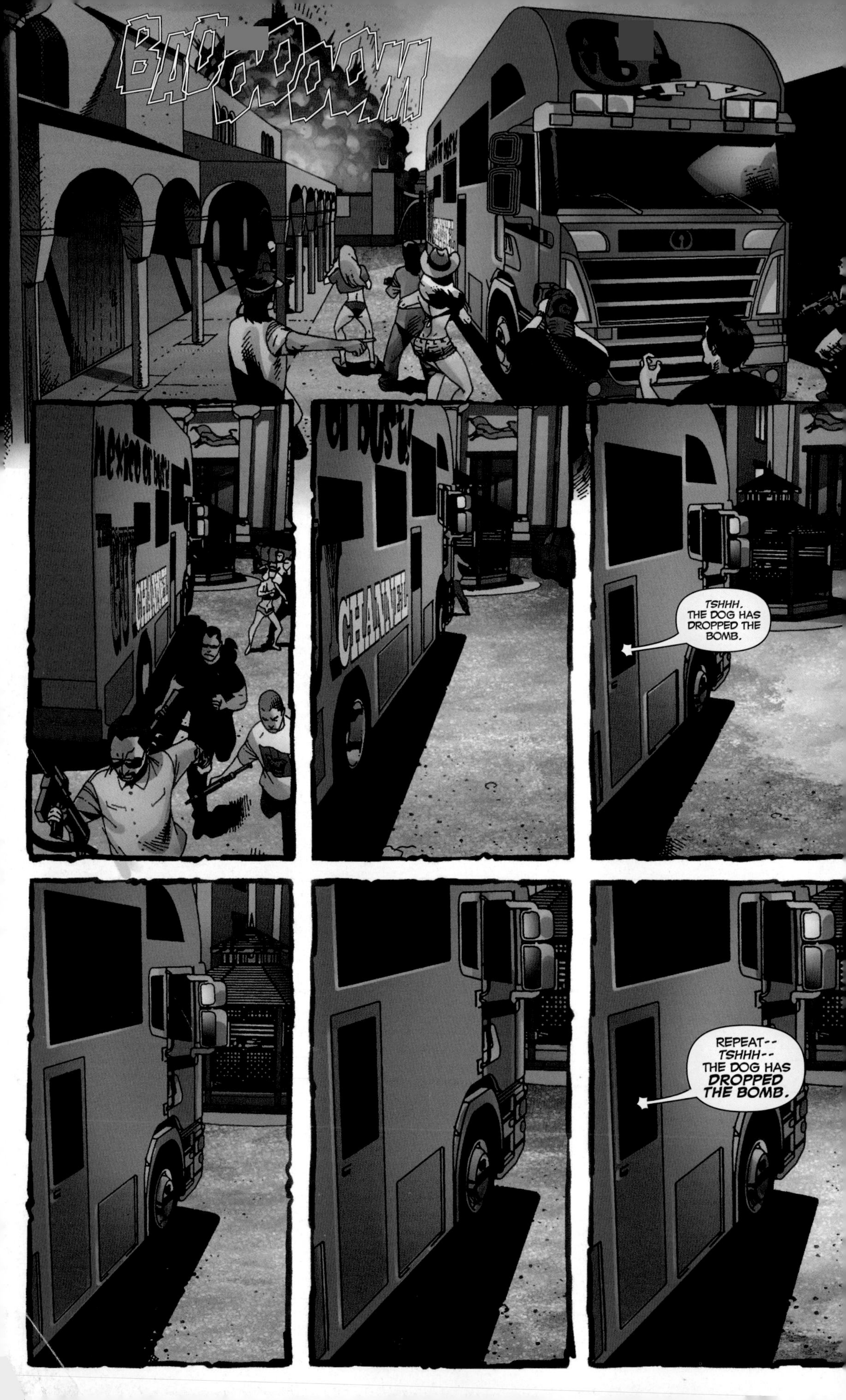
TSHHH. THE DOG HAS DROPPED THE BOMB.
REPEAT-- TSHHH-- THE DOG HAS DROPPED THE BOMB.

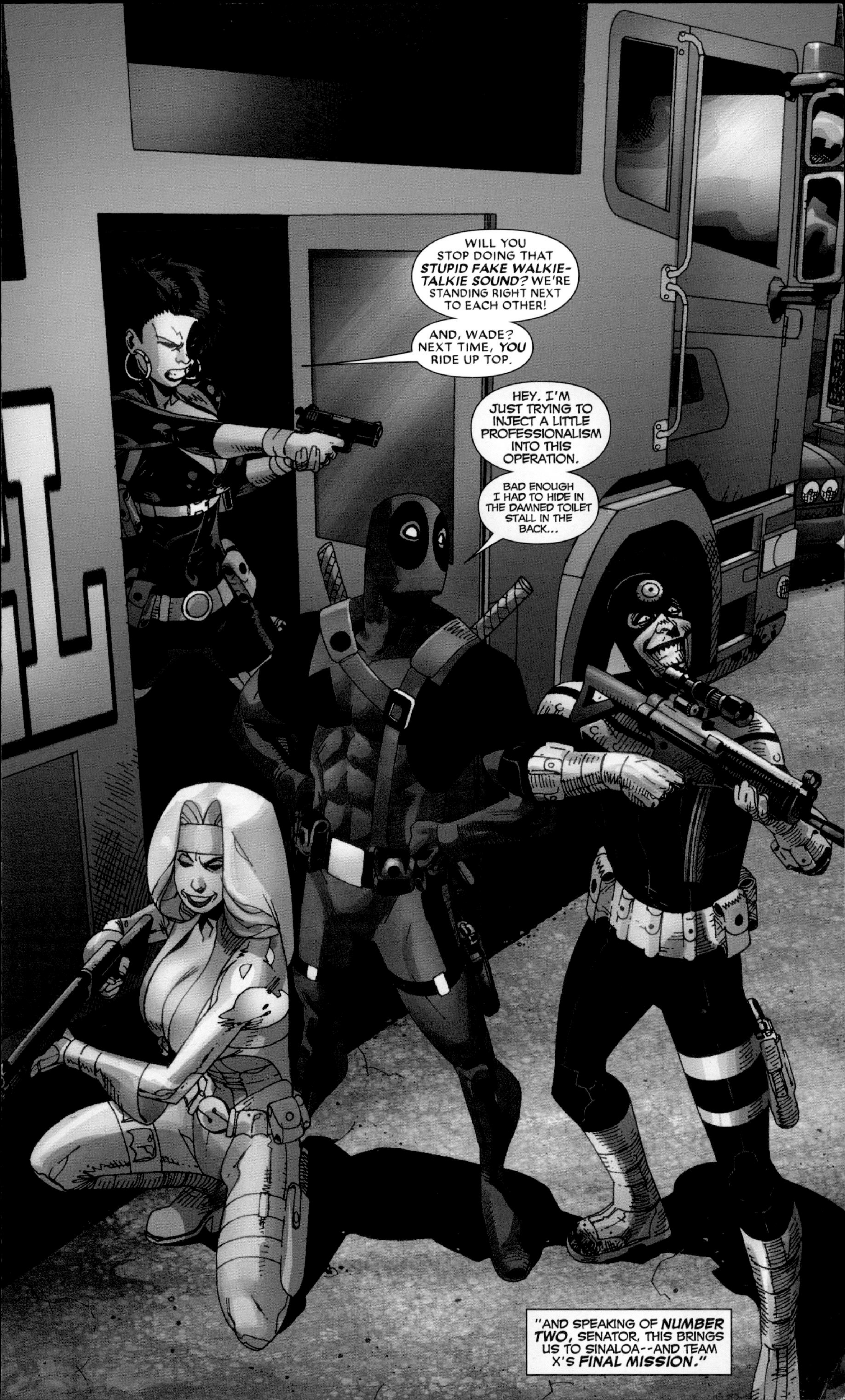
WILL YOU STOP DOING THAT STUPID FAKE WALKIE-TALKIE SOUND? WE'RE STANDING RIGHT NEXT TO EACH OTHER!
AND, WADE? NEXT TIME, YOU RIDE UP TOP.
HEY. I'M JUST TRYING TO INJECT A LITTLE PROFESSIONALISM INTO THIS OPERATION.
BAD ENOUGH I HAD TO HIDE IN THE DAMNED TOILET STALL IN THE BACK...
"AND SPEAKING OF NUMBER TWO, SENATOR, THIS BRINGS US TO SINALOA--AND TEAM X'S FINAL MISSION."

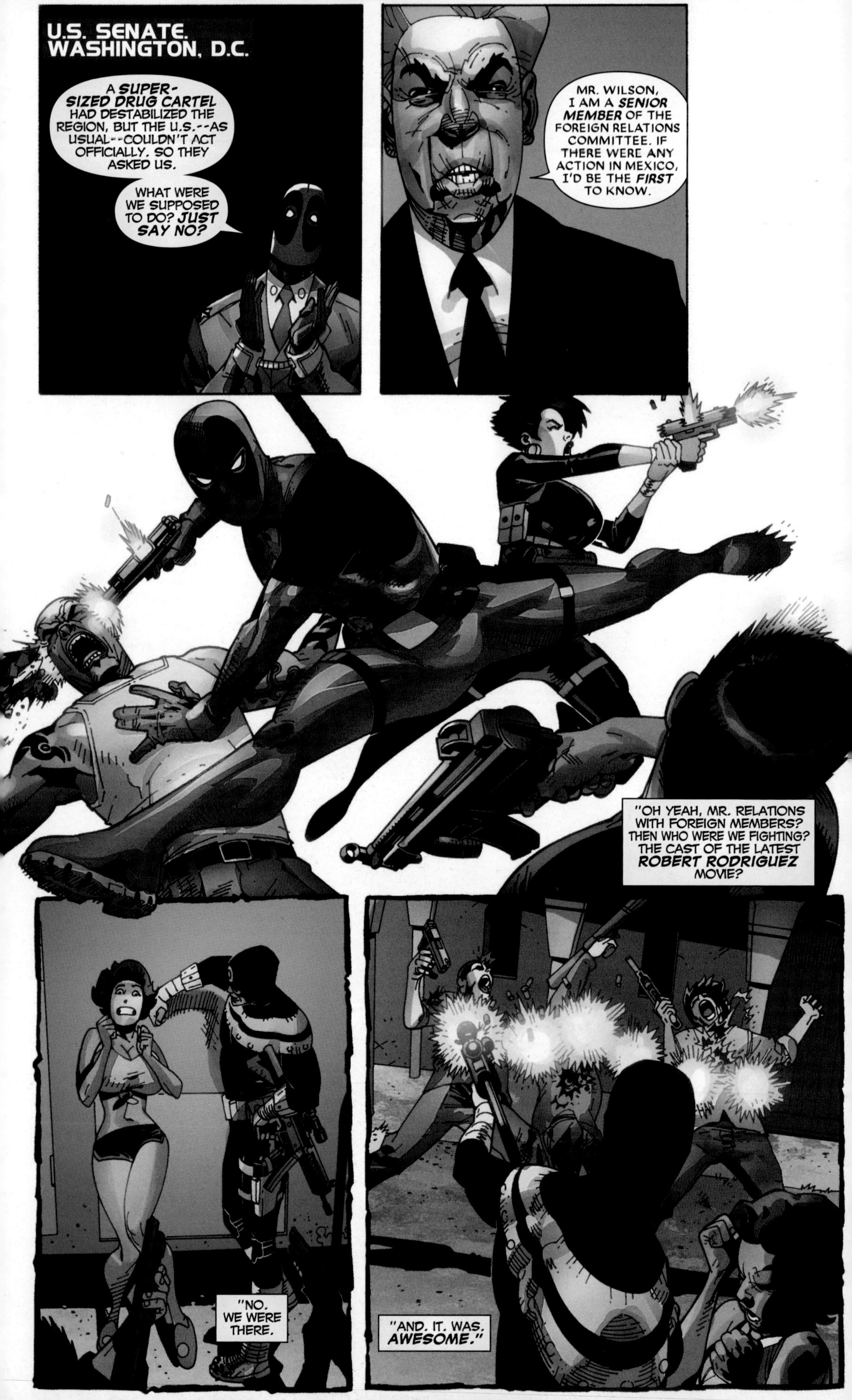
U.S. SENATE.
WASHINGTON, D.C.
A SUPER-SIZED DRUG CARTEL HAD DESTABILIZED THE REGION, BUT THE U.S.--AS USUAL--COULDN'T ACT OFFICIALLY. SO THEY ASKED US.
WHAT WERE WE SUPPOSED TO DO? JUST SAY NO?
MR. WILSON, I AM A SENIOR MEMBER OF THE FOREIGN RELATIONS COMMITTEE. IF THERE WERE ANY ACTION IN MEXICO, I'D BE THE FIRST TO KNOW.
"OH YEAH, MR. RELATIONS WITH FOREIGN MEMBERS? THEN WHO WERE WE FIGHTING? THE CAST OF THE LATEST ROBERT RODRIGUEZ MOVIE?
"NO. WE WERE THERE.
"AND. IT. WAS. AWESOME."

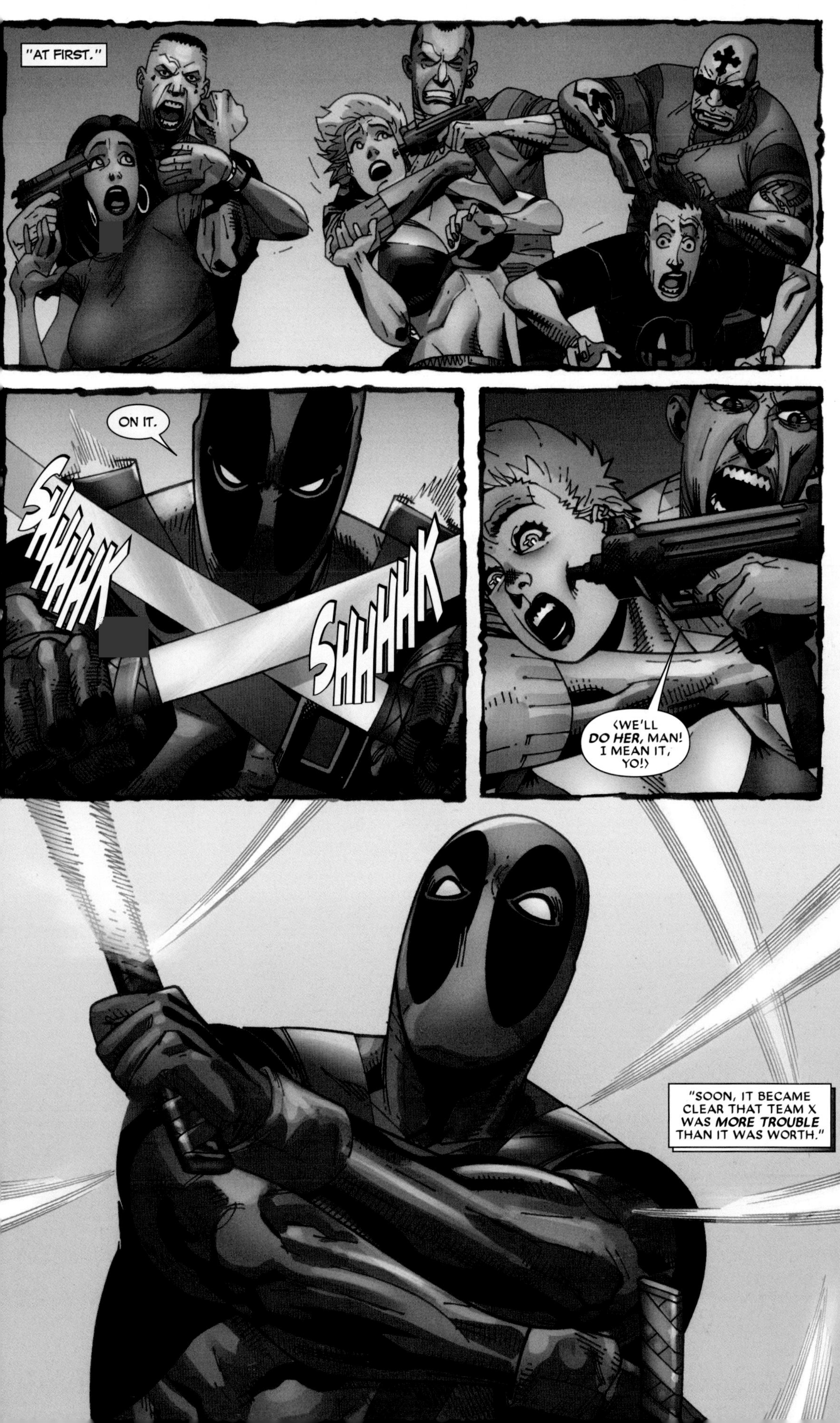
"AT FIRST."
ON IT.
SHHHHK
SHHHHK
‹WE'LL DO HER, MAN! I MEAN IT, YO!›
"SOON, IT BECAME CLEAR THAT TEAM X WAS MORE TROUBLE THAN IT WAS WORTH."

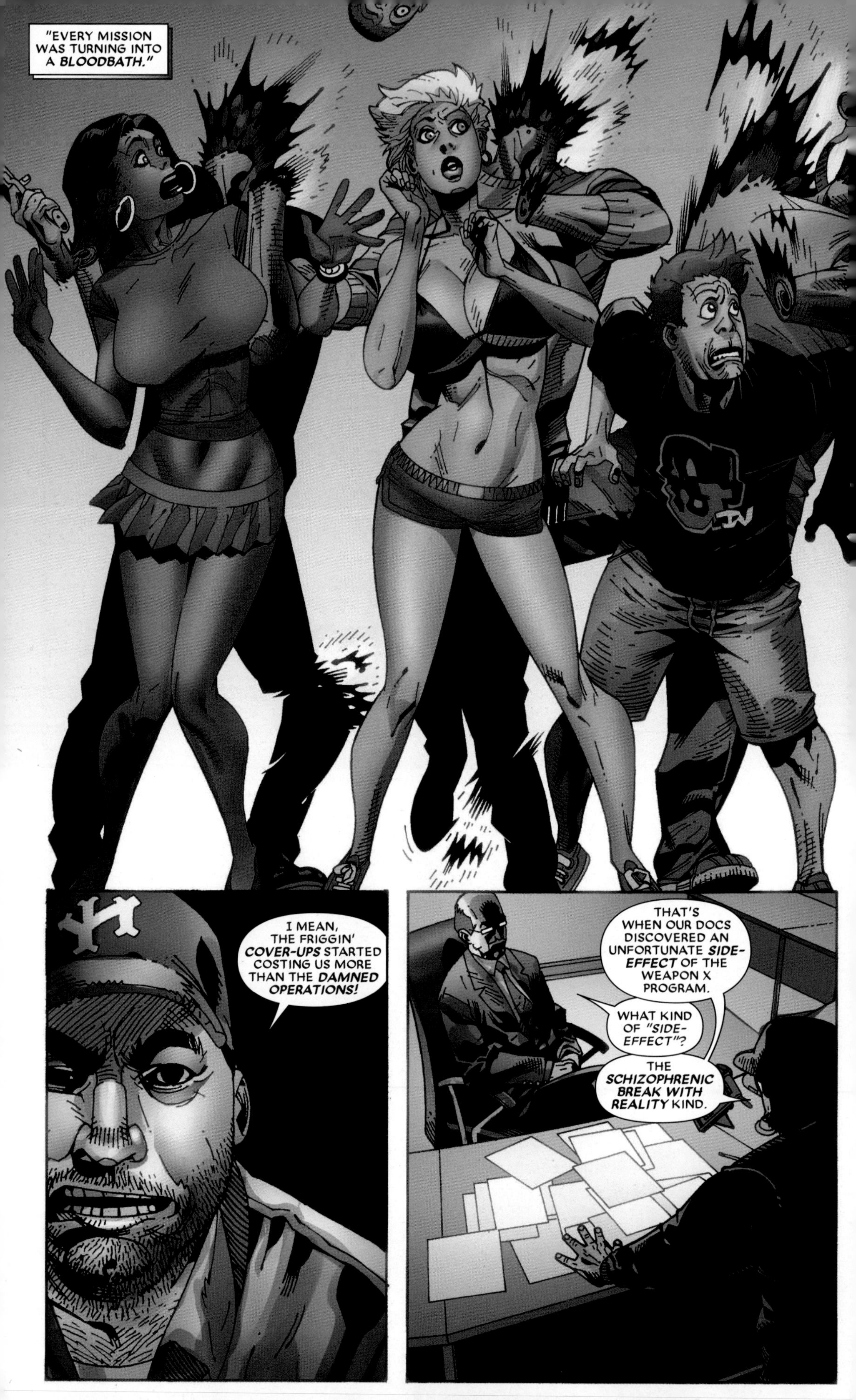
"EVERY MISSION WAS TURNING INTO A BLOODBATH."
I MEAN, THE FRIGGIN' COVER-UPS STARTED COSTING US MORE THAN THE DAMNED OPERATIONS!
THAT'S WHEN OUR DOCS DISCOVERED AN UNFORTUNATE SIDE-EFFECT OF THE WEAPON X PROGRAM.
WHAT KIND OF "SIDE-EFFECT"?
THE SCHIZOPHRENIC BREAK WITH REALITY KIND.

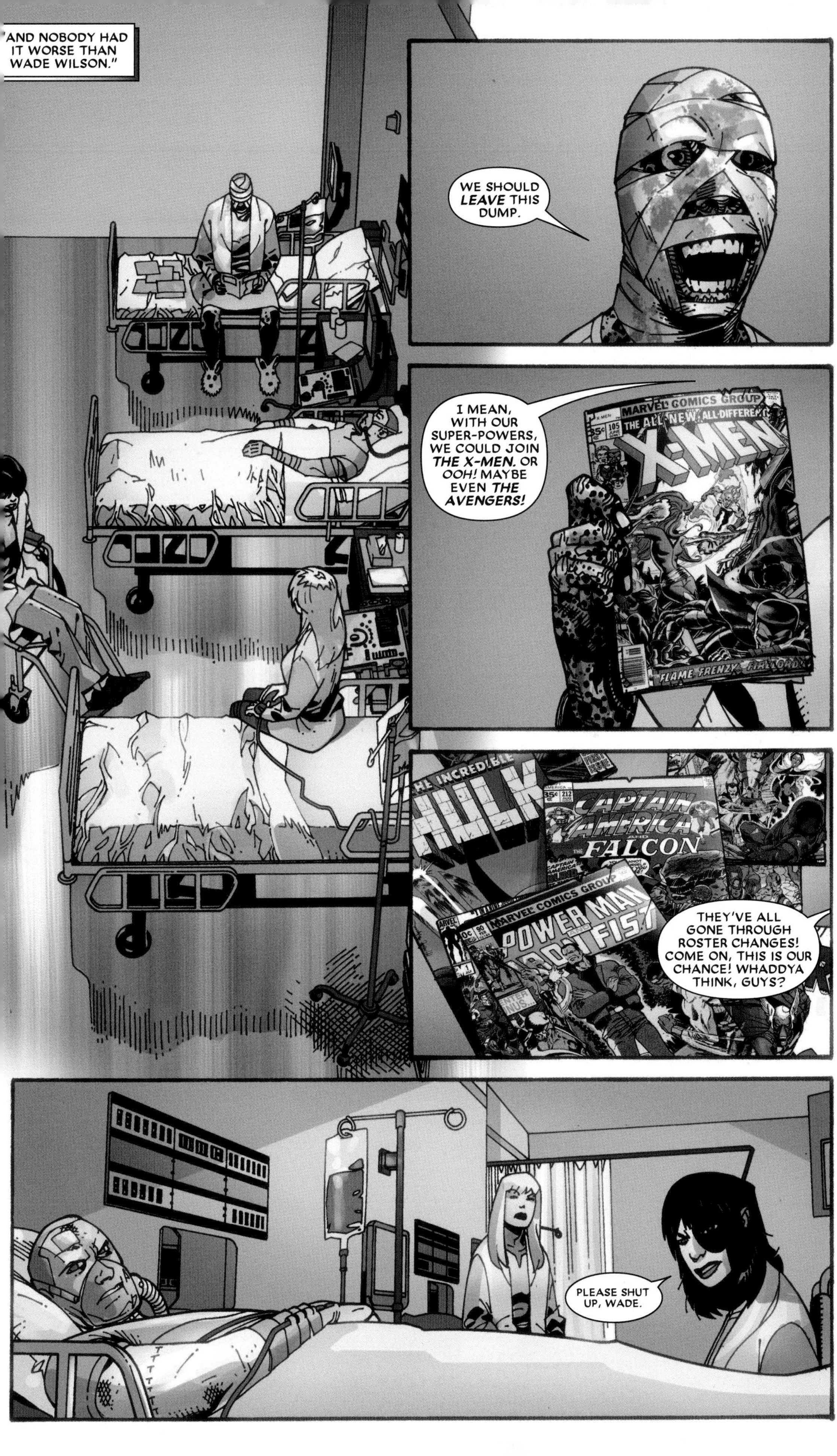

"AND NOBODY HAD IT WORSE THAN WADE WILSON."
WE SHOULD *LEAVE* THIS DUMP.
I MEAN, WITH OUR SUPER-POWERS, WE COULD JOIN *THE X-MEN.* OR *OOH!* MAYBE EVEN *THE AVENGERS!*
MARVEL COMICS GROUP
X-MEN
THE INCREDIBLE HULK
CAPTAIN AMERICA AND THE FALCON
POWER MAN
THEY'VE ALL GONE THROUGH ROSTER CHANGES! COME ON, THIS IS OUR CHANCE! WHADDYA THINK, GUYS?
PLEASE SHUT UP, WADE.

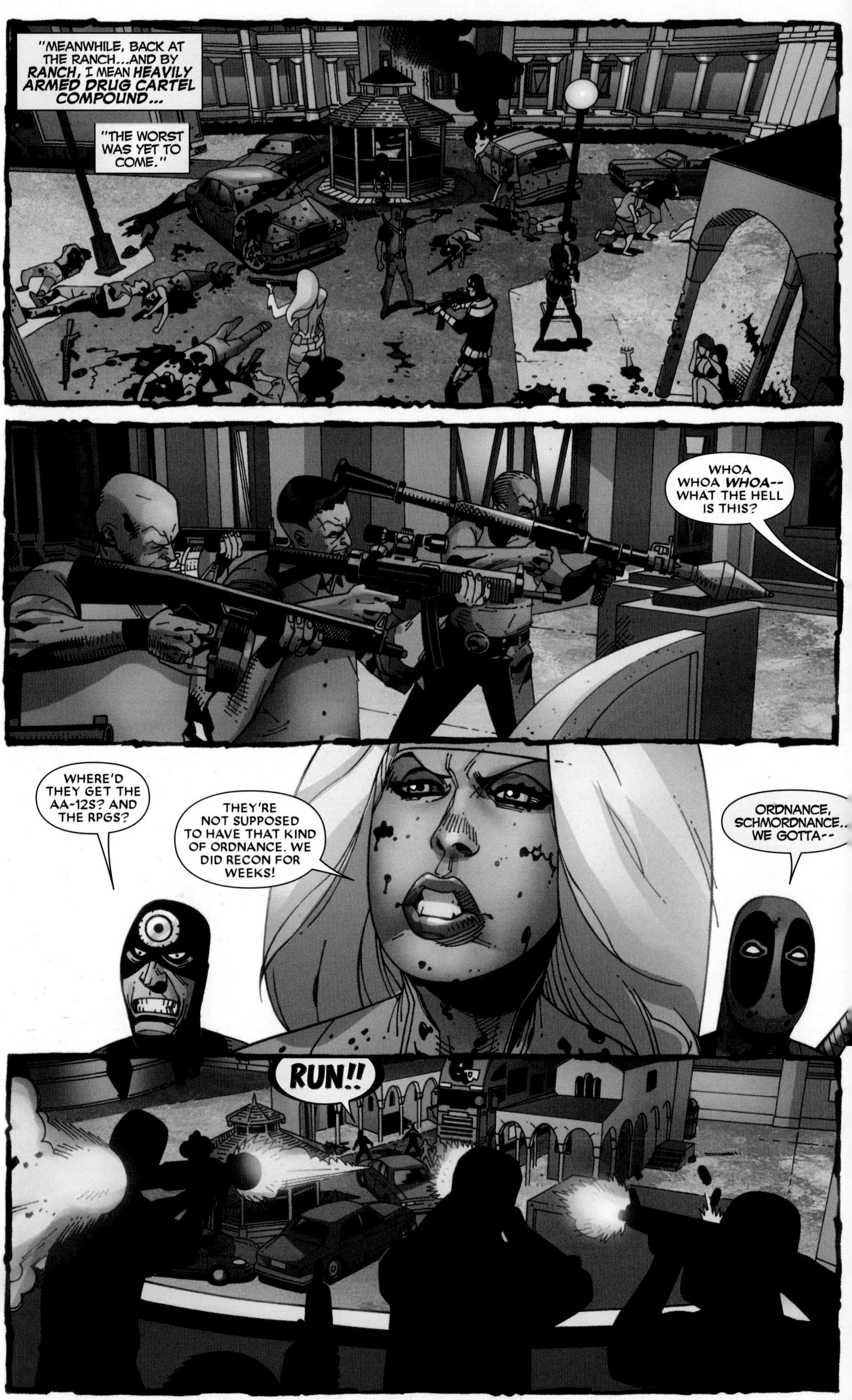
"MEANWHILE, BACK AT THE RANCH...AND BY RANCH, I MEAN HEAVILY ARMED DRUG CARTEL COMPOUND...
"THE WORST WAS YET TO COME."
WHOA WHOA WHOA-- WHAT THE HELL IS THIS?
WHERE'D THEY GET THE AA-12S? AND THE RPGS?
THEY'RE NOT SUPPOSED TO HAVE THAT KIND OF ORDNANCE. WE DID RECON FOR WEEKS!
ORDNANCE, SCHMORDNANCE... WE GOTTA--
RUN!!

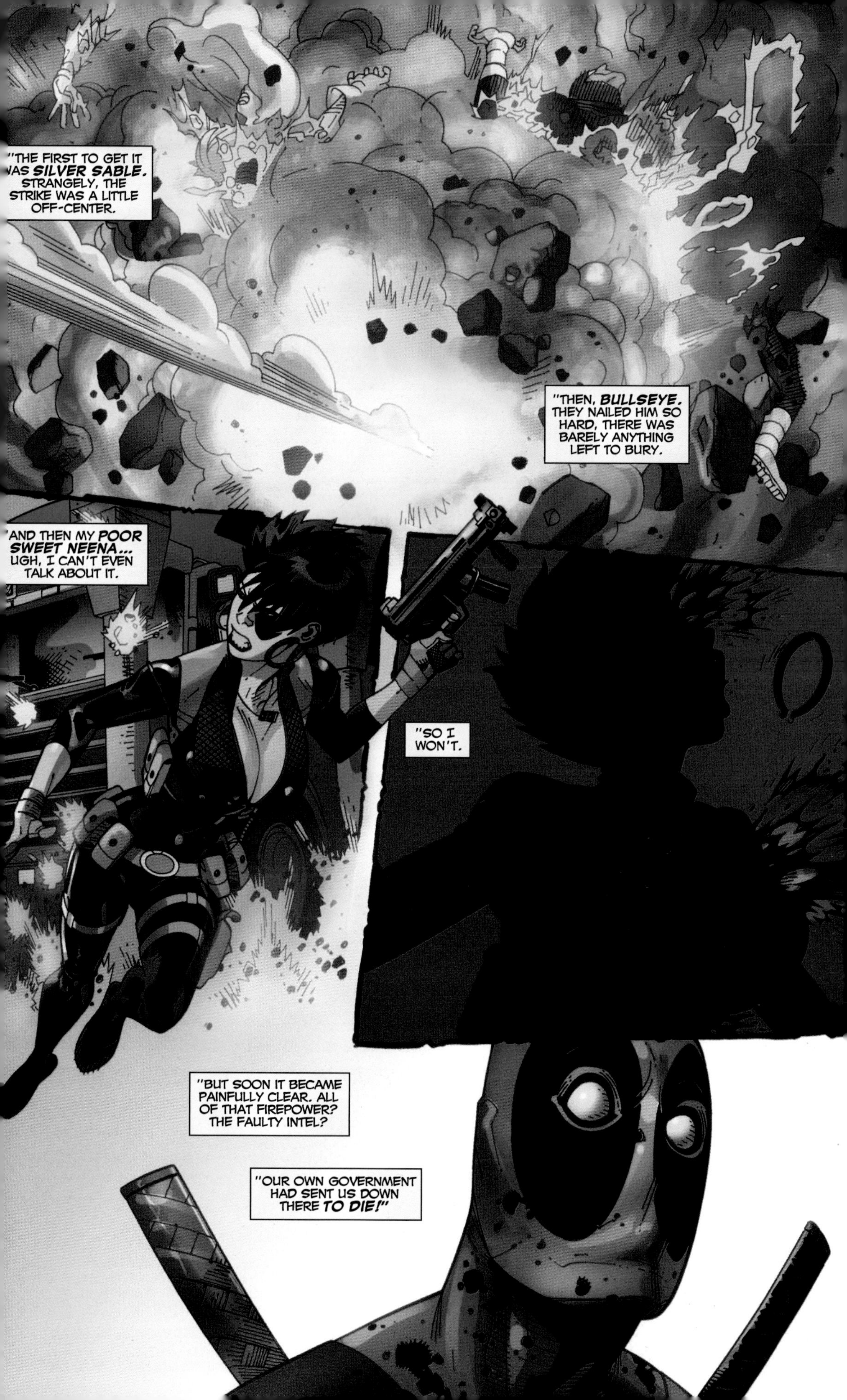
"THE FIRST TO GET IT WAS SILVER SABLE. STRANGELY, THE STRIKE WAS A LITTLE OFF-CENTER.
"THEN, BULLSEYE. THEY NAILED HIM SO HARD, THERE WAS BARELY ANYTHING LEFT TO BURY.
"AND THEN MY POOR SWEET NEENA... UGH, I CAN'T EVEN TALK ABOUT IT.
"SO I WON'T.
"BUT SOON IT BECAME PAINFULLY CLEAR. ALL OF THAT FIREPOWER? THE FAULTY INTEL?
"OUR OWN GOVERNMENT HAD SENT US DOWN THERE TO DIE!"

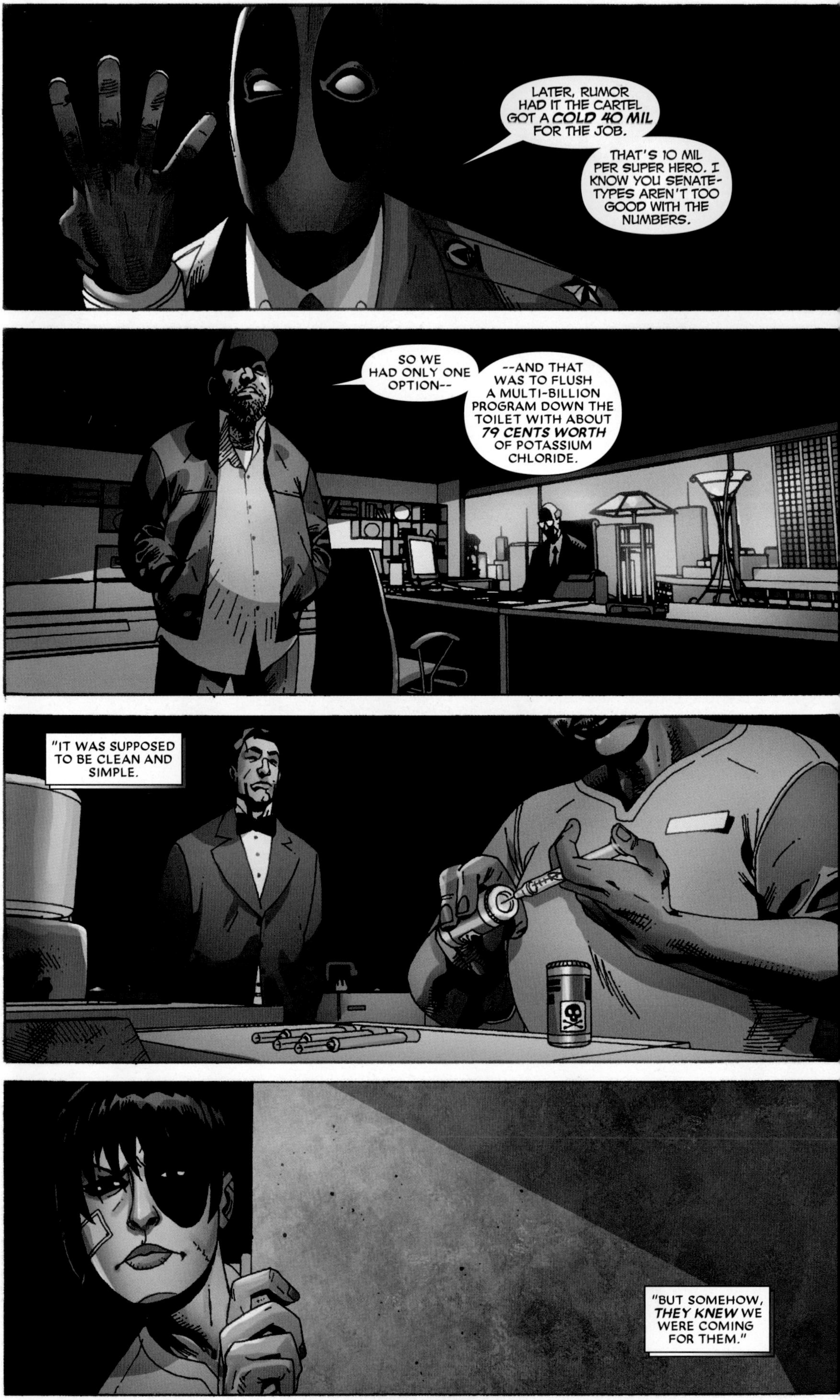

LATER, RUMOR HAD IT THE CARTEL GOT A COLD 40 MIL FOR THE JOB.
THAT'S 10 MIL PER SUPER HERO. I KNOW YOU SENATE-TYPES AREN'T TOO GOOD WITH THE NUMBERS.
SO WE HAD ONLY ONE OPTION--
--AND THAT WAS TO FLUSH A MULTI-BILLION PROGRAM DOWN THE TOILET WITH ABOUT 79 CENTS WORTH OF POTASSIUM CHLORIDE.
"IT WAS SUPPOSED TO BE CLEAN AND SIMPLE.
"BUT SOMEHOW, THEY KNEW WE WERE COMING FOR THEM."

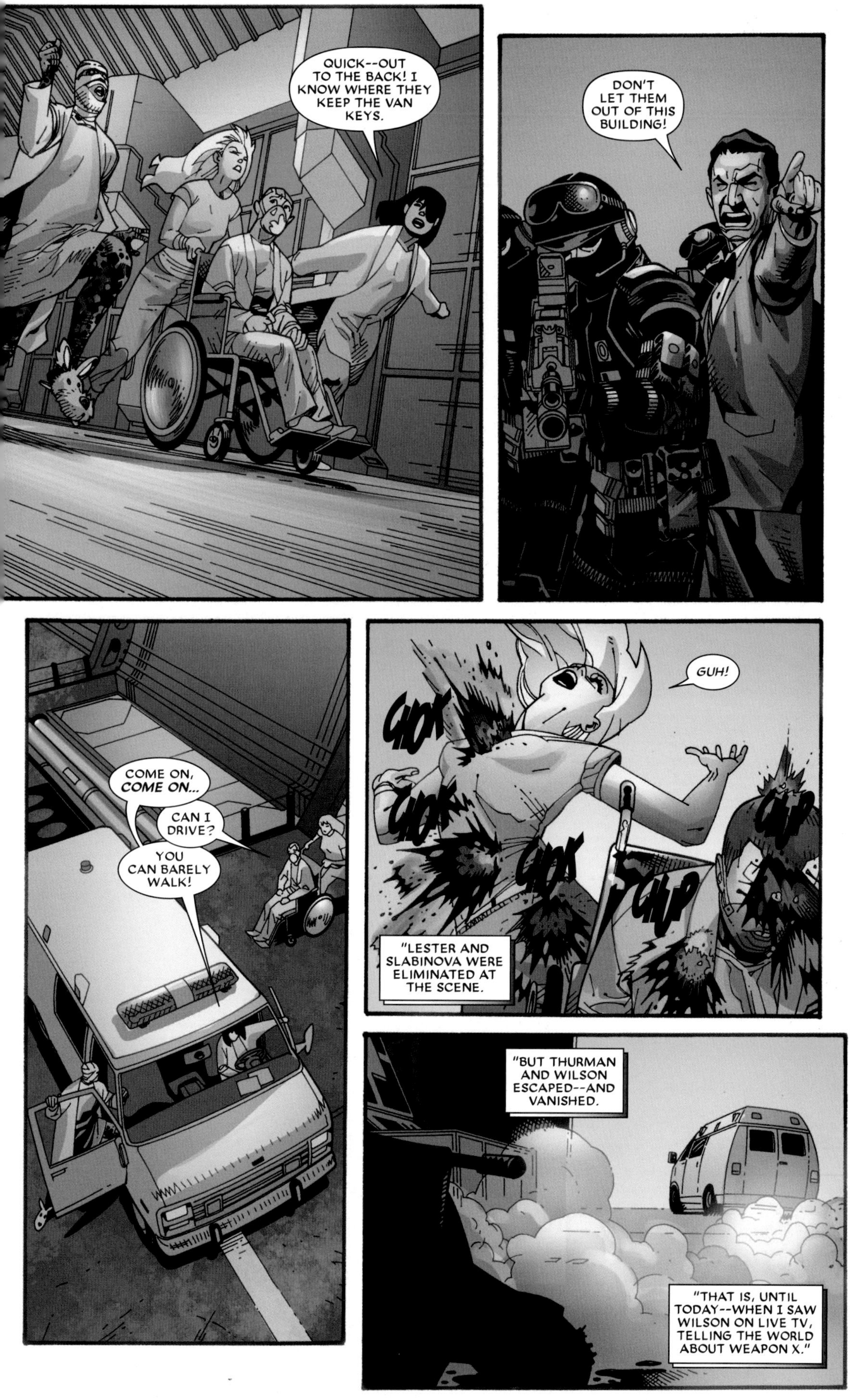
QUICK--OUT TO THE BACK! I KNOW WHERE THEY KEEP THE VAN KEYS.
DON'T LET THEM OUT OF THIS BUILDING!
COME ON, *COME ON...*
CAN I DRIVE?
YOU CAN BARELY WALK!
GUH!
"LESTER AND SLABINOVA WERE ELIMINATED AT THE SCENE.
"BUT THURMAN AND WILSON ESCAPED--AND VANISHED.
"THAT IS, UNTIL TODAY--WHEN I SAW WILSON ON LIVE TV, TELLING THE WORLD ABOUT WEAPON X."

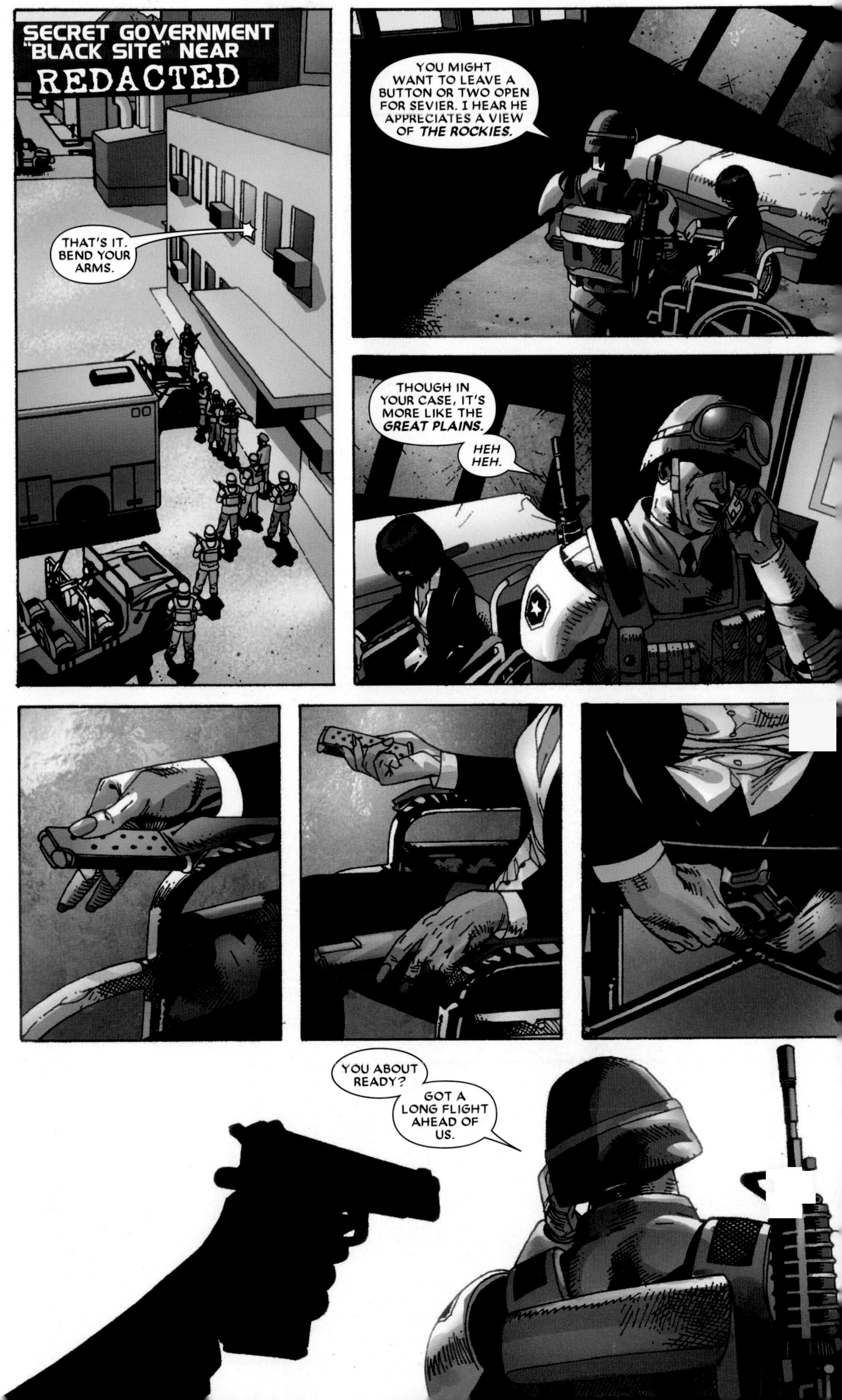
SECRET GOVERNMENT "BLACK SITE" NEAR REDACTED
THAT'S IT. BEND YOUR ARMS.
YOU MIGHT WANT TO LEAVE A BUTTON OR TWO OPEN FOR SEVIER. I HEAR HE APPRECIATES A VIEW OF THE ROCKIES.
THOUGH IN YOUR CASE, IT'S MORE LIKE THE GREAT PLAINS.
HEH HEH.
YOU ABOUT READY?
GOT A LONG FLIGHT AHEAD OF US.

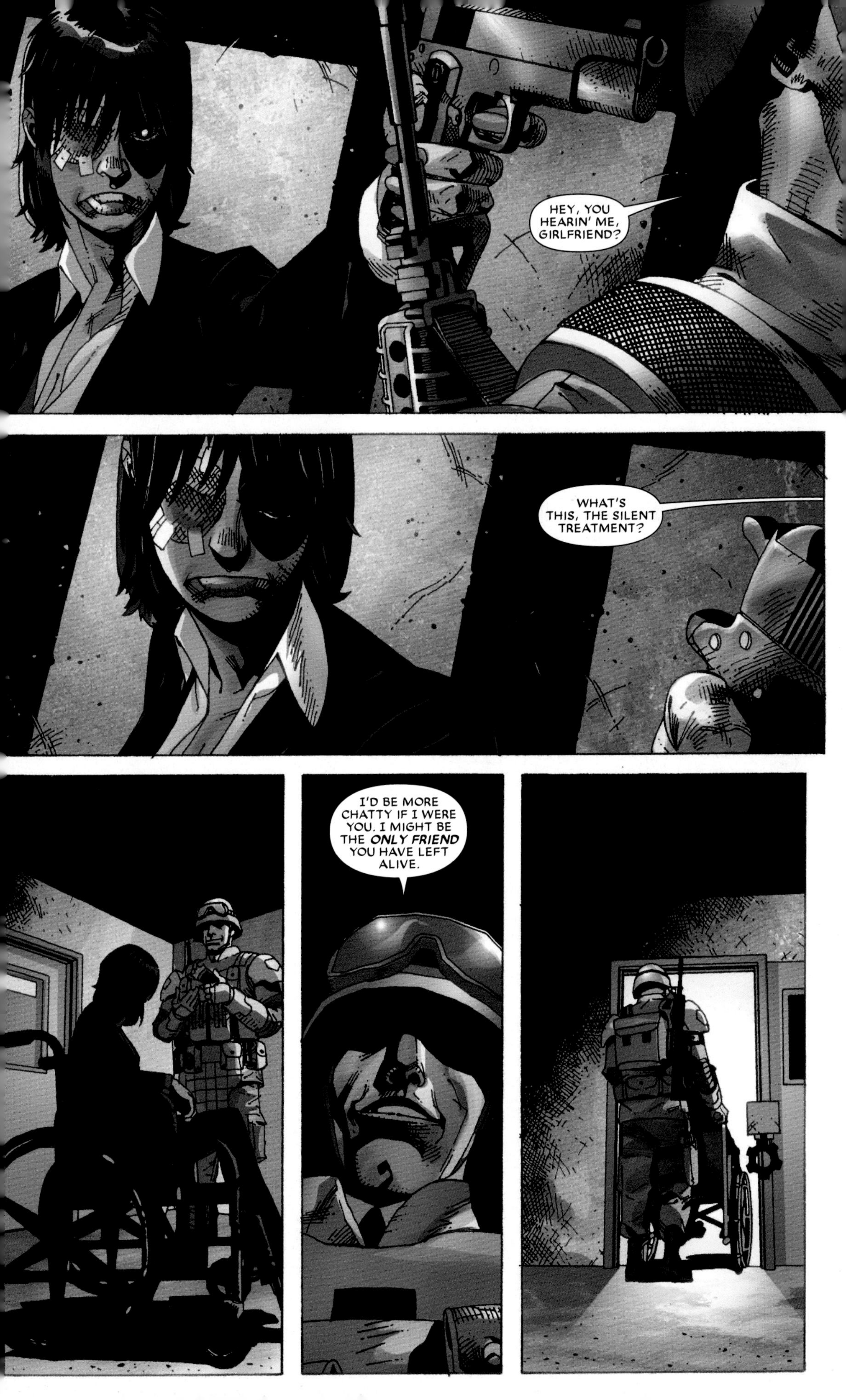
HEY, YOU HEARIN' ME, GIRLFRIEND?
WHAT'S THIS, THE SILENT TREATMENT?
I'D BE MORE CHATTY IF I WERE YOU. I MIGHT BE THE *ONLY FRIEND* YOU HAVE LEFT ALIVE.

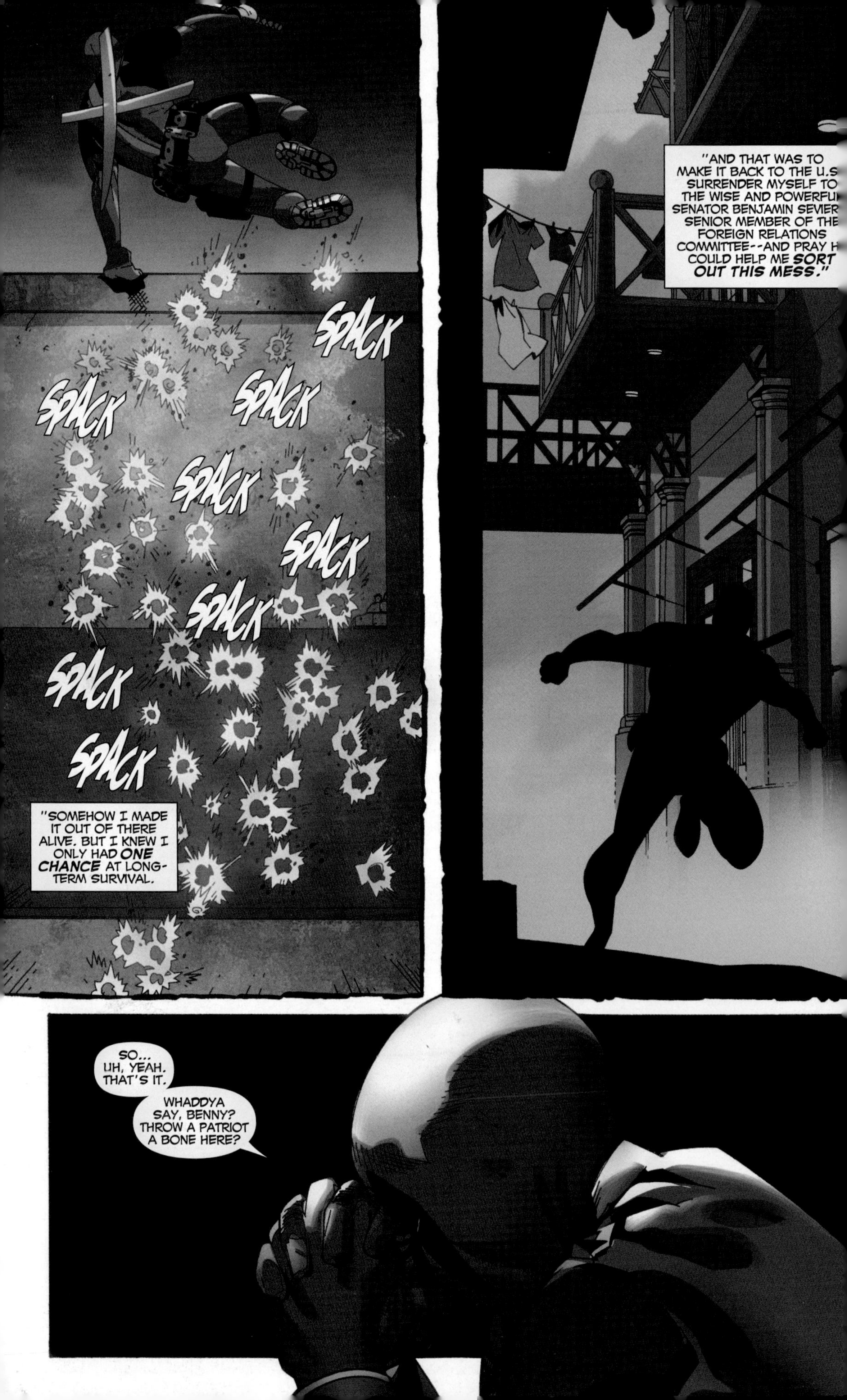
SPACK
SPACK
SPACK
SPACK
SPACK
SPACK
SPACK
SPACK
"SOMEHOW I MADE IT OUT OF THERE ALIVE. BUT I KNEW I ONLY HAD ONE CHANCE AT LONG-TERM SURVIVAL.
"AND THAT WAS TO MAKE IT BACK TO THE U.S SURRENDER MYSELF TO THE WISE AND POWERFU SENATOR BENJAMIN SEVIER SENIOR MEMBER OF THE FOREIGN RELATIONS COMMITTEE--AND PRAY H COULD HELP ME SORT OUT THIS MESS."
SO... UH, YEAH. THAT'S IT.
WHADDYA SAY, BENNY? THROW A PATRIOT A BONE HERE?

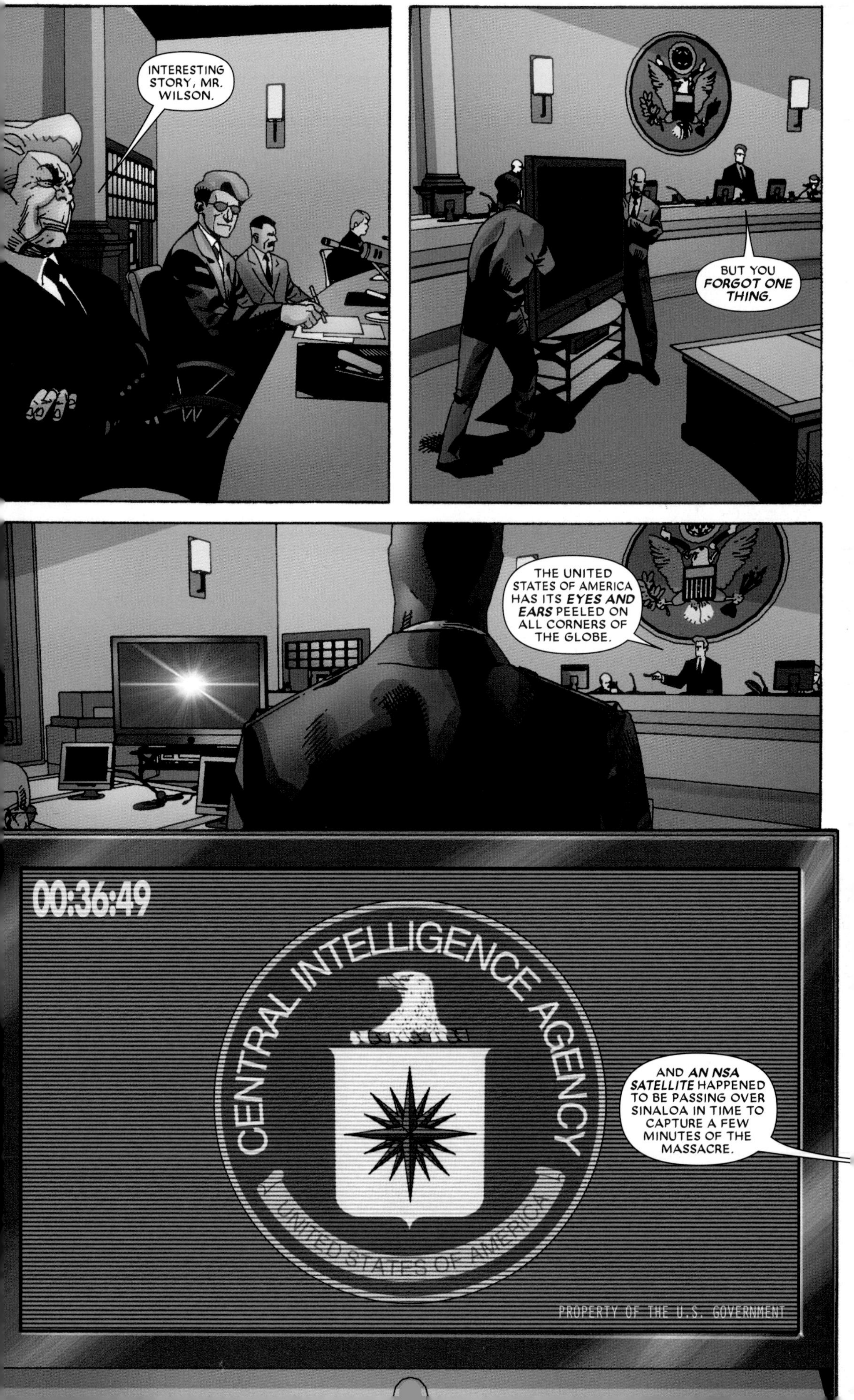
INTERESTING STORY, MR. WILSON.
BUT YOU *FORGOT ONE THING.*
THE UNITED STATES OF AMERICA HAS ITS *EYES AND EARS* PEELED ON ALL CORNERS OF THE GLOBE.
00:36:49
CENTRAL INTELLIGENCE AGENCY
UNITED STATES OF AMERICA
PROPERTY OF THE U.S. GOVERNMENT
AND *AN NSA SATELLITE* HAPPENED TO BE PASSING OVER SINALOA IN TIME TO CAPTURE A FEW MINUTES OF THE MASSACRE.

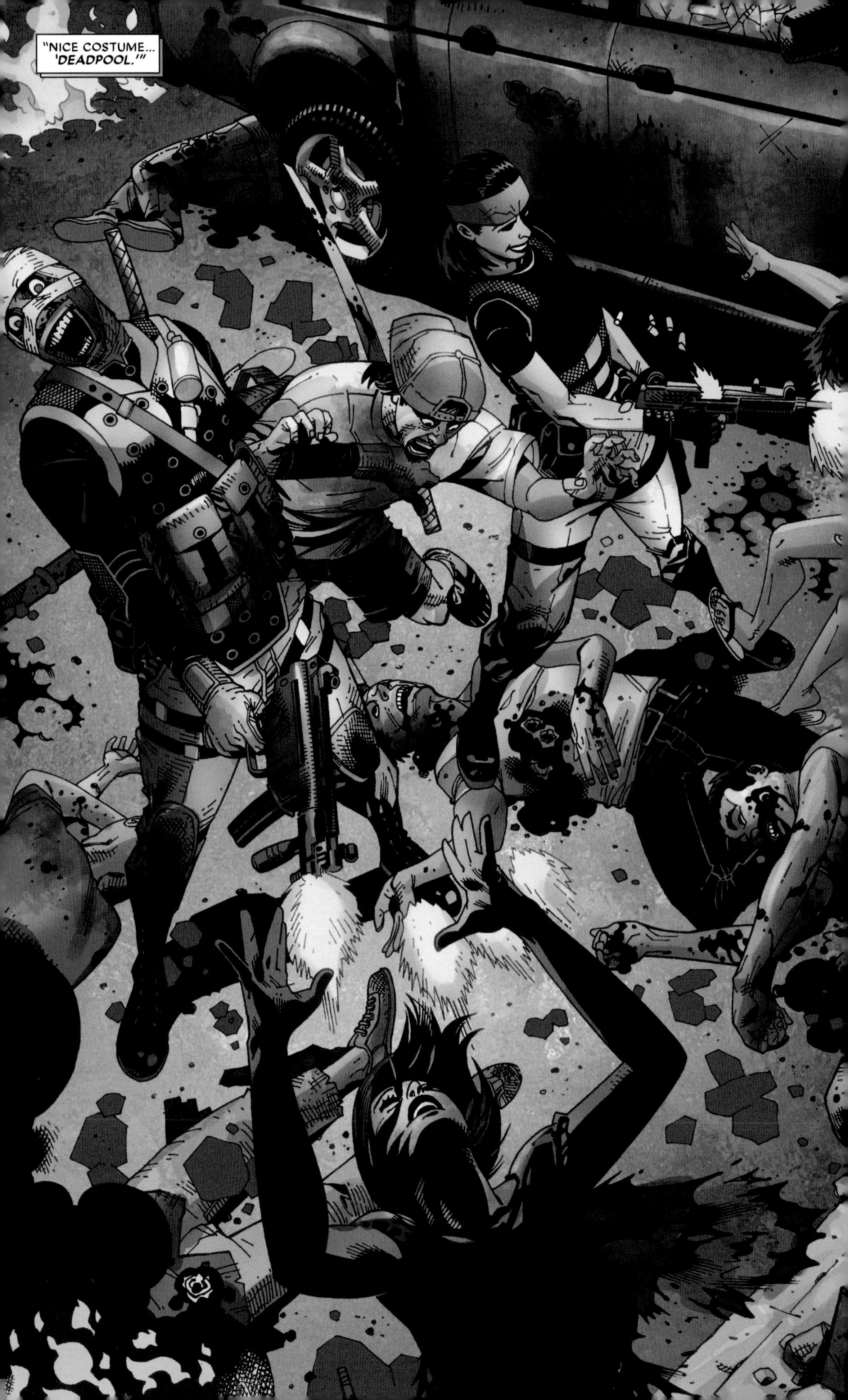
"NICE COSTUME... 'DEADPOOL.'"

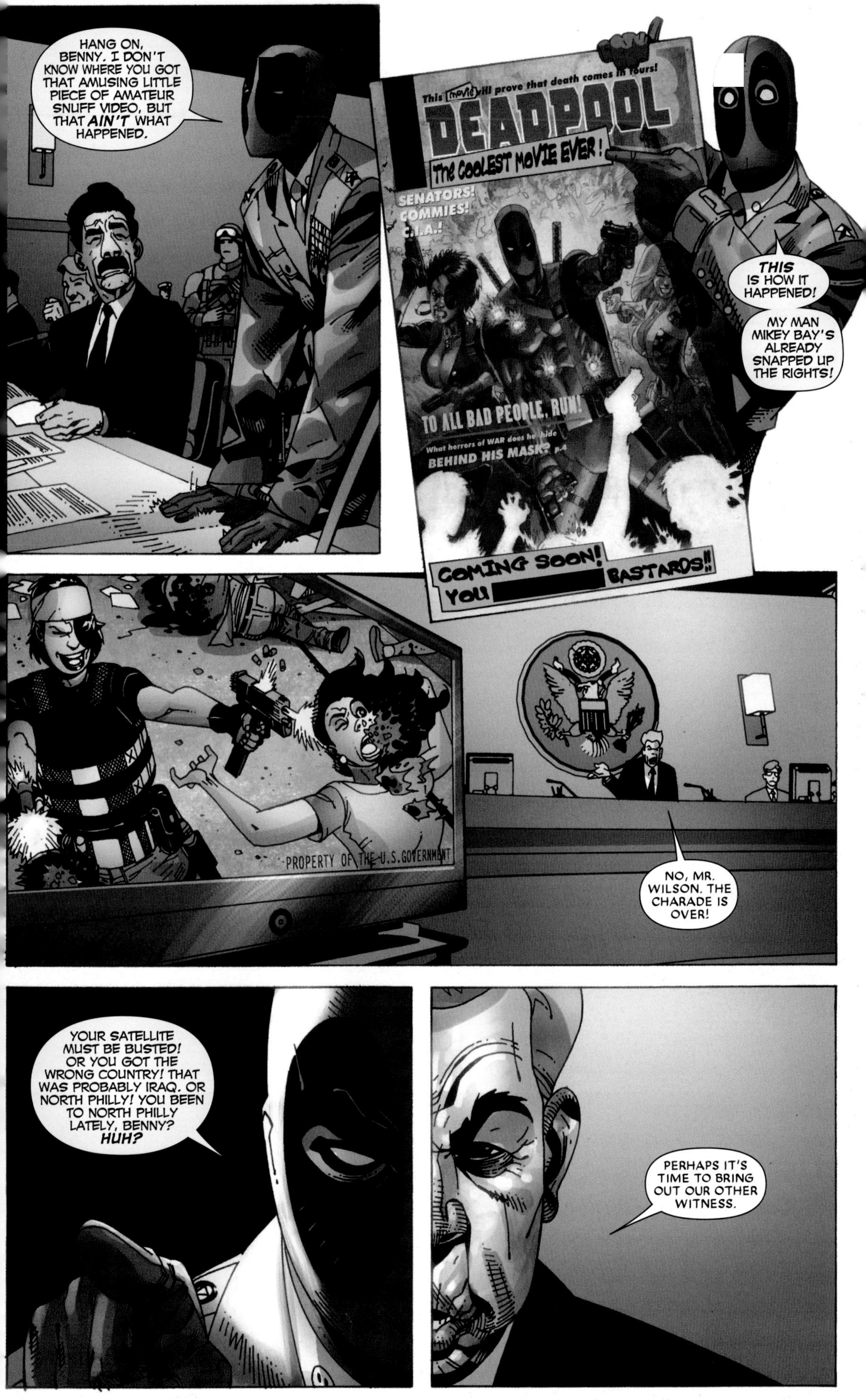
HANG ON, BENNY. I DON'T KNOW WHERE YOU GOT THAT AMUSING LITTLE PIECE OF AMATEUR SNUFF VIDEO, BUT THAT AIN'T WHAT HAPPENED.
This movie will prove that death comes in fours!
DEADPOOL
The COOLEST MOVIE EVER!
SENATORS! COMMIES! C.I.A.!
TO ALL BAD PEOPLE, RUN!
What horrors of WAR does he hide BEHIND HIS MASK? p.4
COMING SOON! YOU [redacted] BASTARDS!!
THIS IS HOW IT HAPPENED!
MY MAN MIKEY BAY'S ALREADY SNAPPED UP THE RIGHTS!
PROPERTY OF THE U.S. GOVERNMENT
NO, MR. WILSON. THE CHARADE IS OVER!
YOUR SATELLITE MUST BE BUSTED! OR YOU GOT THE WRONG COUNTRY! THAT WAS PROBABLY IRAQ. OR NORTH PHILLY! YOU BEEN TO NORTH PHILLY LATELY, BENNY? HUH?
PERHAPS IT'S TIME TO BRING OUT OUR OTHER WITNESS.

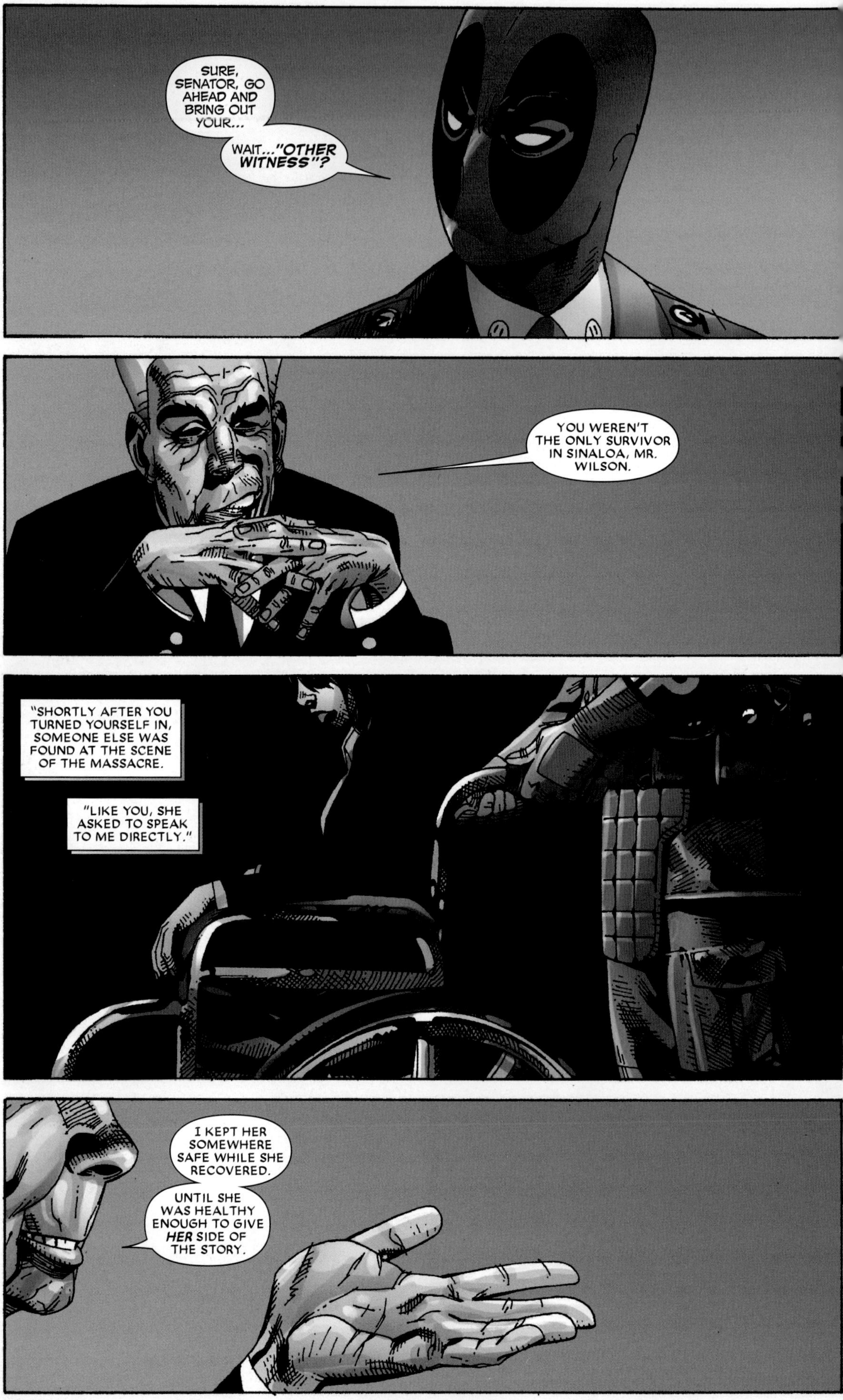
SURE, SENATOR, GO AHEAD AND BRING OUT YOUR...
WAIT..."OTHER WITNESS"?
YOU WEREN'T THE ONLY SURVIVOR IN SINALOA, MR. WILSON.
"SHORTLY AFTER YOU TURNED YOURSELF IN, SOMEONE ELSE WAS FOUND AT THE SCENE OF THE MASSACRE.
"LIKE YOU, SHE ASKED TO SPEAK TO ME DIRECTLY."
I KEPT HER SOMEWHERE SAFE WHILE SHE RECOVERED.
UNTIL SHE WAS HEALTHY ENOUGH TO GIVE HER SIDE OF THE STORY.

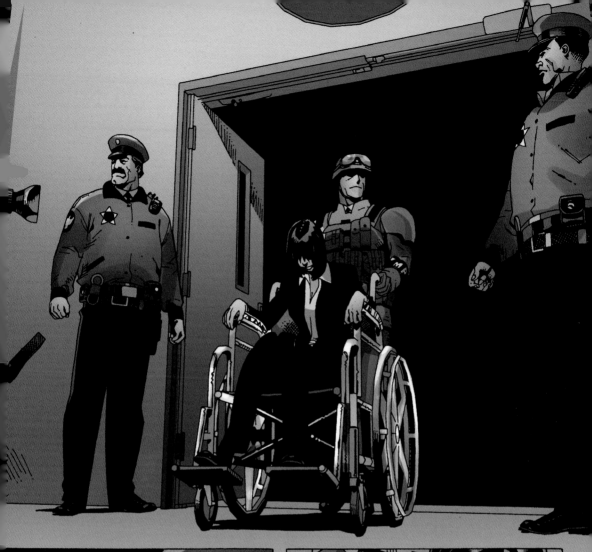

NEENA?

MY GOD...YOU'RE ALIVE.

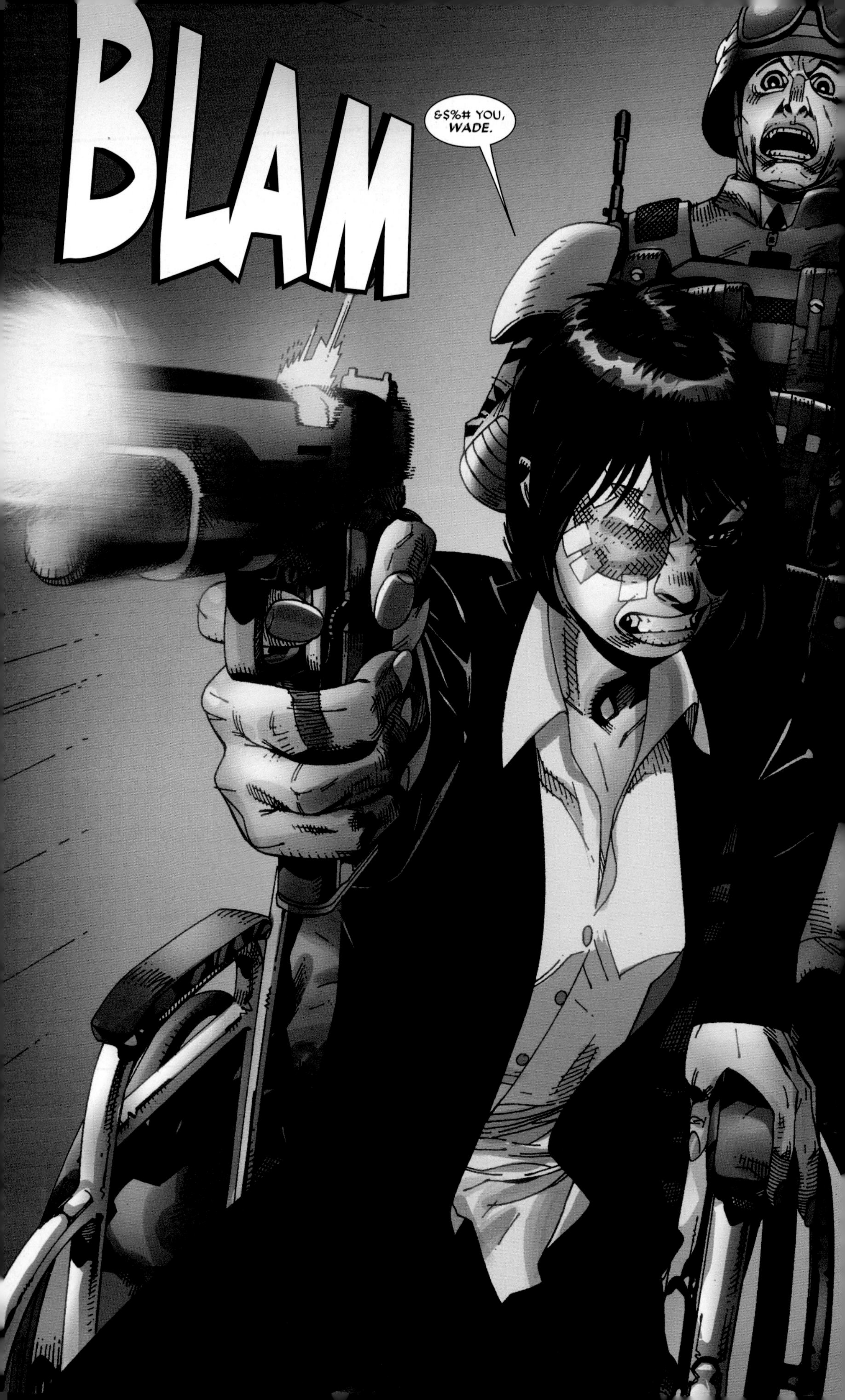
BLAM
&$%# YOU, WADE.

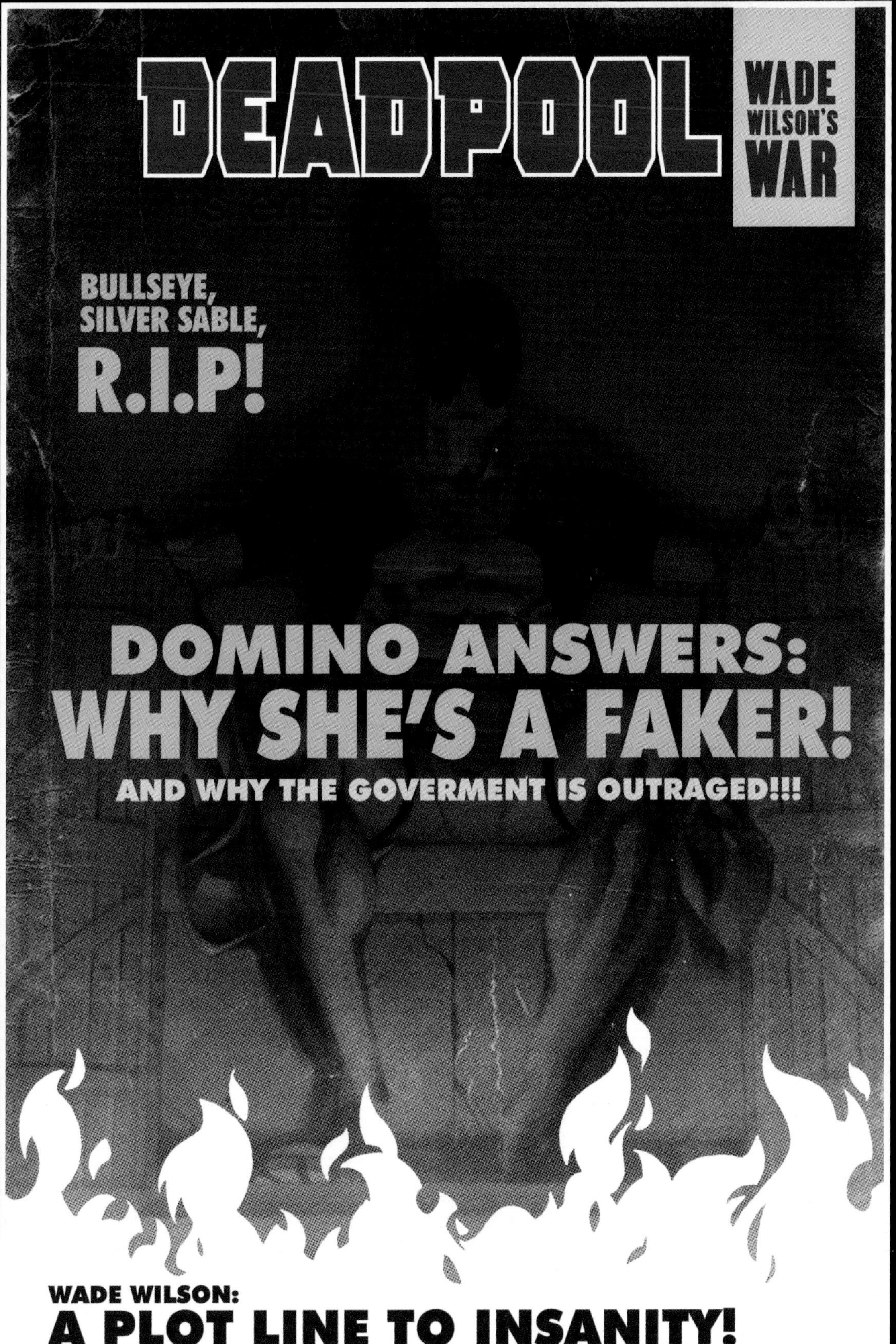
DEADPOOL
WADE WILSON'S WAR
BULLSEYE, SILVER SABLE, R.I.P!
DOMINO ANSWERS: WHY SHE'S A FAKER!
AND WHY THE GOVERMENT IS OUTRAGED!!!
WADE WILSON: A PLOT LINE TO INSANITY!

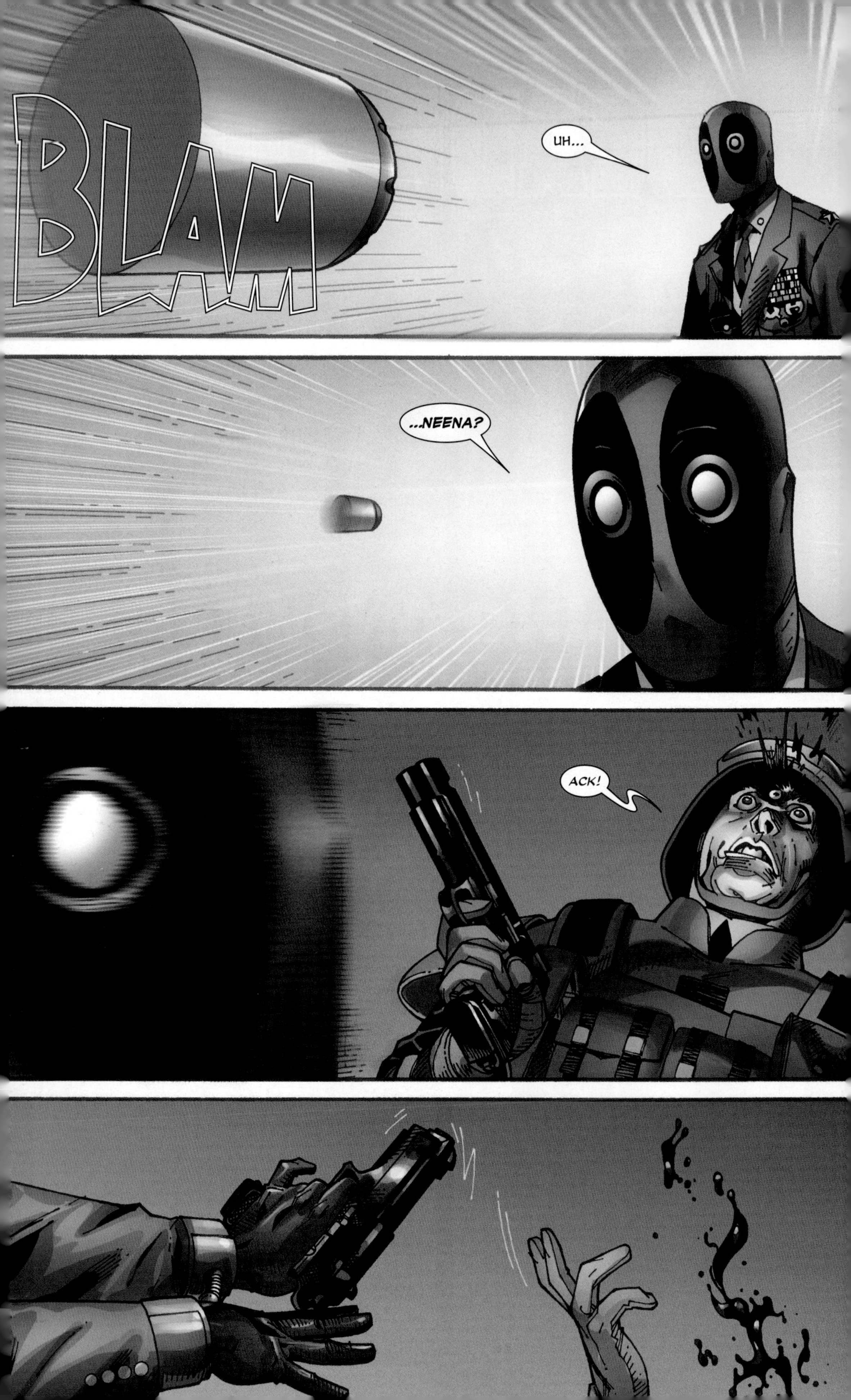
BLAM
UH...
...NEENA?
ACK!

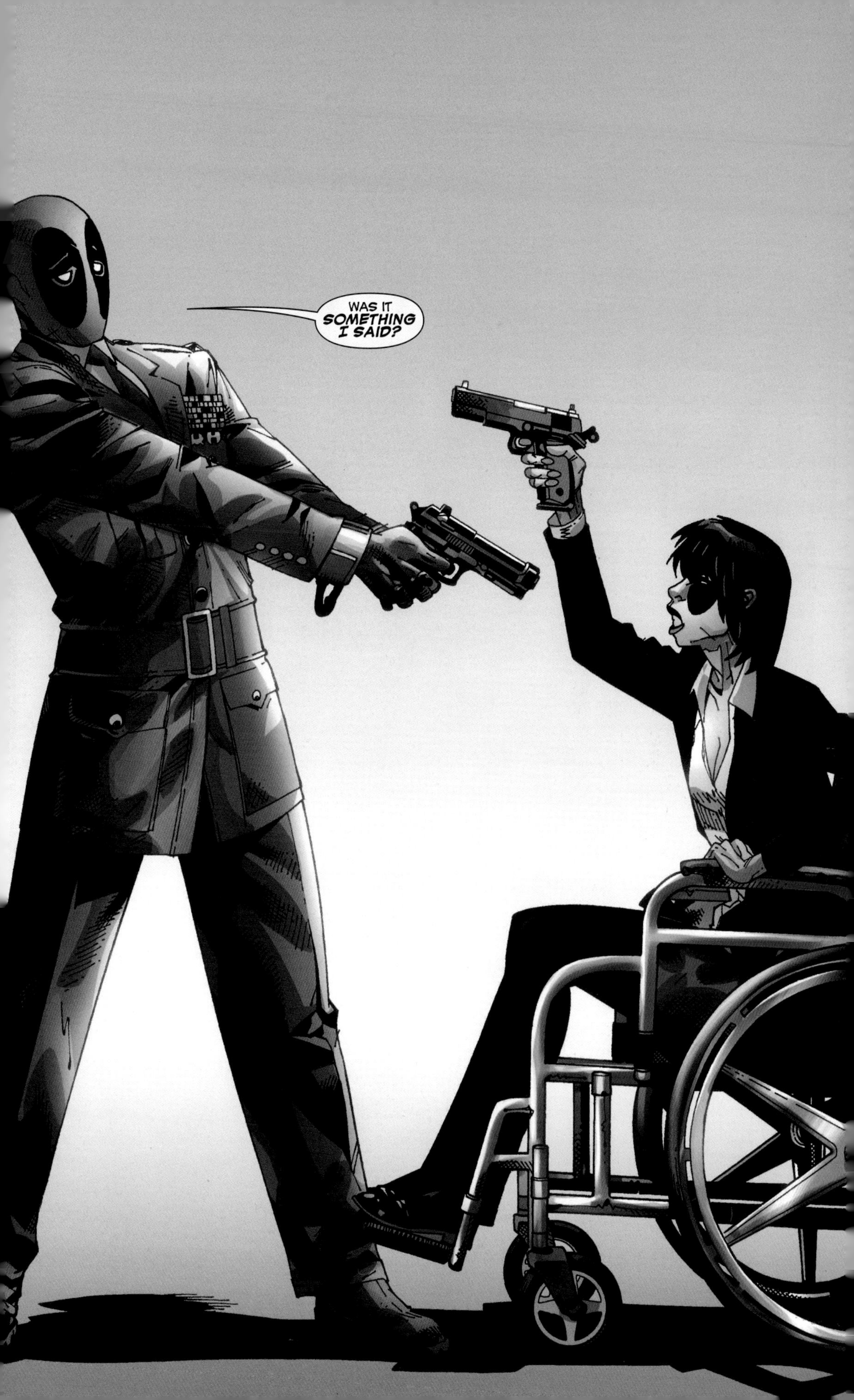
WAS IT SOMETHING I SAID?

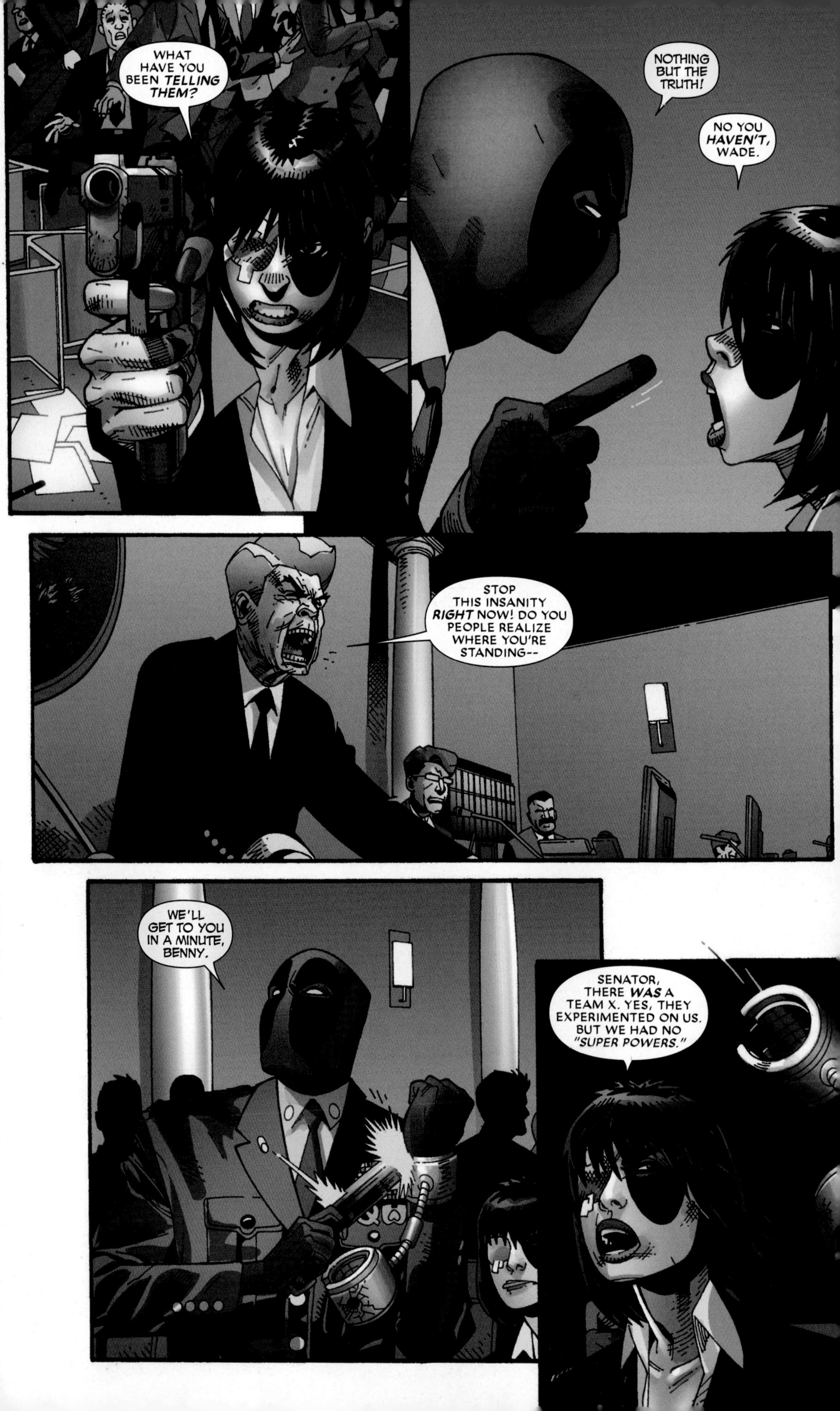
WHAT HAVE YOU BEEN TELLING THEM?
NOTHING BUT THE TRUTH!
NO YOU HAVEN'T, WADE.
STOP THIS INSANITY RIGHT NOW! DO YOU PEOPLE REALIZE WHERE YOU'RE STANDING--
WE'LL GET TO YOU IN A MINUTE, BENNY.
SENATOR, THERE WAS A TEAM X. YES, THEY EXPERIMENTED ON US. BUT WE HAD NO "SUPER POWERS."

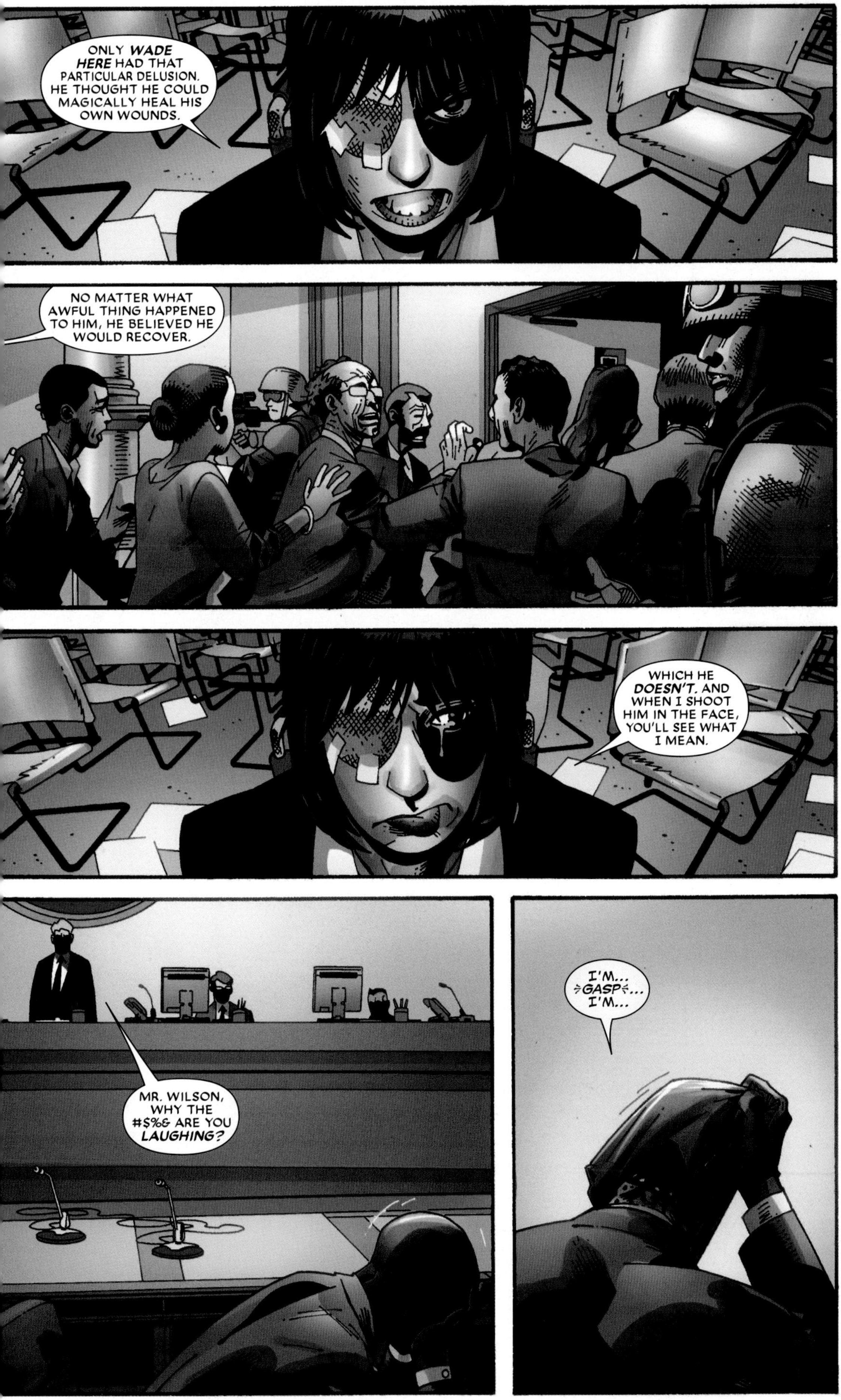
ONLY WADE HERE HAD THAT PARTICULAR DELUSION. HE THOUGHT HE COULD MAGICALLY HEAL HIS OWN WOUNDS.
NO MATTER WHAT AWFUL THING HAPPENED TO HIM, HE BELIEVED HE WOULD RECOVER.
WHICH HE DOESN'T. AND WHEN I SHOOT HIM IN THE FACE, YOU'LL SEE WHAT I MEAN.
MR. WILSON, WHY THE #$%& ARE YOU LAUGHING?
I'M... GASP... I'M...

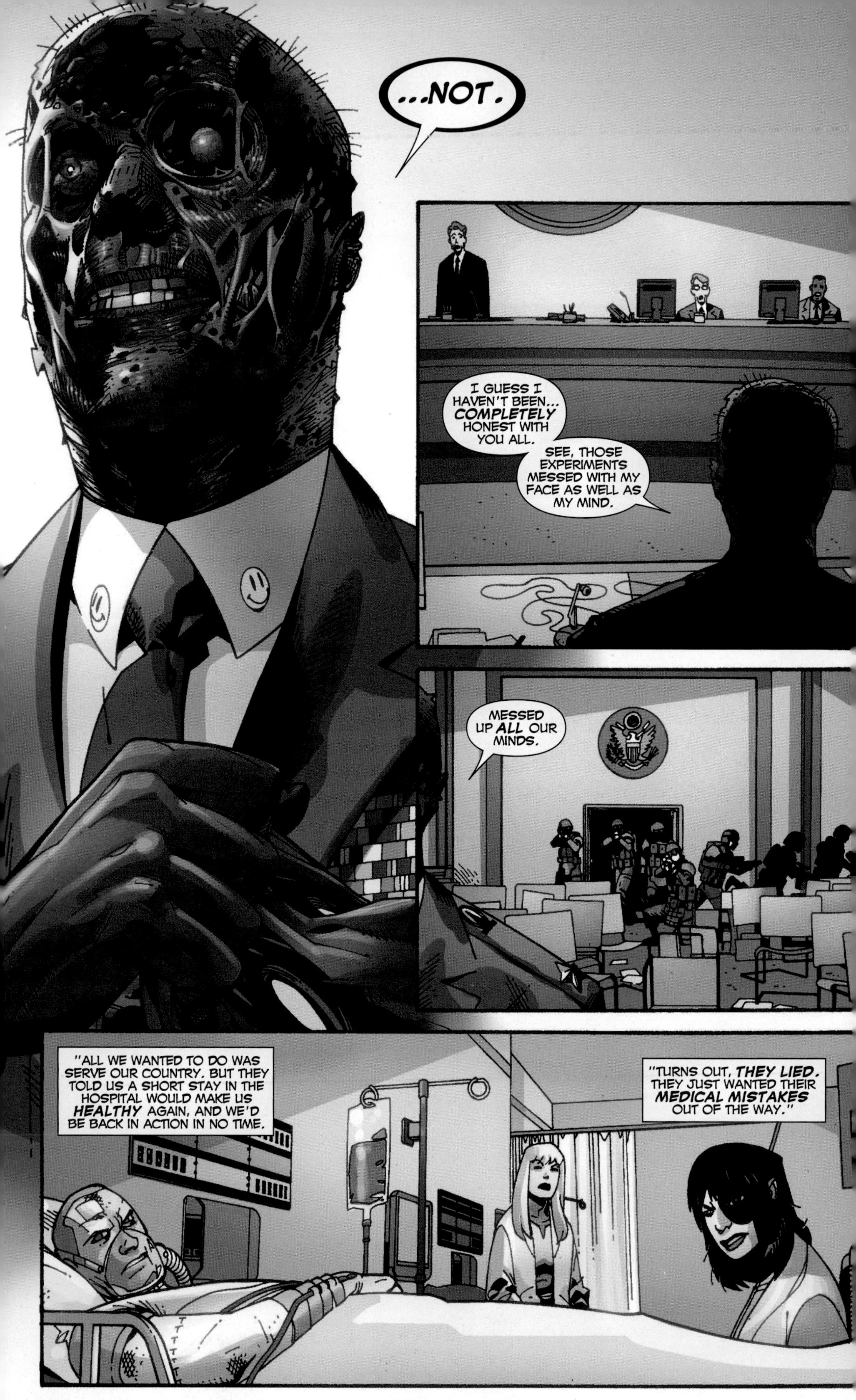
...NOT.
I GUESS I HAVEN'T BEEN... COMPLETELY HONEST WITH YOU ALL.
SEE, THOSE EXPERIMENTS MESSED WITH MY FACE AS WELL AS MY MIND.
MESSED UP ALL OUR MINDS.
"ALL WE WANTED TO DO WAS SERVE OUR COUNTRY. BUT THEY TOLD US A SHORT STAY IN THE HOSPITAL WOULD MAKE US HEALTHY AGAIN, AND WE'D BE BACK IN ACTION IN NO TIME.
"TURNS OUT, THEY LIED. THEY JUST WANTED THEIR MEDICAL MISTAKES OUT OF THE WAY."

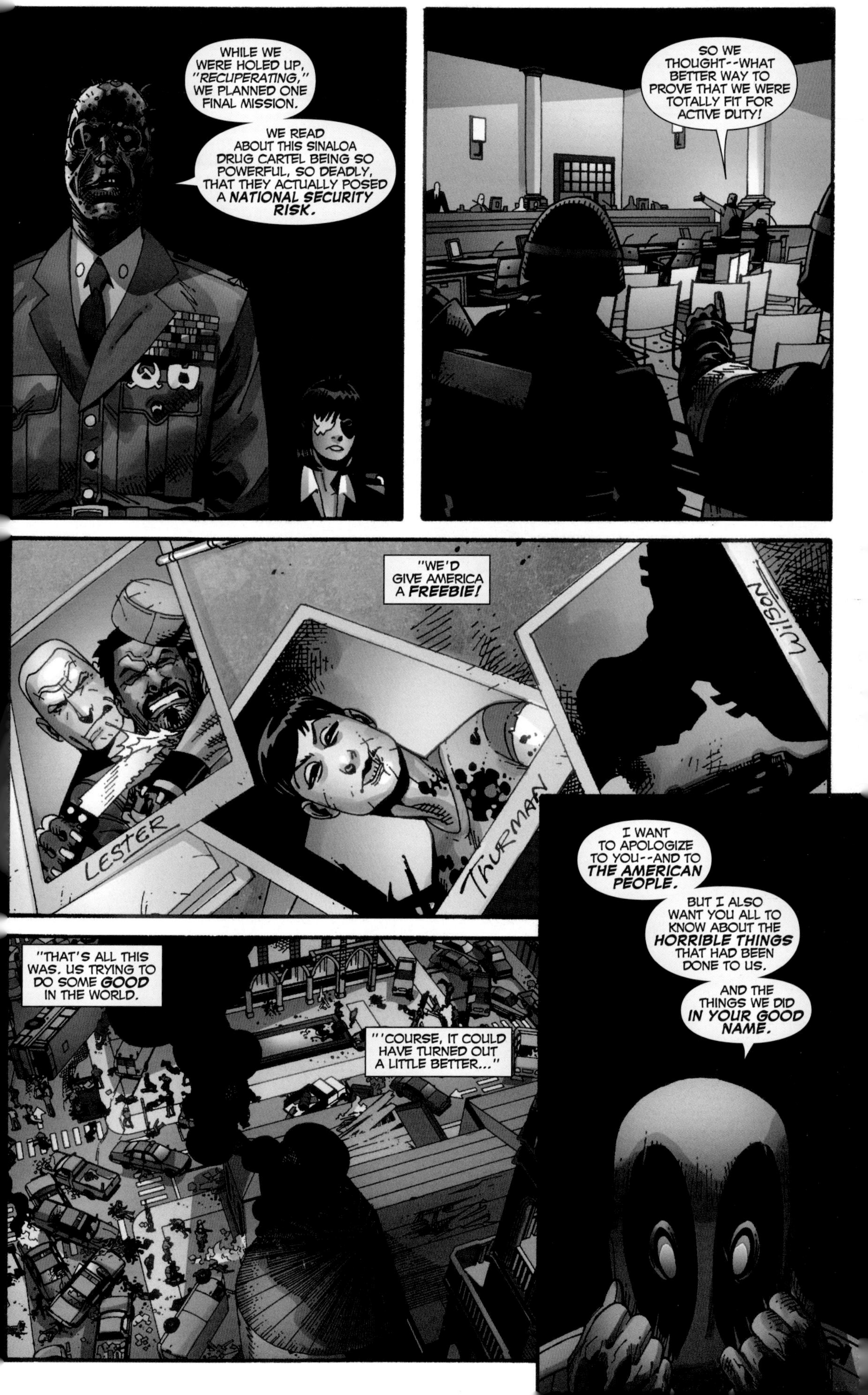
WHILE WE WERE HOLED UP, "RECUPERATING," WE PLANNED ONE FINAL MISSION.
WE READ ABOUT THIS SINALOA DRUG CARTEL BEING SO POWERFUL, SO DEADLY, THAT THEY ACTUALLY POSED A NATIONAL SECURITY RISK.
SO WE THOUGHT--WHAT BETTER WAY TO PROVE THAT WE WERE TOTALLY FIT FOR ACTIVE DUTY!
"WE'D GIVE AMERICA A FREEBIE!
LESTER
THURMAN
WILSON
"THAT'S ALL THIS WAS. US TRYING TO DO SOME GOOD IN THE WORLD.
"'COURSE, IT COULD HAVE TURNED OUT A LITTLE BETTER..."
I WANT TO APOLOGIZE TO YOU--AND TO THE AMERICAN PEOPLE.
BUT I ALSO WANT YOU ALL TO KNOW ABOUT THE HORRIBLE THINGS THAT HAD BEEN DONE TO US.
AND THE THINGS WE DID IN YOUR GOOD NAME.

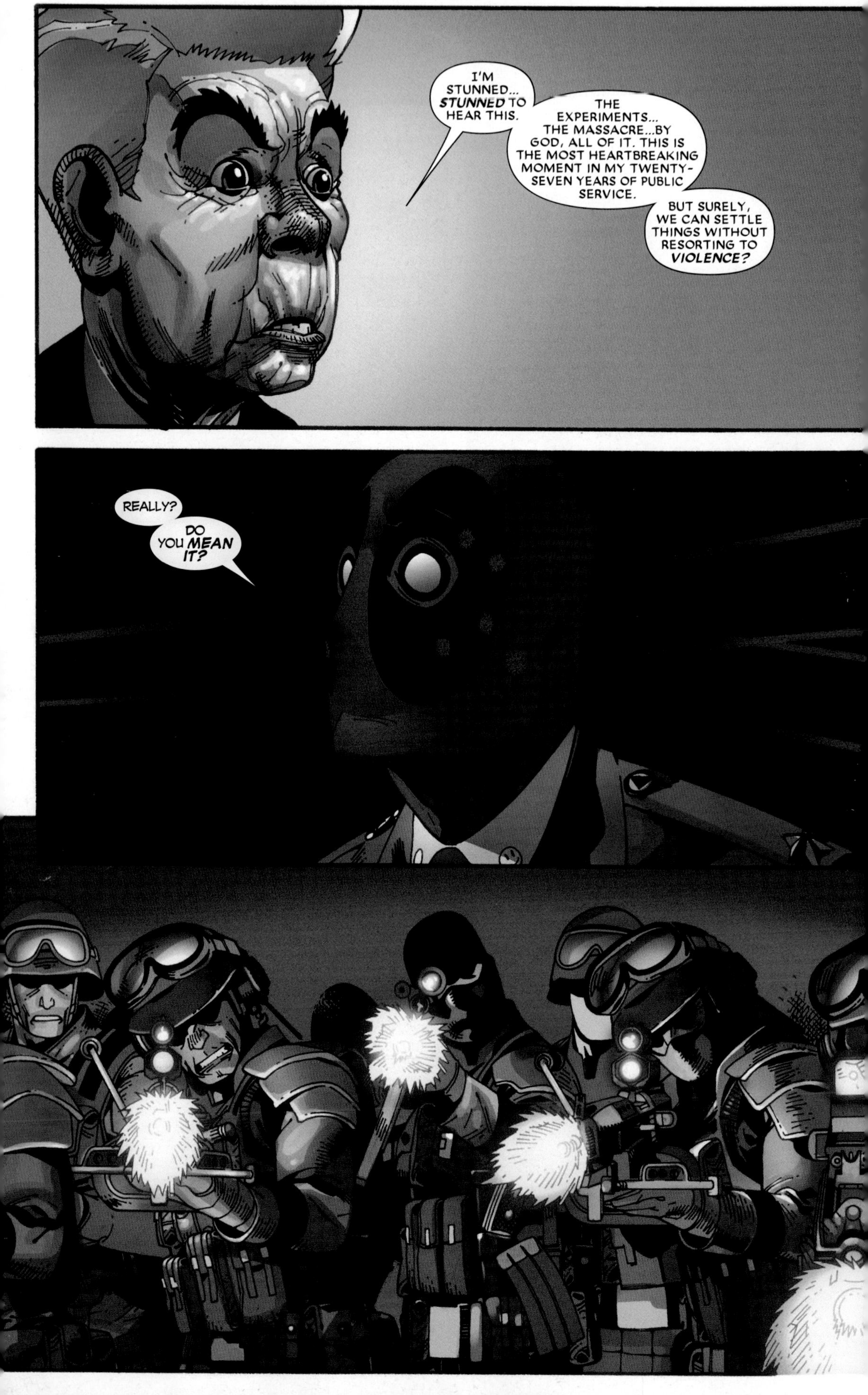
I'M STUNNED... STUNNED TO HEAR THIS.
THE EXPERIMENTS... THE MASSACRE...BY GOD, ALL OF IT. THIS IS THE MOST HEARTBREAKING MOMENT IN MY TWENTY-SEVEN YEARS OF PUBLIC SERVICE.
BUT SURELY, WE CAN SETTLE THINGS WITHOUT RESORTING TO VIOLENCE?
REALLY?
DO YOU MEAN IT?

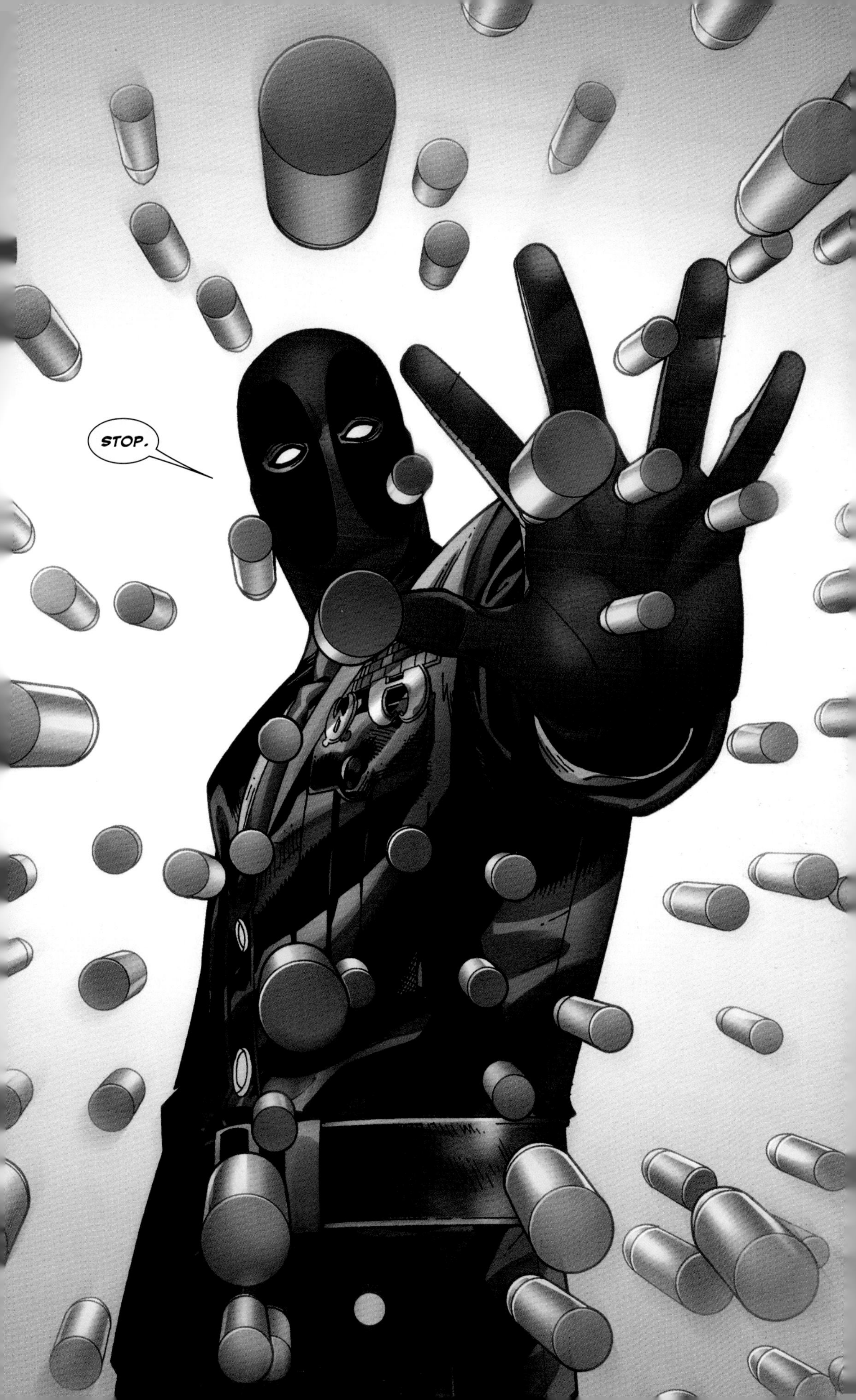
STOP.

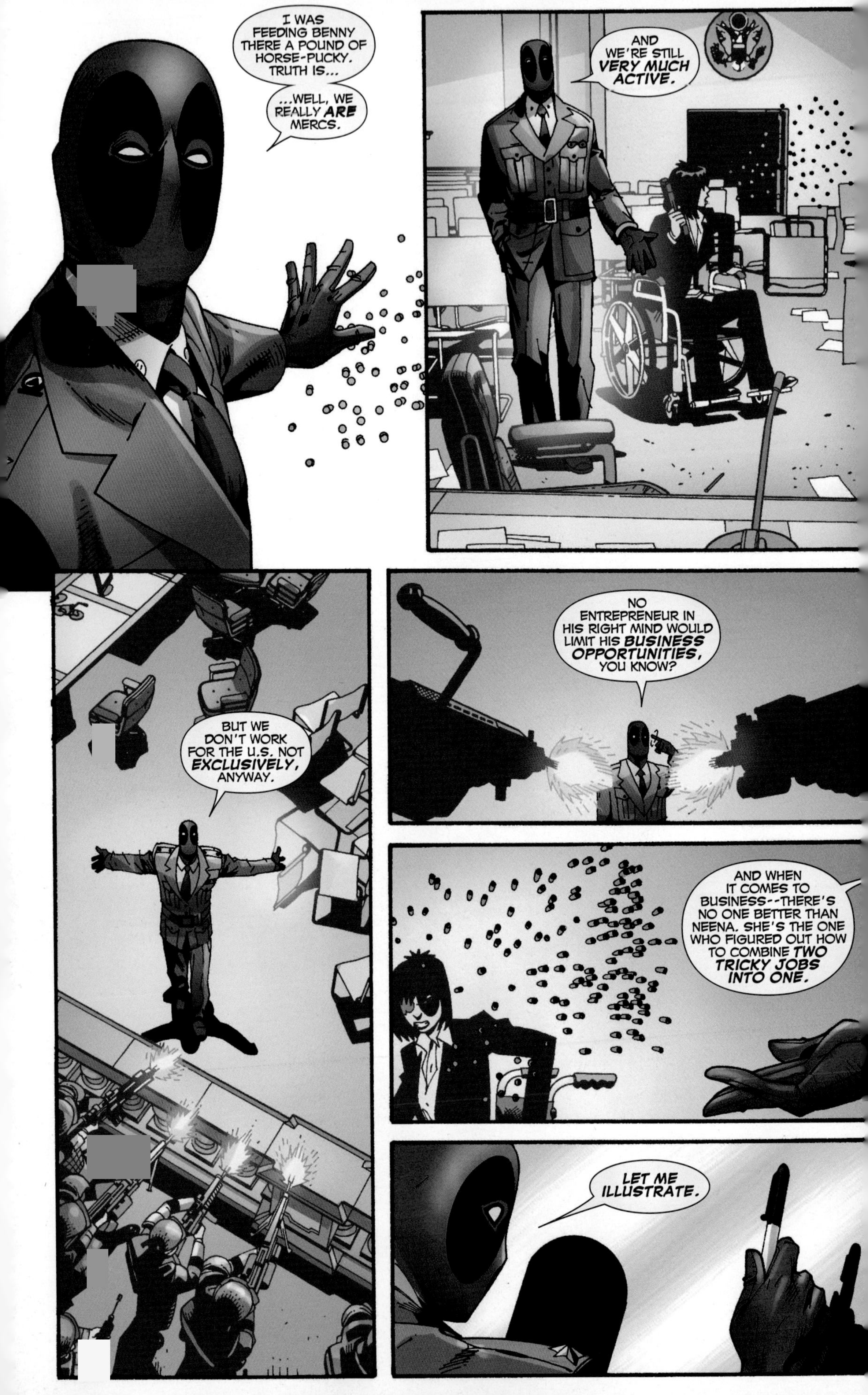
I WAS FEEDING BENNY THERE A POUND OF HORSE-PUCKY. TRUTH IS...
...WELL, WE REALLY ARE MERCS.
AND WE'RE STILL VERY MUCH ACTIVE.
BUT WE DON'T WORK FOR THE U.S. NOT EXCLUSIVELY, ANYWAY.
NO ENTREPRENEUR IN HIS RIGHT MIND WOULD LIMIT HIS BUSINESS OPPORTUNITIES, YOU KNOW?
AND WHEN IT COMES TO BUSINESS--THERE'S NO ONE BETTER THAN NEENA. SHE'S THE ONE WHO FIGURED OUT HOW TO COMBINE TWO TRICKY JOBS INTO ONE.
LET ME ILLUSTRATE.

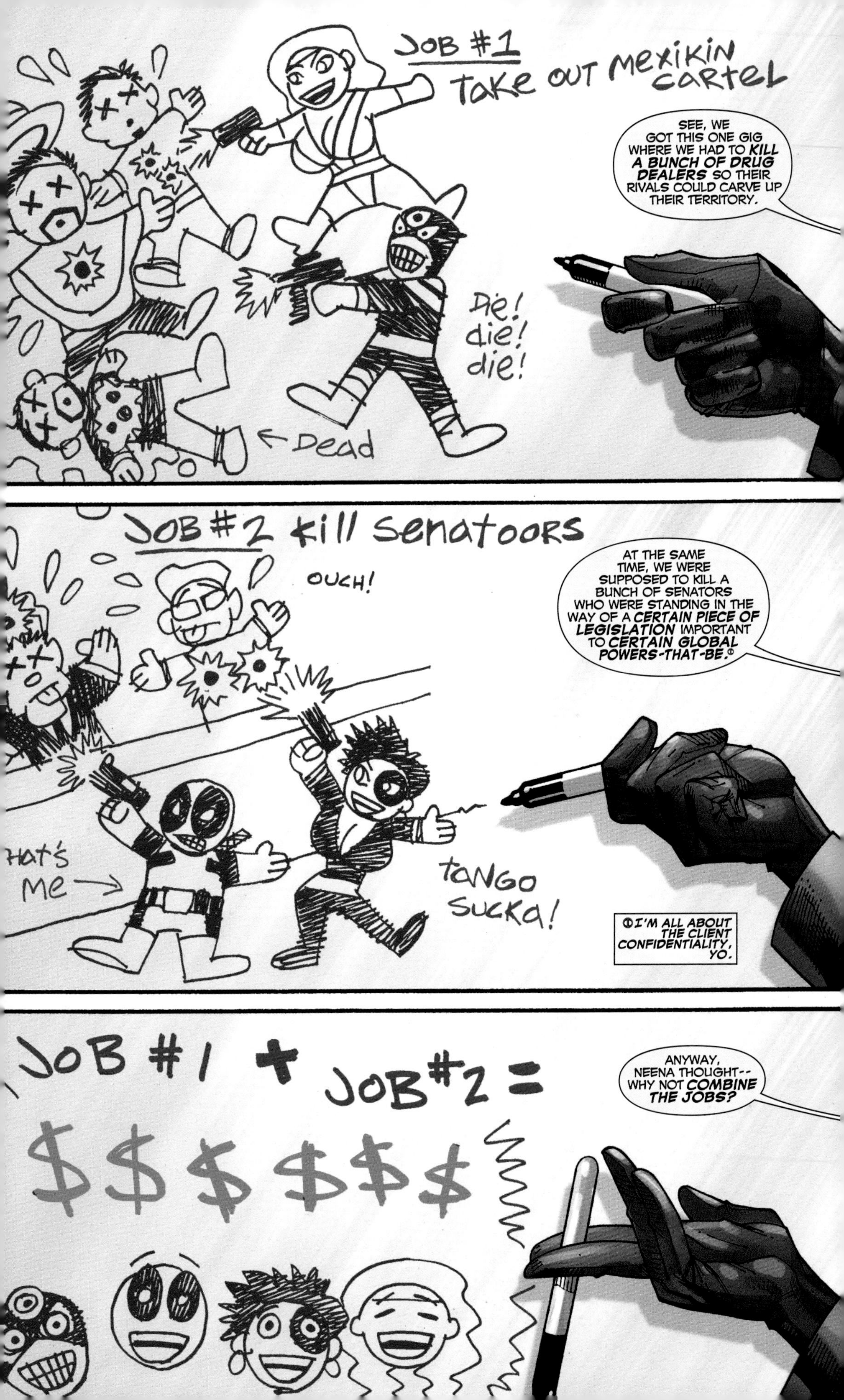
JOB #1
Take out mexikin cartel
SEE, WE GOT THIS ONE GIG WHERE WE HAD TO KILL A BUNCH OF DRUG DEALERS SO THEIR RIVALS COULD CARVE UP THEIR TERRITORY.
Die! die! die!
← Dead
JOB #2 kill senatoors
OUCH!
AT THE SAME TIME, WE WERE SUPPOSED TO KILL A BUNCH OF SENATORS WHO WERE STANDING IN THE WAY OF A CERTAIN PIECE OF LEGISLATION IMPORTANT TO CERTAIN GLOBAL POWERS-THAT-BE.①
Hat's me →
TANGO SUCKA!
① I'M ALL ABOUT THE CLIENT CONFIDENTIALITY, YO.
JOB #1 + JOB #2 =
ANYWAY, NEENA THOUGHT-- WHY NOT COMBINE THE JOBS?
$ $ $ $ $ $

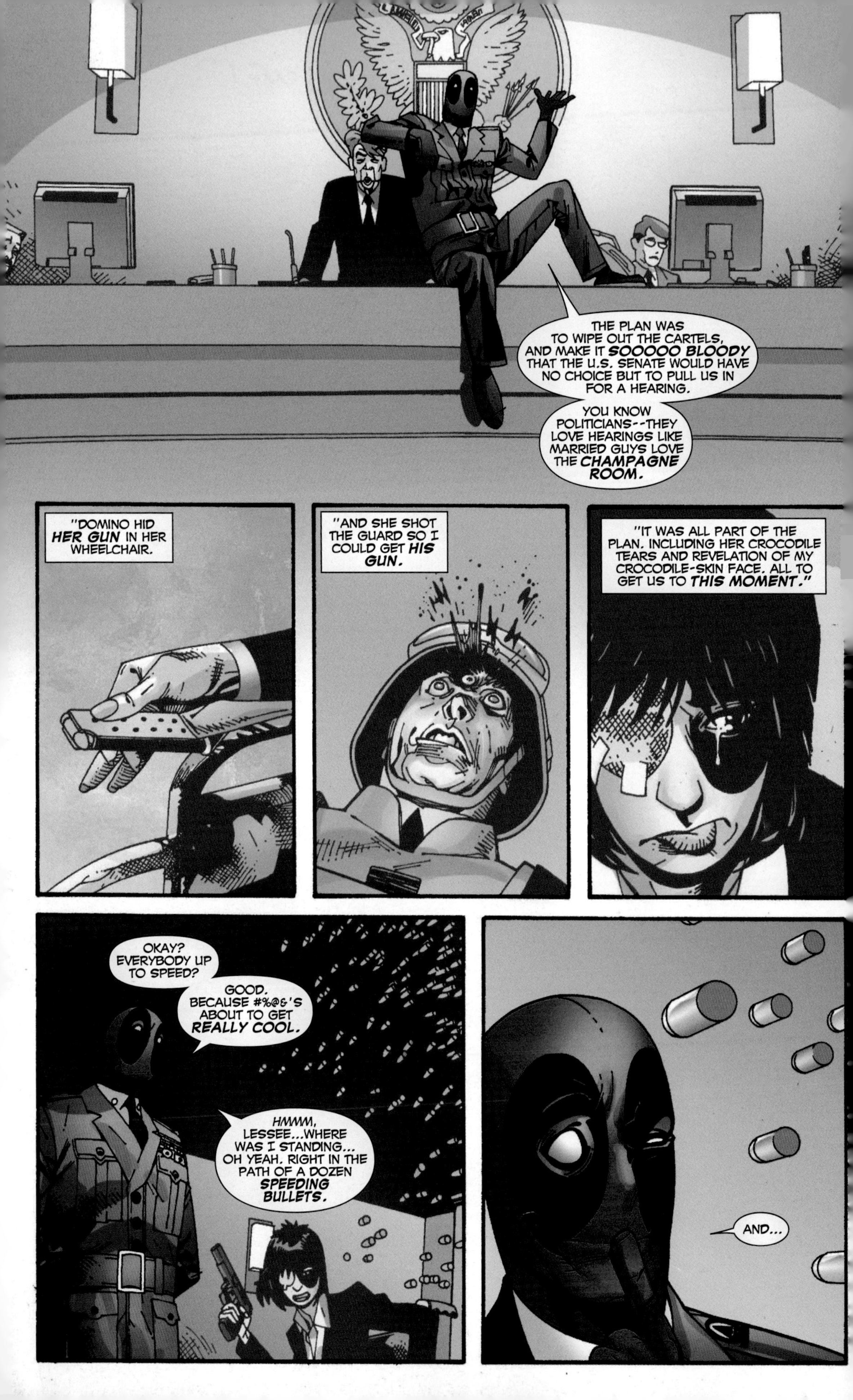
THE PLAN WAS TO WIPE OUT THE CARTELS, AND MAKE IT SOOOOO BLOODY THAT THE U.S. SENATE WOULD HAVE NO CHOICE BUT TO PULL US IN FOR A HEARING.
YOU KNOW POLITICIANS--THEY LOVE HEARINGS LIKE MARRIED GUYS LOVE THE CHAMPAGNE ROOM.
"DOMINO HID HER GUN IN HER WHEELCHAIR.
"AND SHE SHOT THE GUARD SO I COULD GET HIS GUN.
"IT WAS ALL PART OF THE PLAN. INCLUDING HER CROCODILE TEARS AND REVELATION OF MY CROCODILE-SKIN FACE. ALL TO GET US TO THIS MOMENT."
OKAY? EVERYBODY UP TO SPEED?
GOOD. BECAUSE #%@&'S ABOUT TO GET REALLY COOL.
HMMM, LESSEE...WHERE WAS I STANDING... OH YEAH. RIGHT IN THE PATH OF A DOZEN SPEEDING BULLETS.
AND...

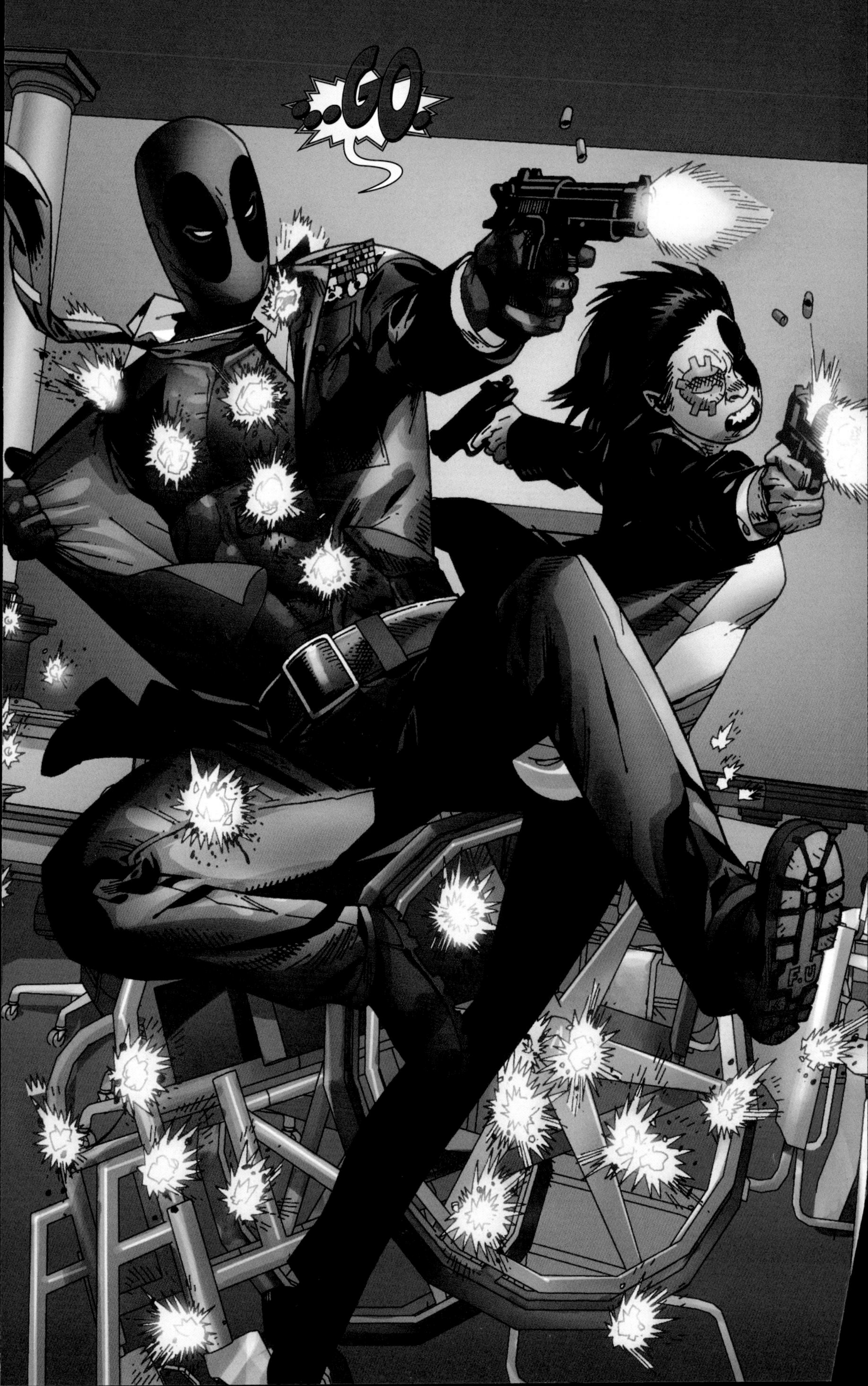
...GO
F.U

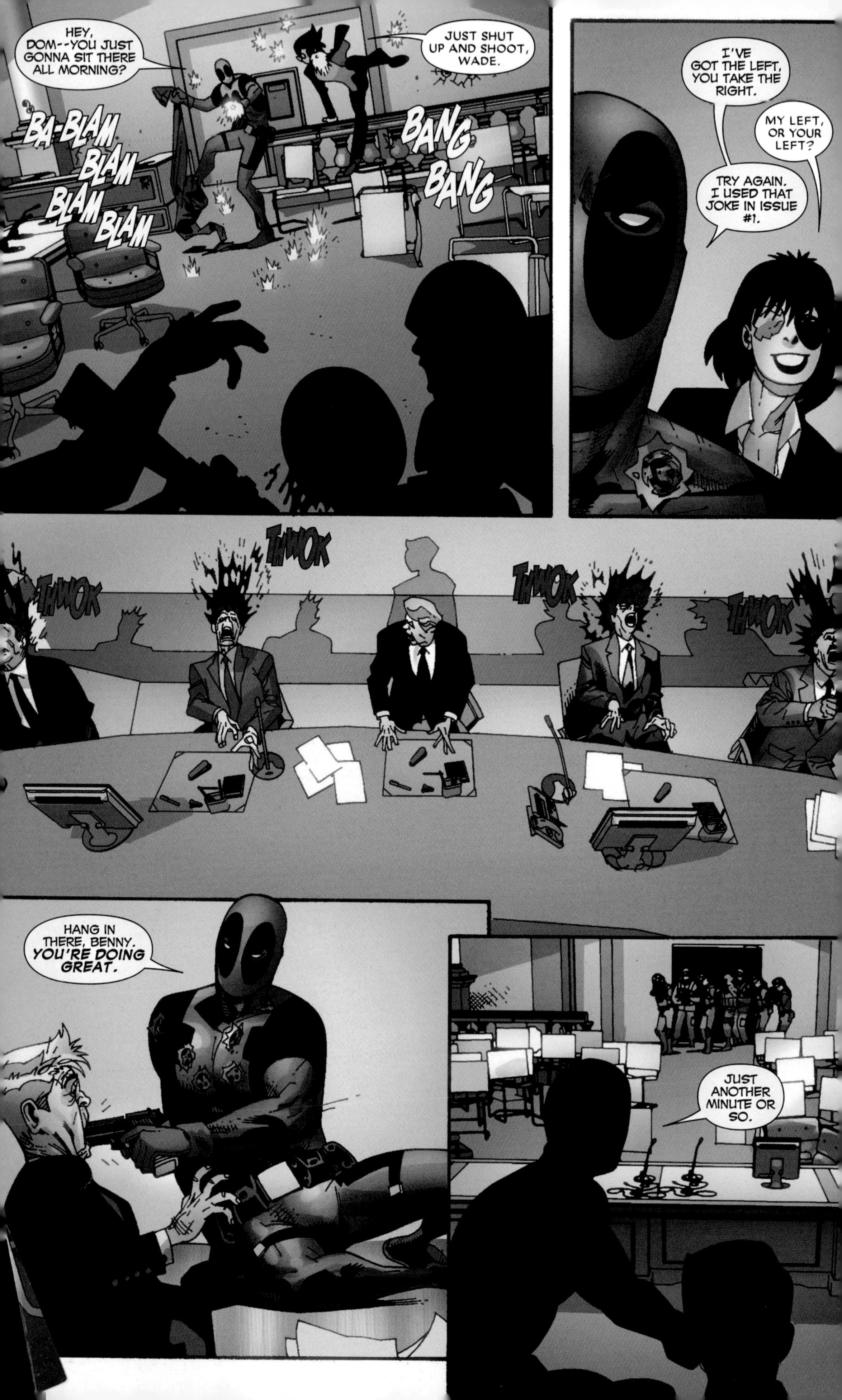

HEY, DOM--YOU JUST GONNA SIT THERE ALL MORNING?
JUST SHUT UP AND SHOOT, WADE.
BA-BLAM BLAM BLAM BLAM
BANG BANG
I'VE GOT THE LEFT, YOU TAKE THE RIGHT.
MY LEFT, OR YOUR LEFT?
TRY AGAIN. I USED THAT JOKE IN ISSUE #1.
THWOK
THWOK
THWOK
THWOK
HANG IN THERE, BENNY. YOU'RE DOING GREAT.
JUST ANOTHER MINUTE OR SO.

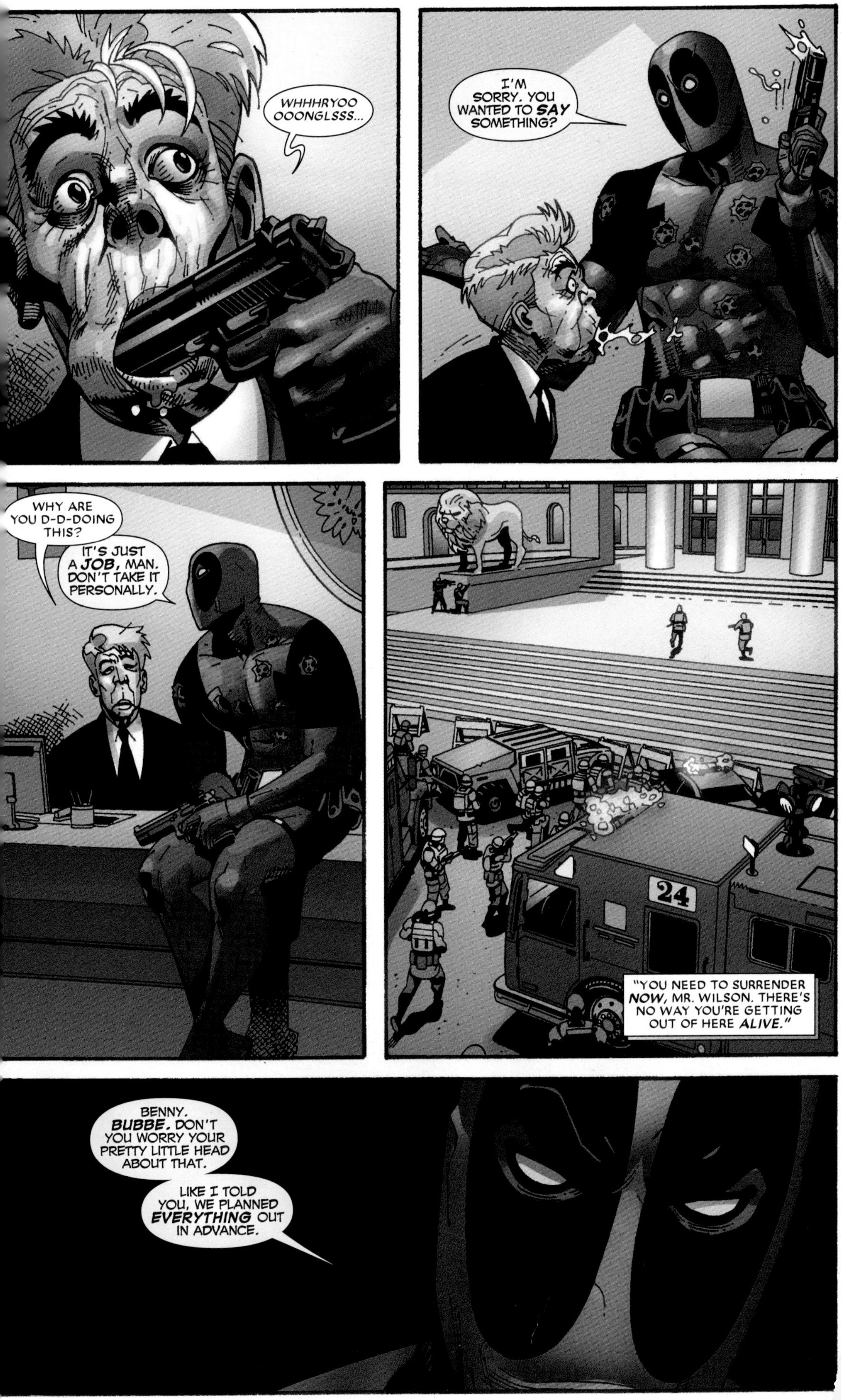
WHHHRYOO OOONGLSSS...
I'M SORRY. YOU WANTED TO SAY SOMETHING?
WHY ARE YOU D-D-DOING THIS?
IT'S JUST A JOB, MAN. DON'T TAKE IT PERSONALLY.
24
"YOU NEED TO SURRENDER NOW, MR. WILSON. THERE'S NO WAY YOU'RE GETTING OUT OF HERE ALIVE."
BENNY. BUBBE. DON'T YOU WORRY YOUR PRETTY LITTLE HEAD ABOUT THAT.
LIKE I TOLD YOU, WE PLANNED EVERYTHING OUT IN ADVANCE.

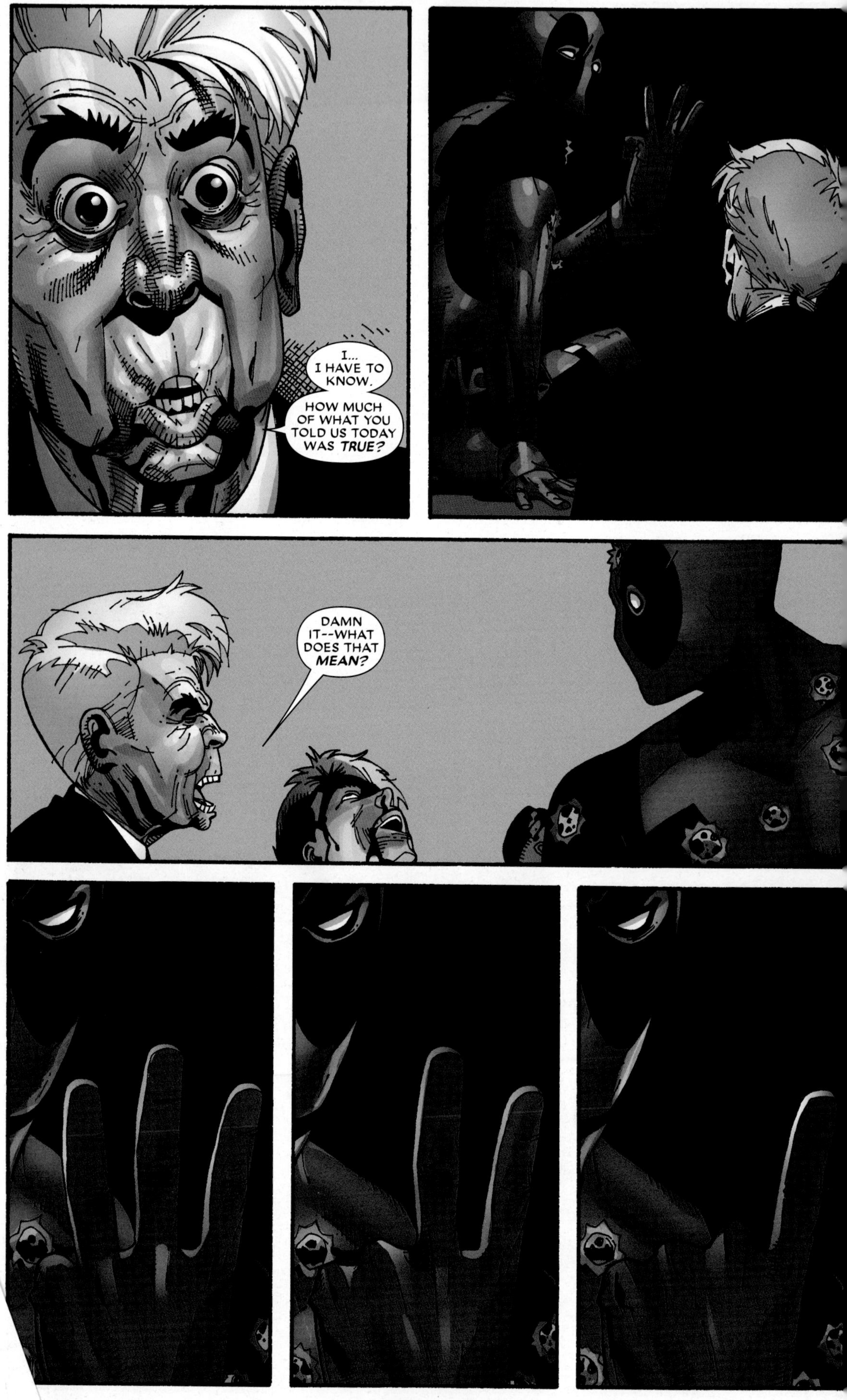
I... I HAVE TO KNOW.
HOW MUCH OF WHAT YOU TOLD US TODAY WAS *TRUE?*
DAMN IT--WHAT DOES THAT *MEAN?*

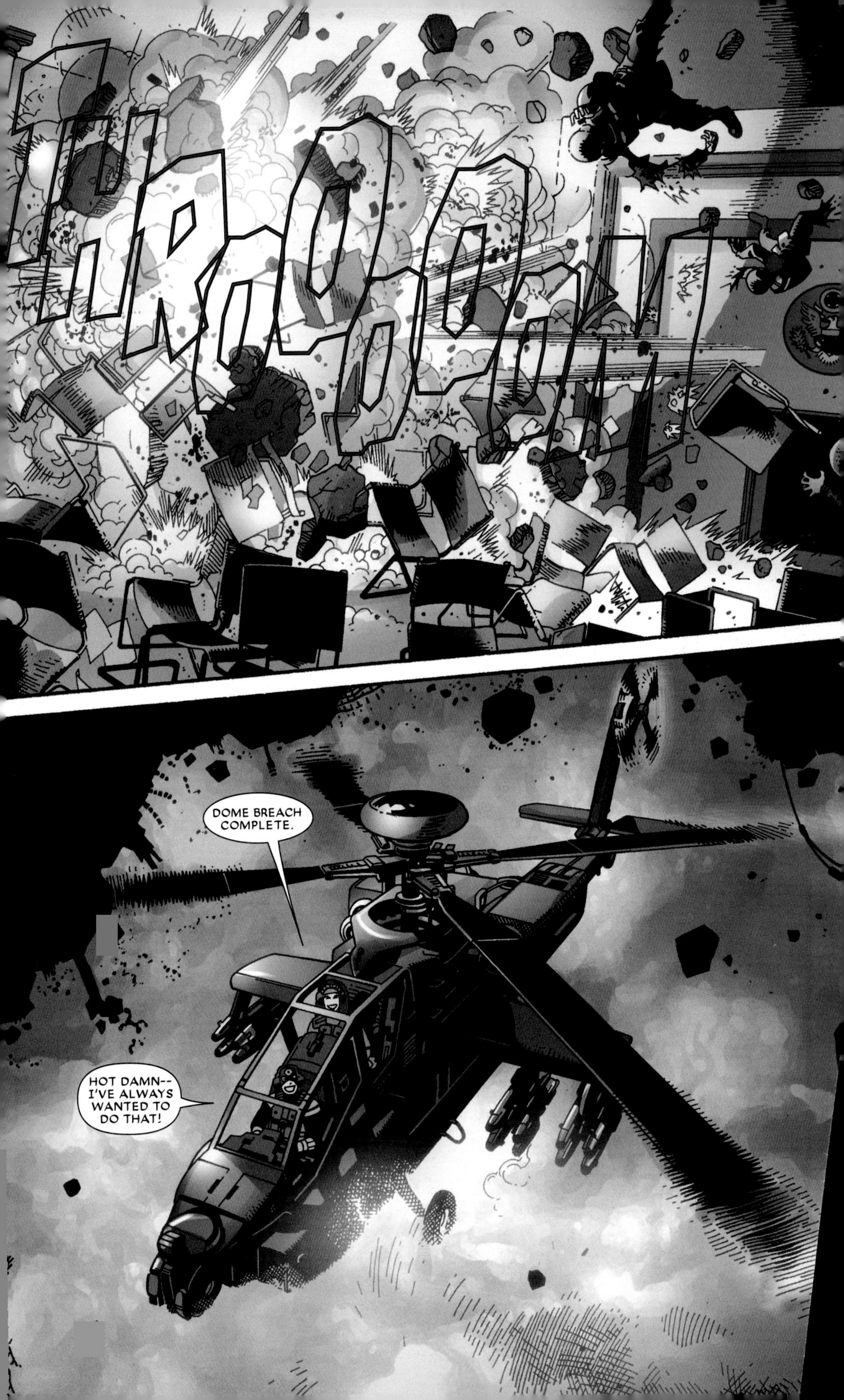
THRROOOOOM
DOME BREACH COMPLETE.
HOT DAMN-- I'VE ALWAYS WANTED TO DO THAT!

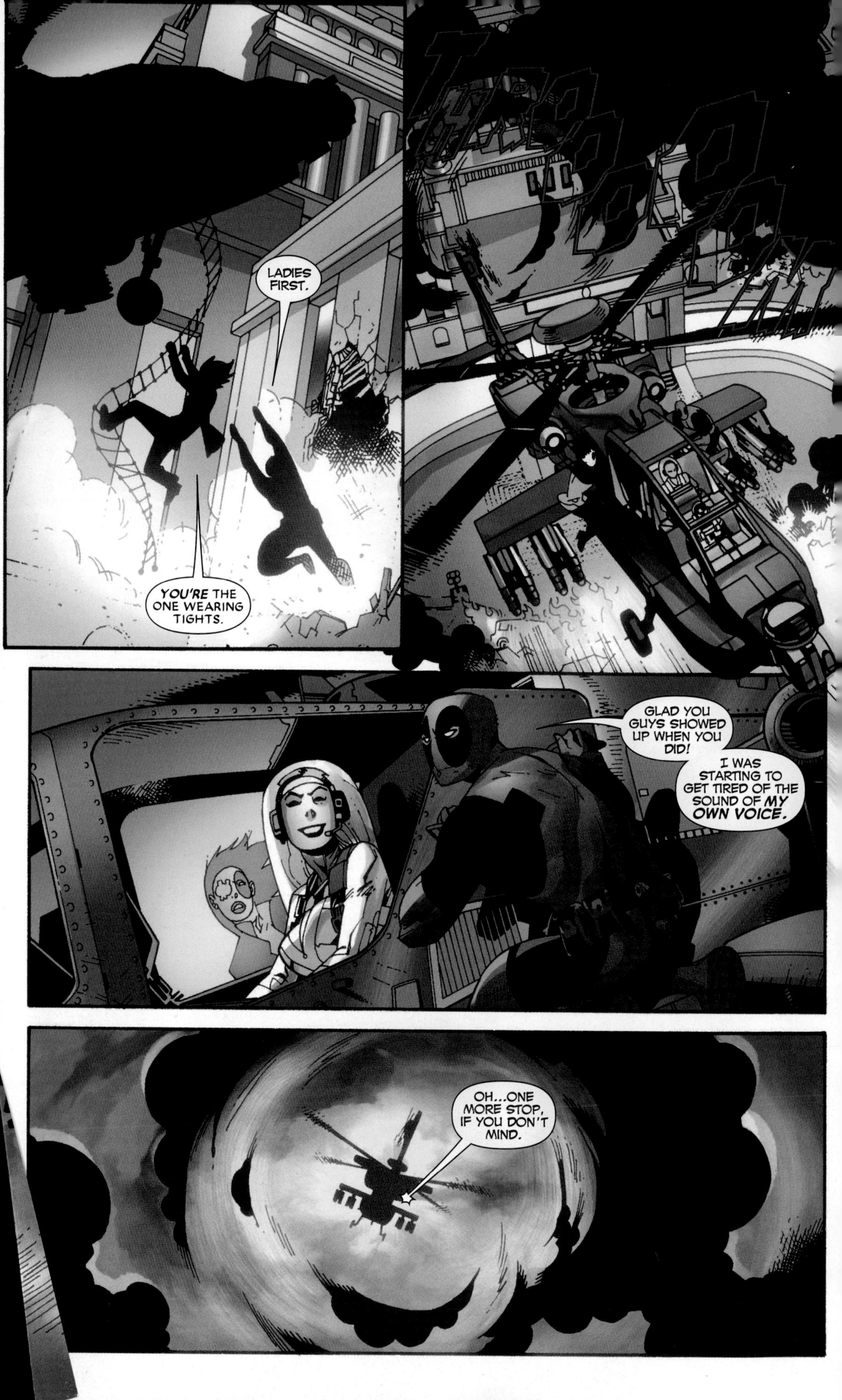
LADIES FIRST.
YOU'RE THE ONE WEARING TIGHTS.
GLAD YOU GUYS SHOWED UP WHEN YOU DID!
I WAS STARTING TO GET TIRED OF THE SOUND OF MY OWN VOICE.
OH...ONE MORE STOP, IF YOU DON'T MIND.

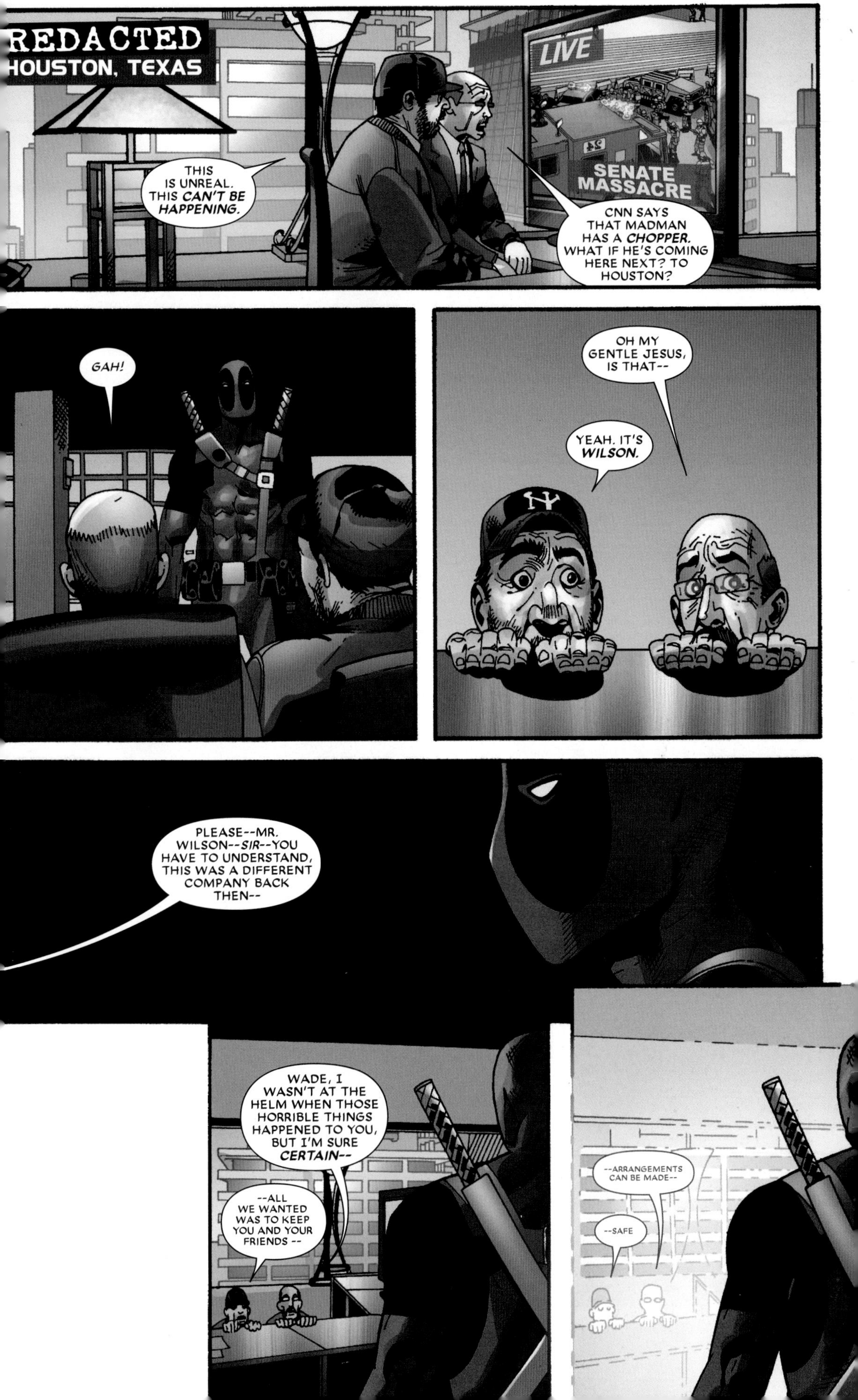
REDACTED
HOUSTON, TEXAS
LIVE
SENATE MASSACRE
THIS IS UNREAL. THIS CAN'T BE HAPPENING.
CNN SAYS THAT MADMAN HAS A CHOPPER. WHAT IF HE'S COMING HERE NEXT? TO HOUSTON?
GAH!
OH MY GENTLE JESUS, IS THAT--
YEAH. IT'S WILSON.
PLEASE--MR. WILSON--SIR--YOU HAVE TO UNDERSTAND, THIS WAS A DIFFERENT COMPANY BACK THEN--
WADE, I WASN'T AT THE HELM WHEN THOSE HORRIBLE THINGS HAPPENED TO YOU, BUT I'M SURE CERTAIN--
--ALL WE WANTED WAS TO KEEP YOU AND YOUR FRIENDS --
--ARRANGEMENTS CAN BE MADE--
--SAFE

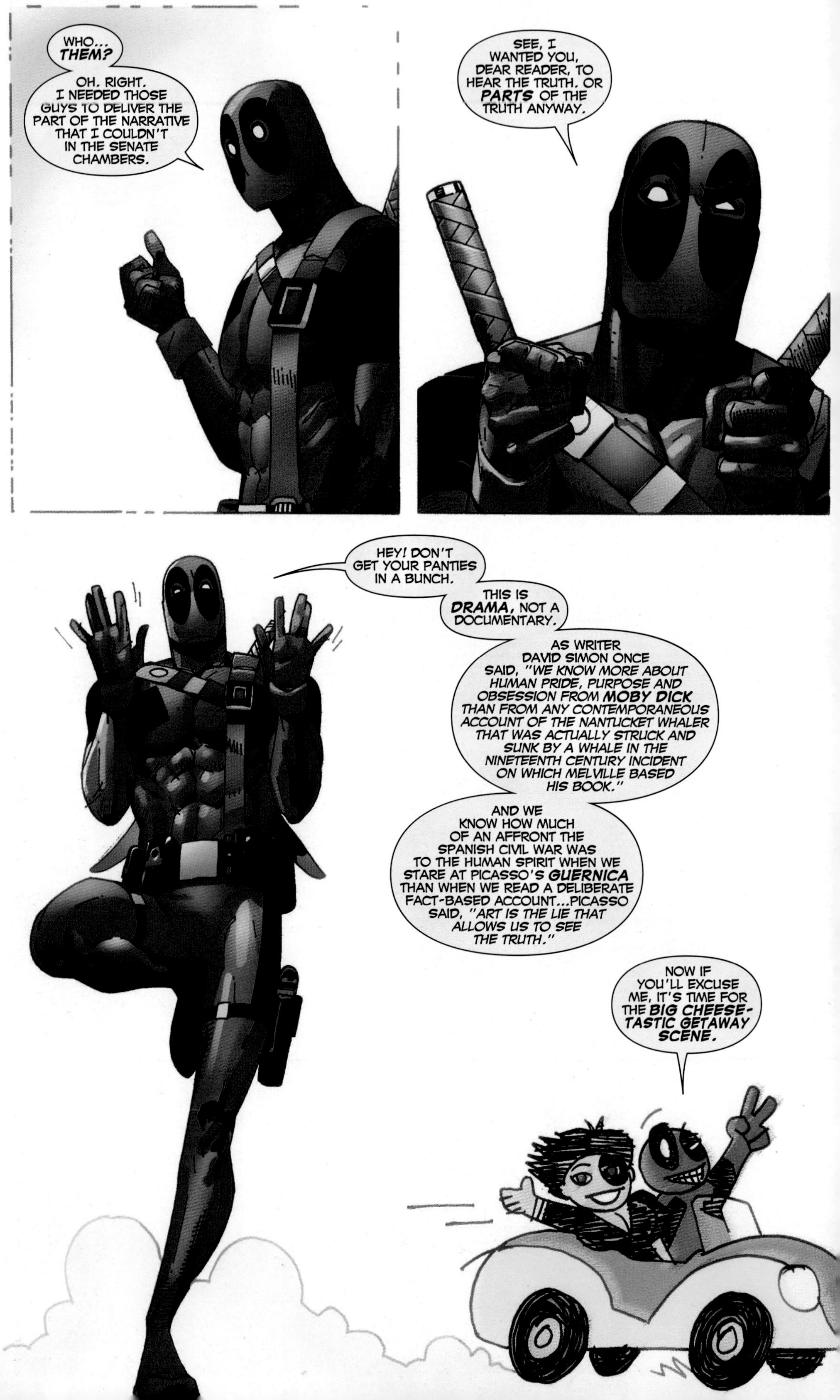

WHO... THEM?
OH. RIGHT. I NEEDED THOSE GUYS TO DELIVER THE PART OF THE NARRATIVE THAT I COULDN'T IN THE SENATE CHAMBERS.
SEE, I WANTED YOU, DEAR READER, TO HEAR THE TRUTH. OR PARTS OF THE TRUTH ANYWAY.
HEY! DON'T GET YOUR PANTIES IN A BUNCH.
THIS IS DRAMA, NOT A DOCUMENTARY.
AS WRITER DAVID SIMON ONCE SAID, "WE KNOW MORE ABOUT HUMAN PRIDE, PURPOSE AND OBSESSION FROM MOBY DICK THAN FROM ANY CONTEMPORANEOUS ACCOUNT OF THE NANTUCKET WHALER THAT WAS ACTUALLY STRUCK AND SUNK BY A WHALE IN THE NINETEENTH CENTURY INCIDENT ON WHICH MELVILLE BASED HIS BOOK."
AND WE KNOW HOW MUCH OF AN AFFRONT THE SPANISH CIVIL WAR WAS TO THE HUMAN SPIRIT WHEN WE STARE AT PICASSO'S GUERNICA THAN WHEN WE READ A DELIBERATE FACT-BASED ACCOUNT...PICASSO SAID, "ART IS THE LIE THAT ALLOWS US TO SEE THE TRUTH."
NOW IF YOU'LL EXCUSE ME, IT'S TIME FOR THE BIG CHEESE-TASTIC GETAWAY SCENE.

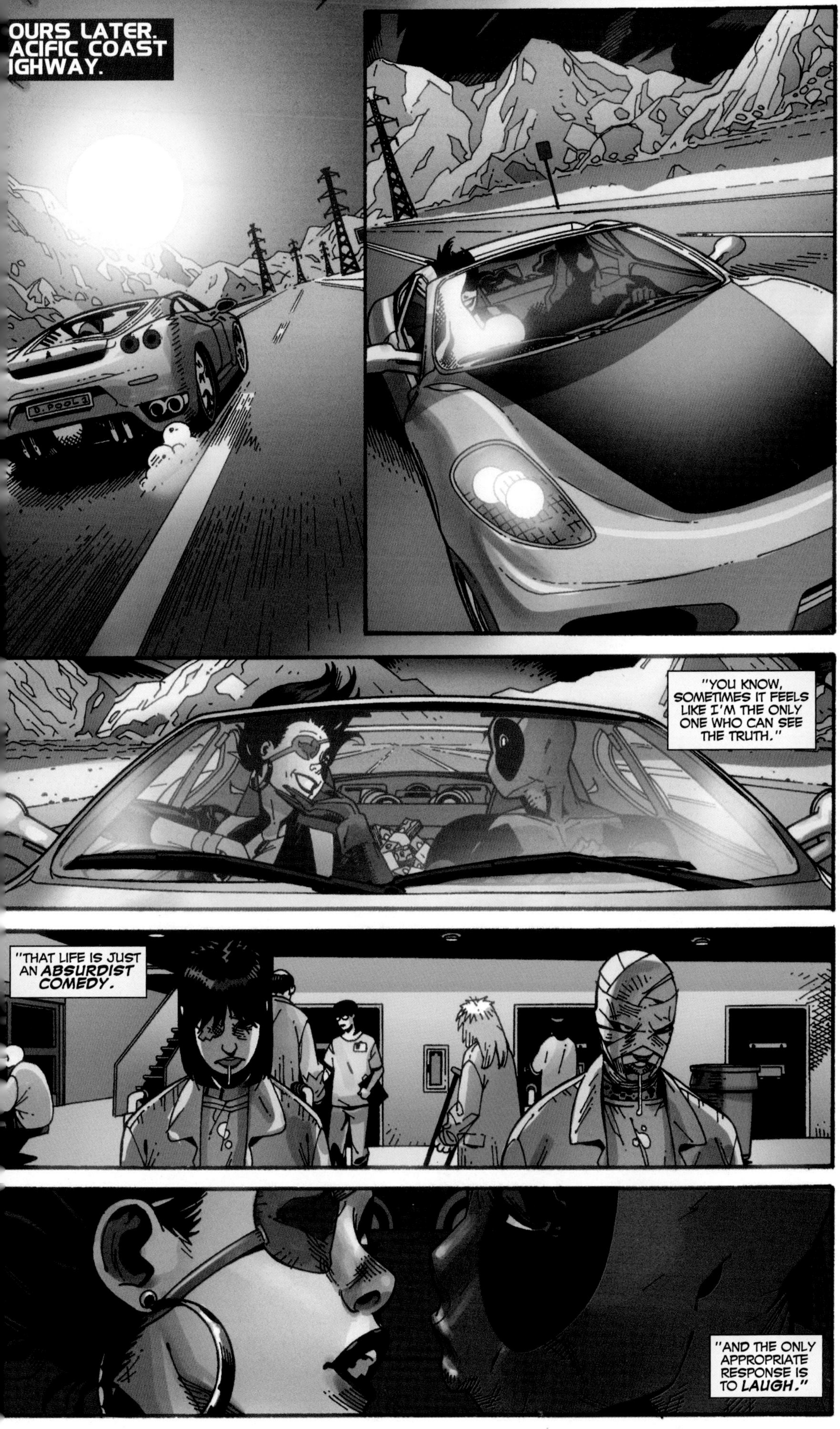
OURS LATER.
ACIFIC COAST
IGHWAY.
D.POOL 1
"YOU KNOW, SOMETIMES IT FEELS LIKE I'M THE ONLY ONE WHO CAN SEE THE TRUTH."
"THAT LIFE IS JUST AN ABSURDIST COMEDY.
"AND THE ONLY APPROPRIATE RESPONSE IS TO LAUGH."

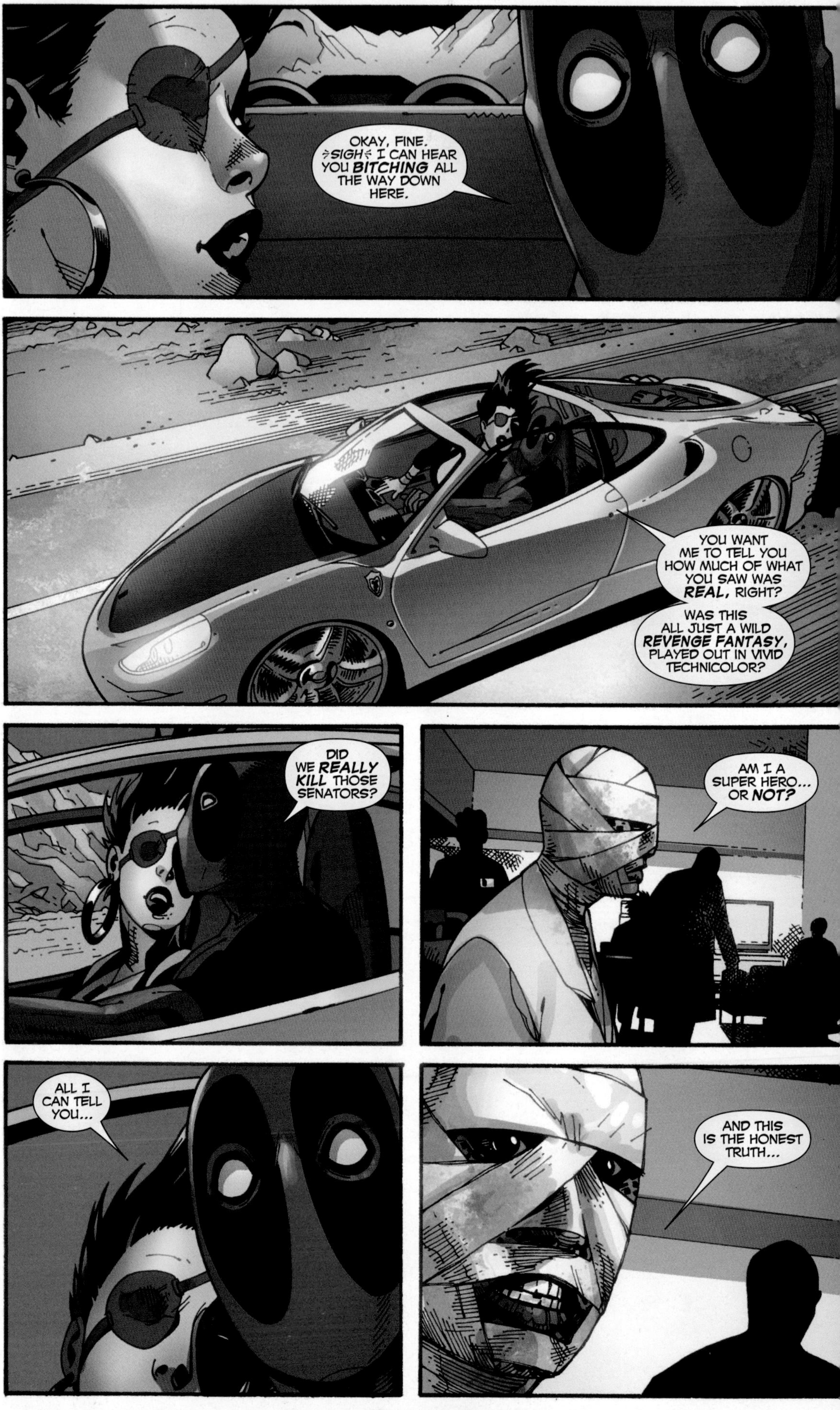

OKAY, FINE. ≯SIGH≮ I CAN HEAR YOU BITCHING ALL THE WAY DOWN HERE.
YOU WANT ME TO TELL YOU HOW MUCH OF WHAT YOU SAW WAS REAL, RIGHT?
WAS THIS ALL JUST A WILD REVENGE FANTASY, PLAYED OUT IN VIVID TECHNICOLOR?
DID WE REALLY KILL THOSE SENATORS?
AM I A SUPER HERO... OR NOT?
ALL I CAN TELL YOU...
AND THIS IS THE HONEST TRUTH...

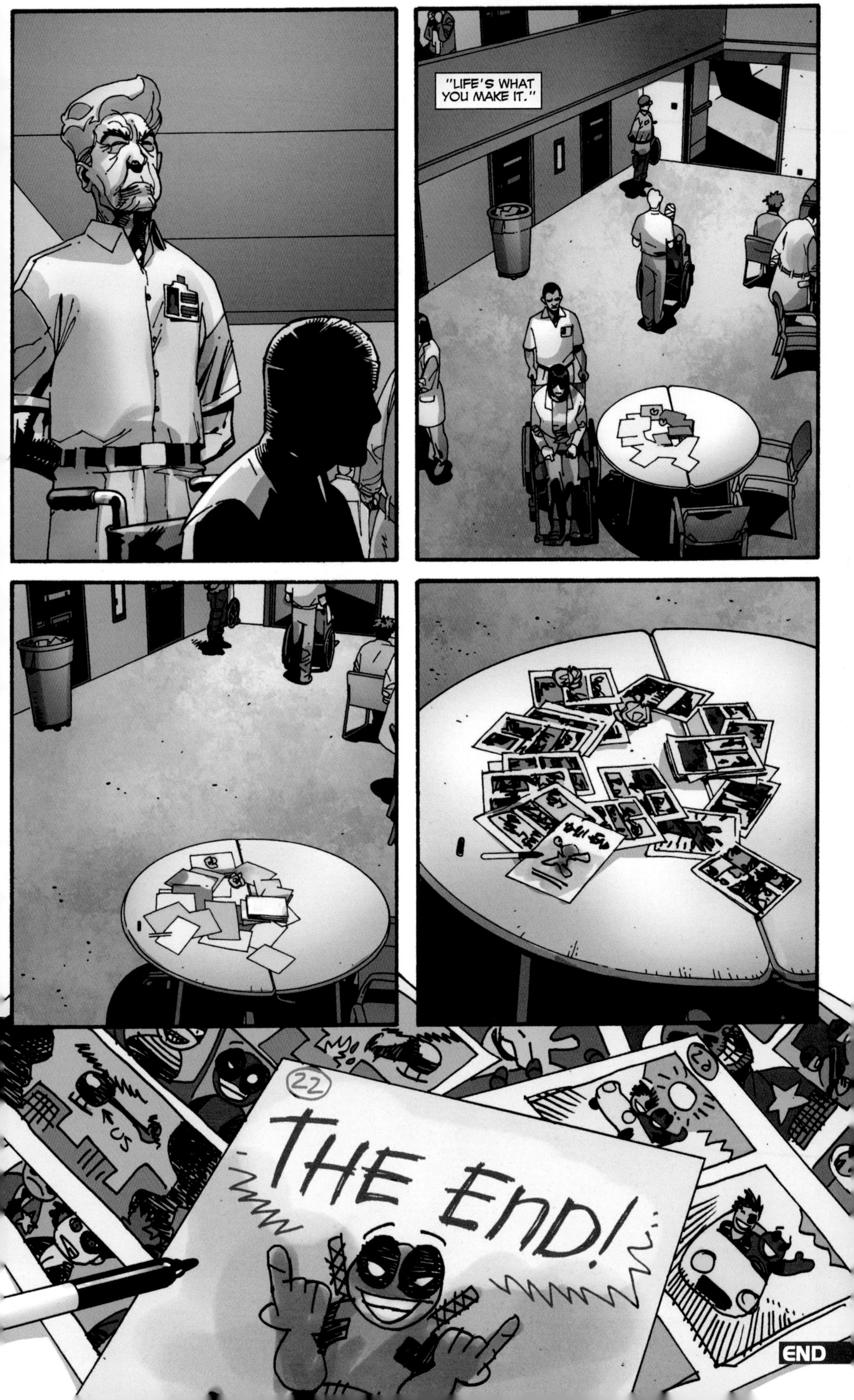
"LIFE'S WHAT YOU MAKE IT."
22
THE END!
END

Series artist Jason Pearson also drew covers for the *Deadpool* ongoing series. Check out his awesome work in this gallery!

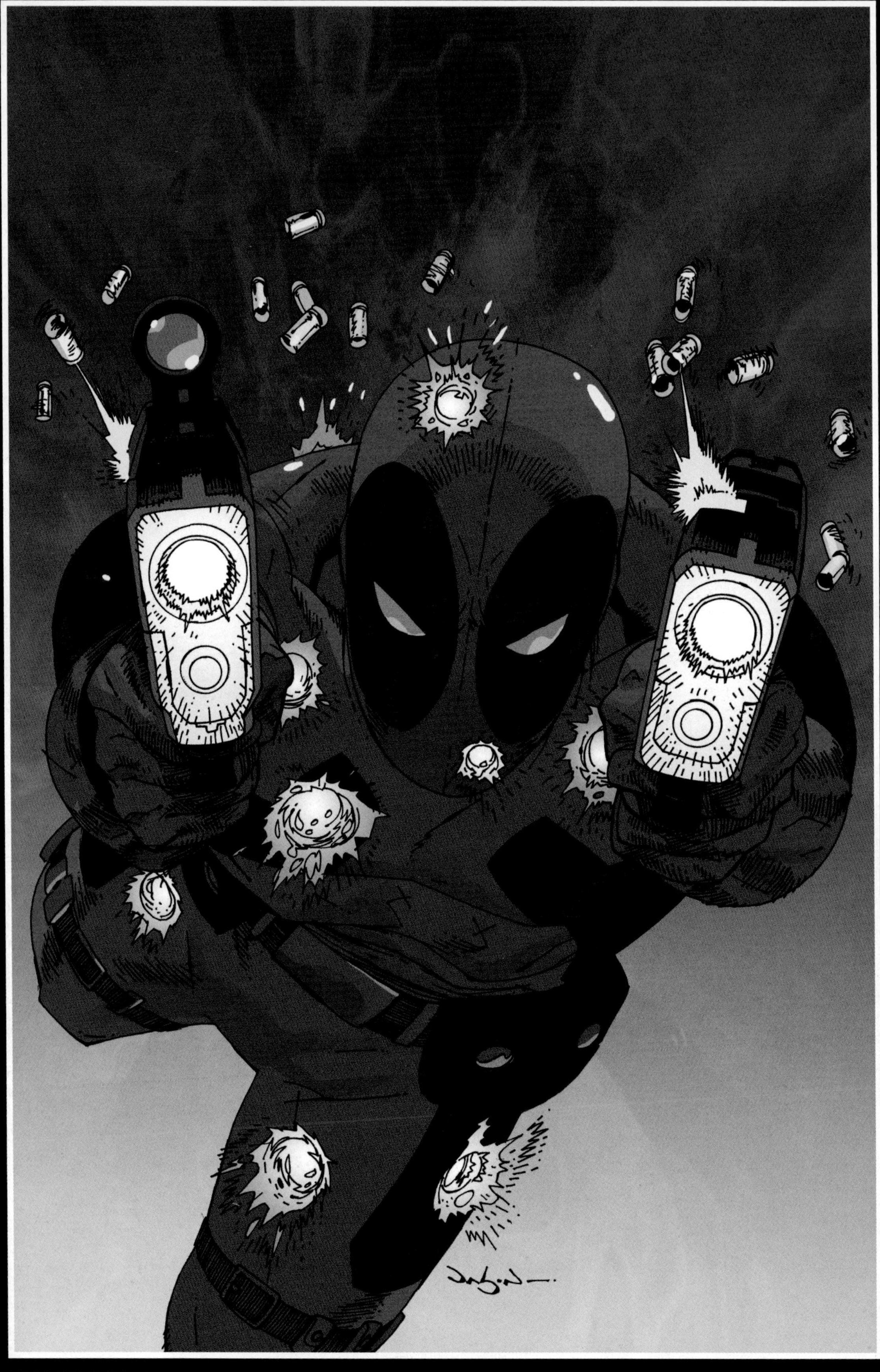

DEADPOOL #4

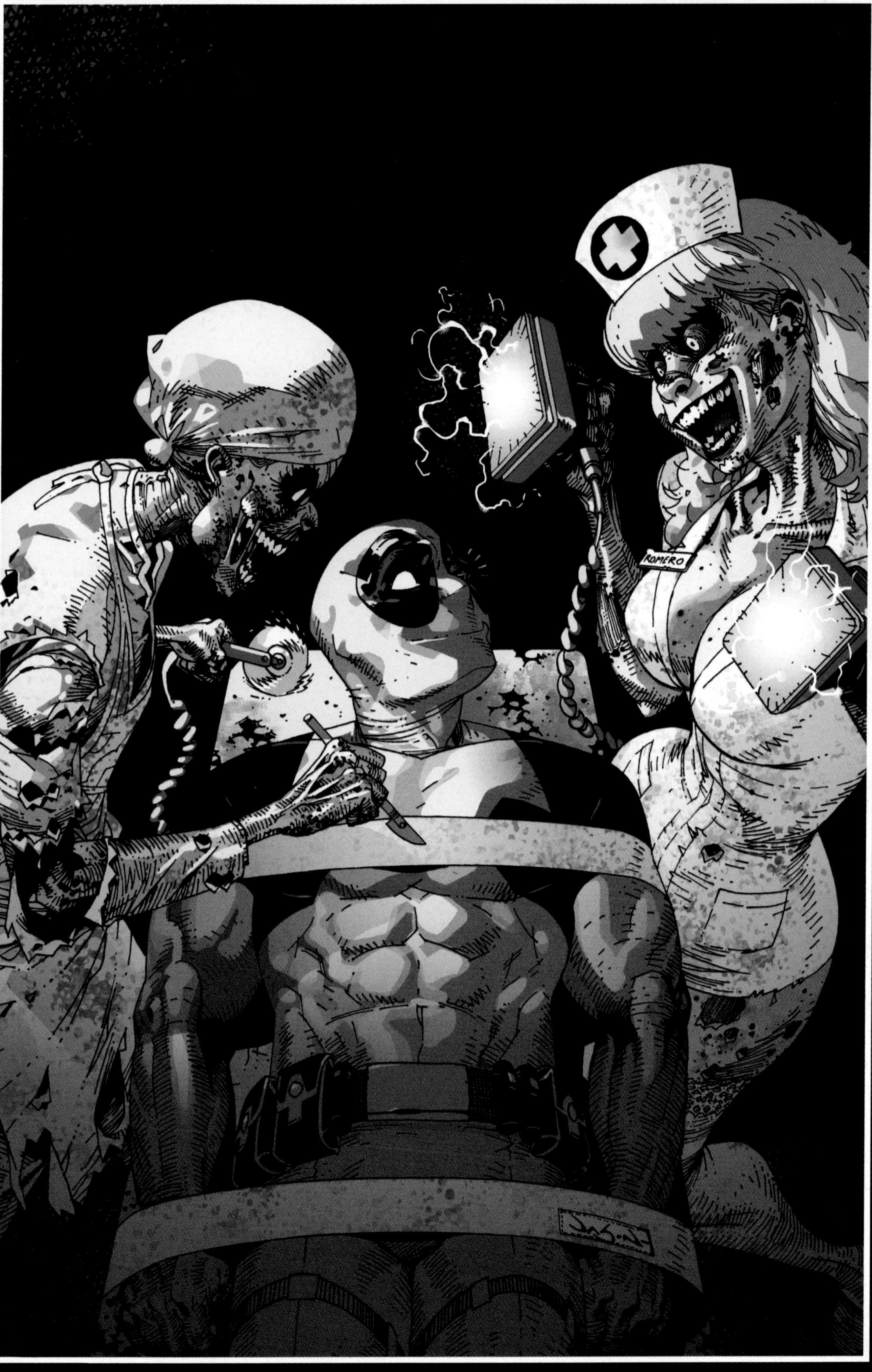
ROMERO

DEADPOOL #5

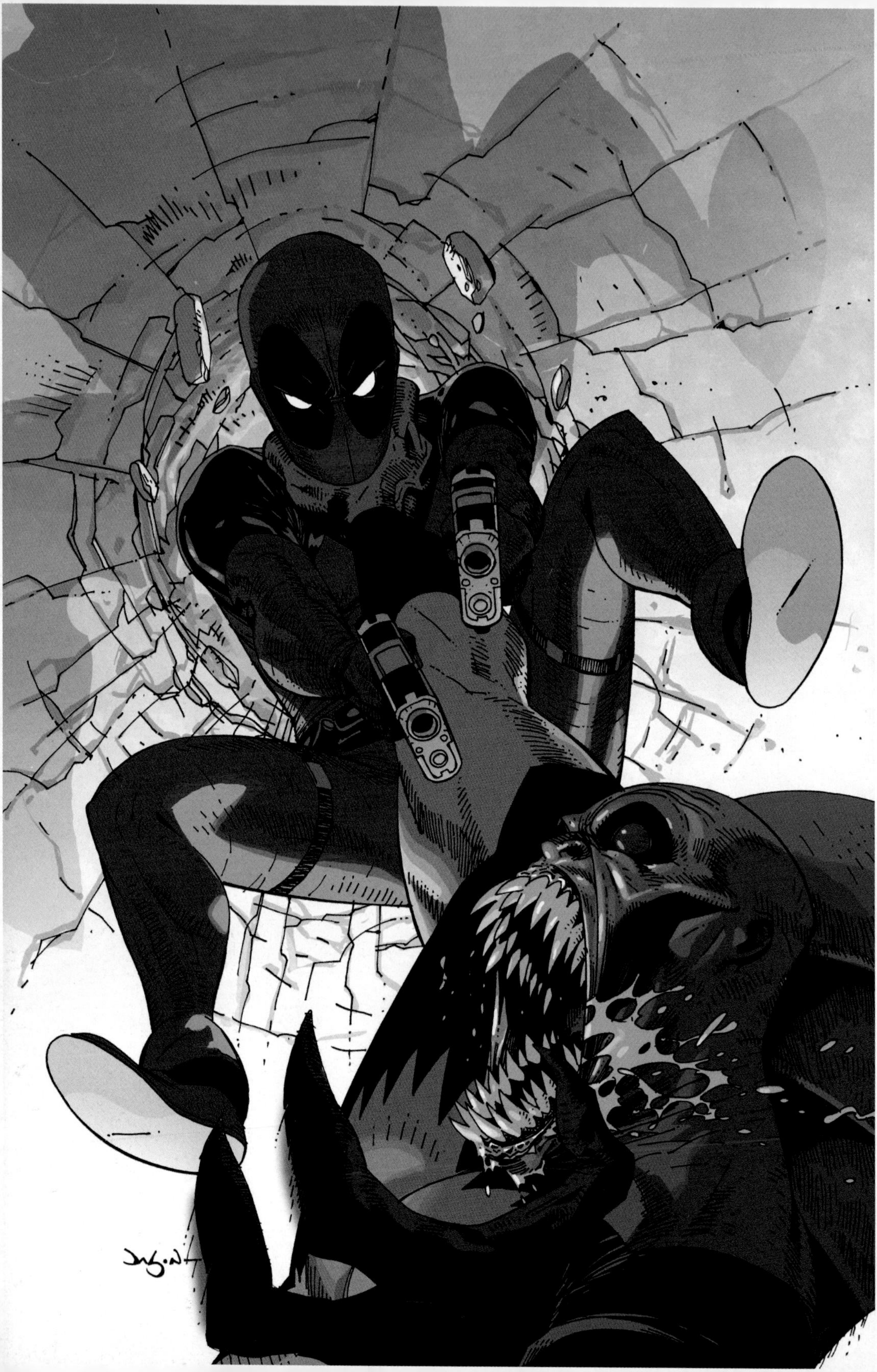

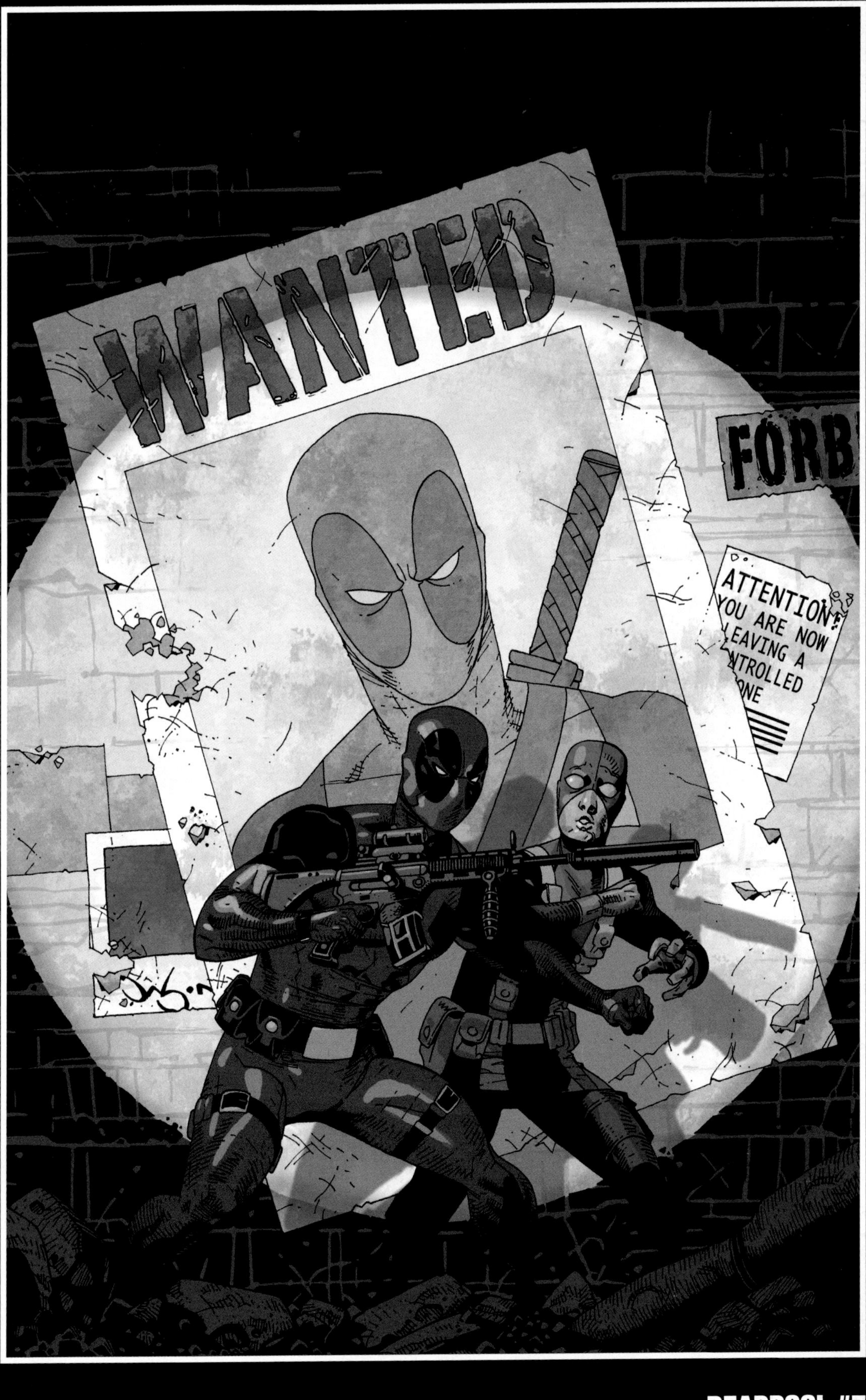
WANTED
FORB
ATTENTION:
YOU ARE NOW
LEAVING A
NTROLLED
ONE

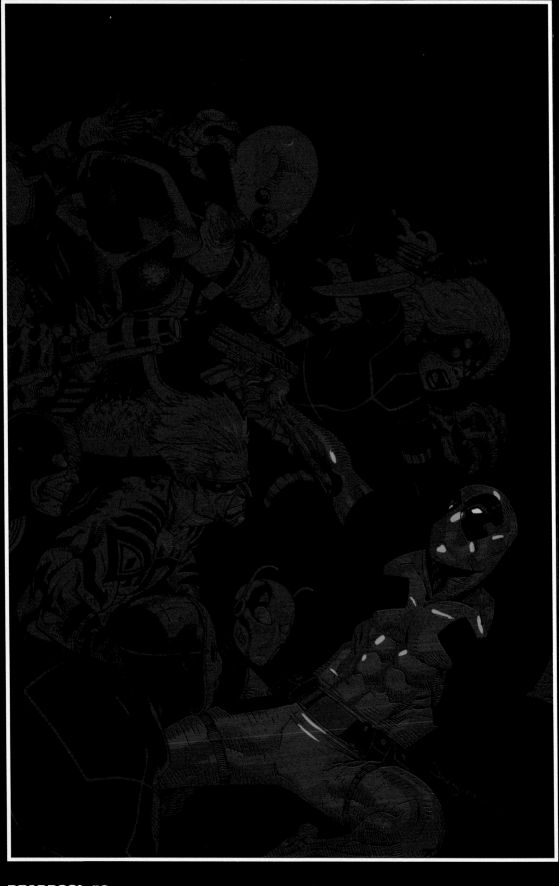

DEADPOOL #8

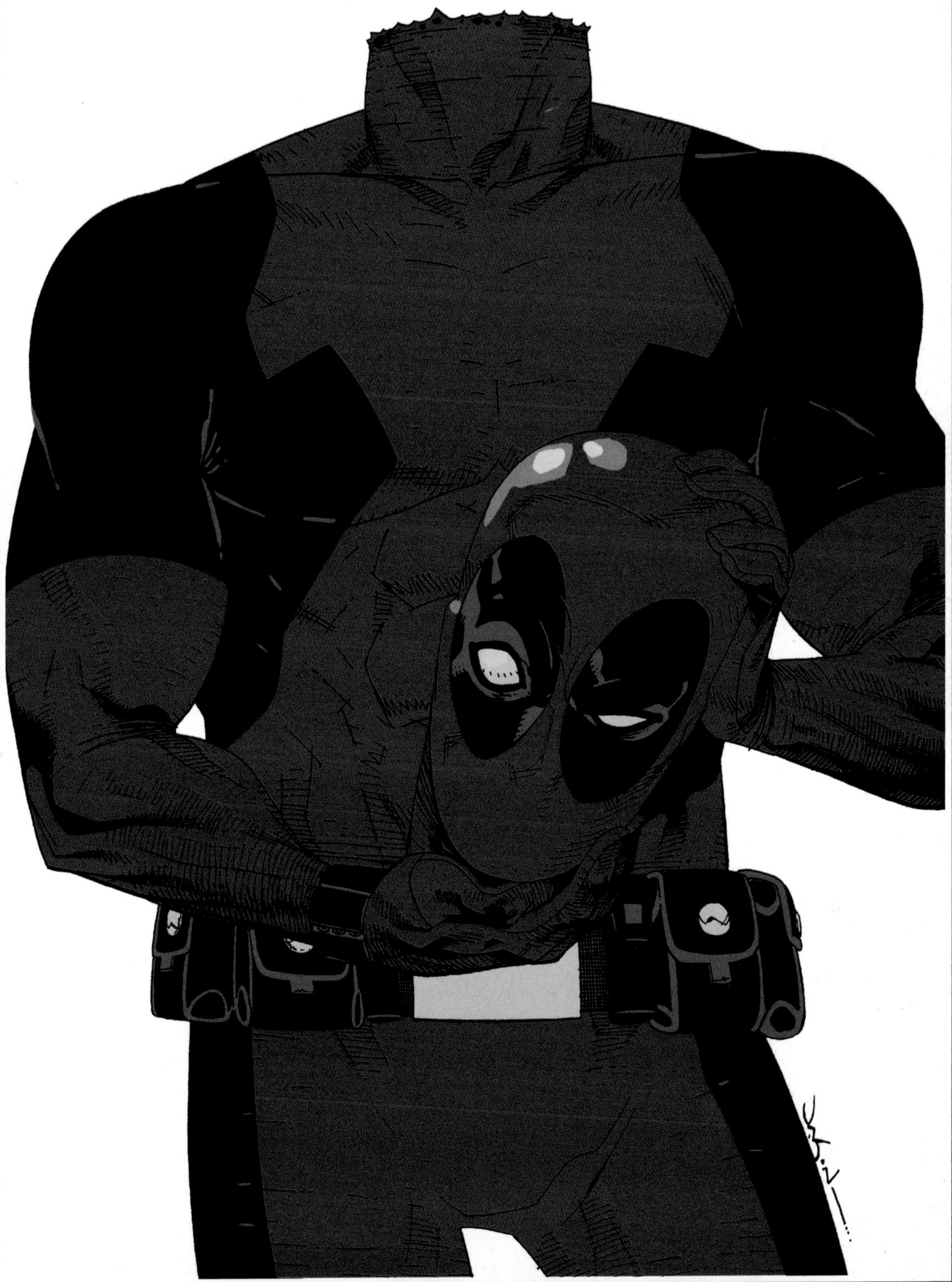

DEADPOOL #9

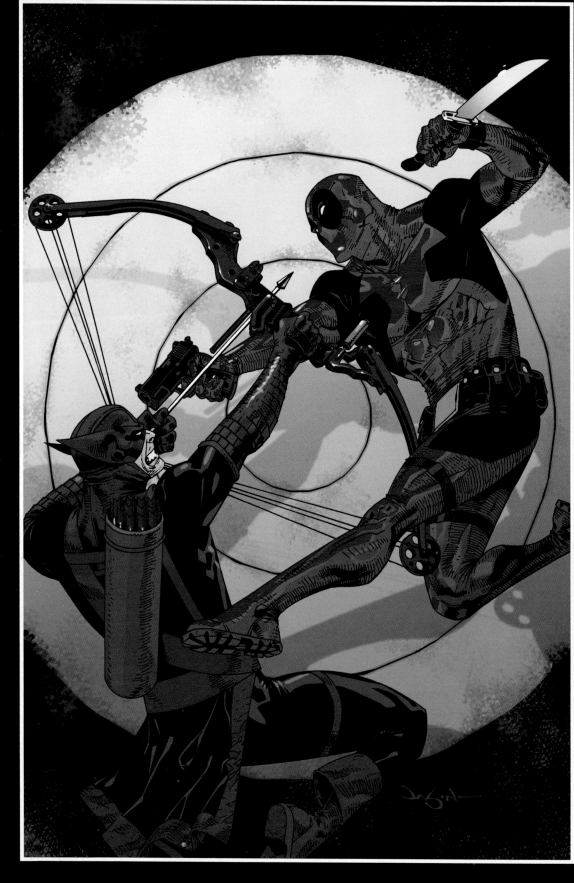

DEADPOOL #10

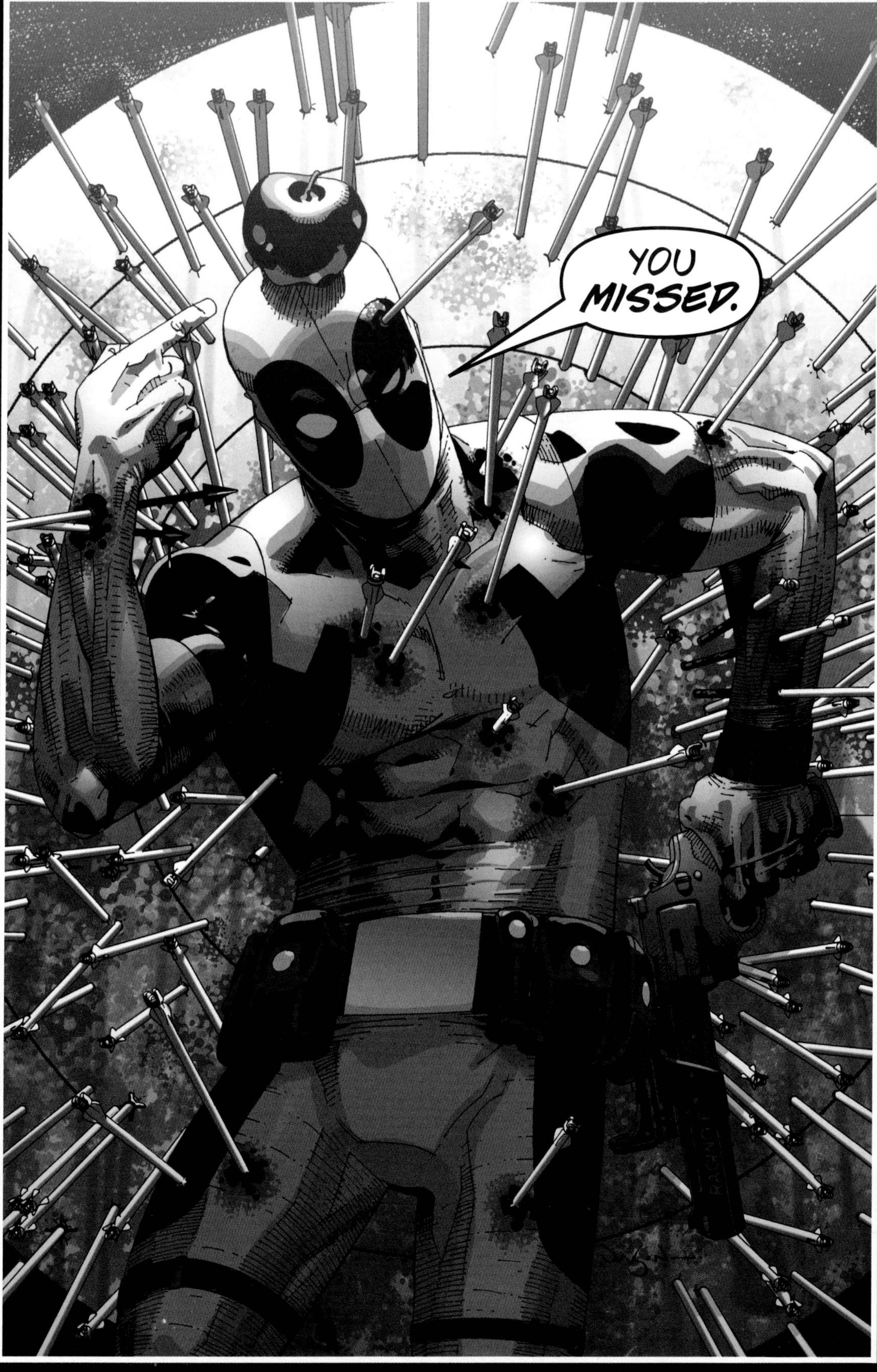
YOU MISSED.

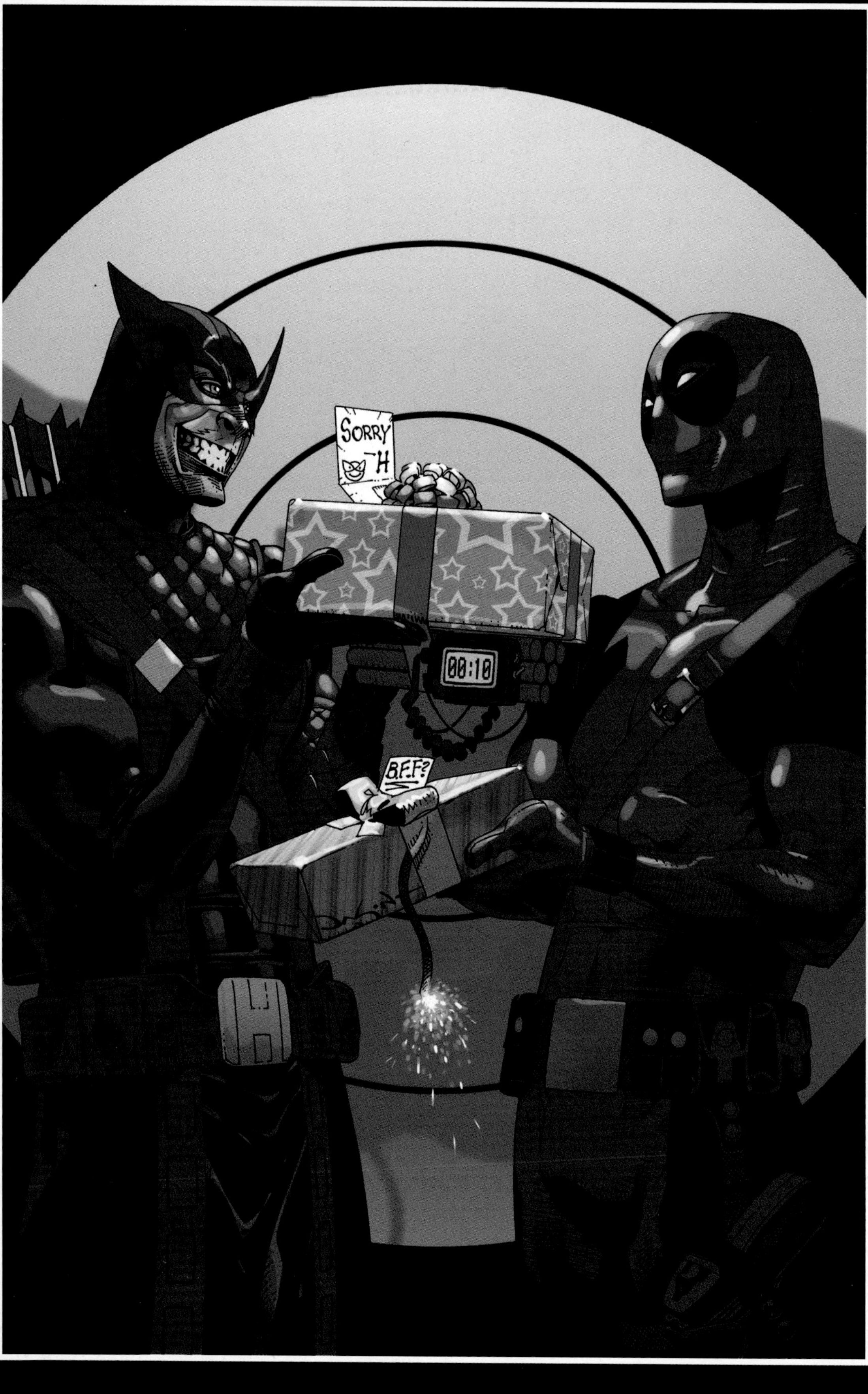
SORRY
-H
00:10
B.F.F?

DEADPOOL #12

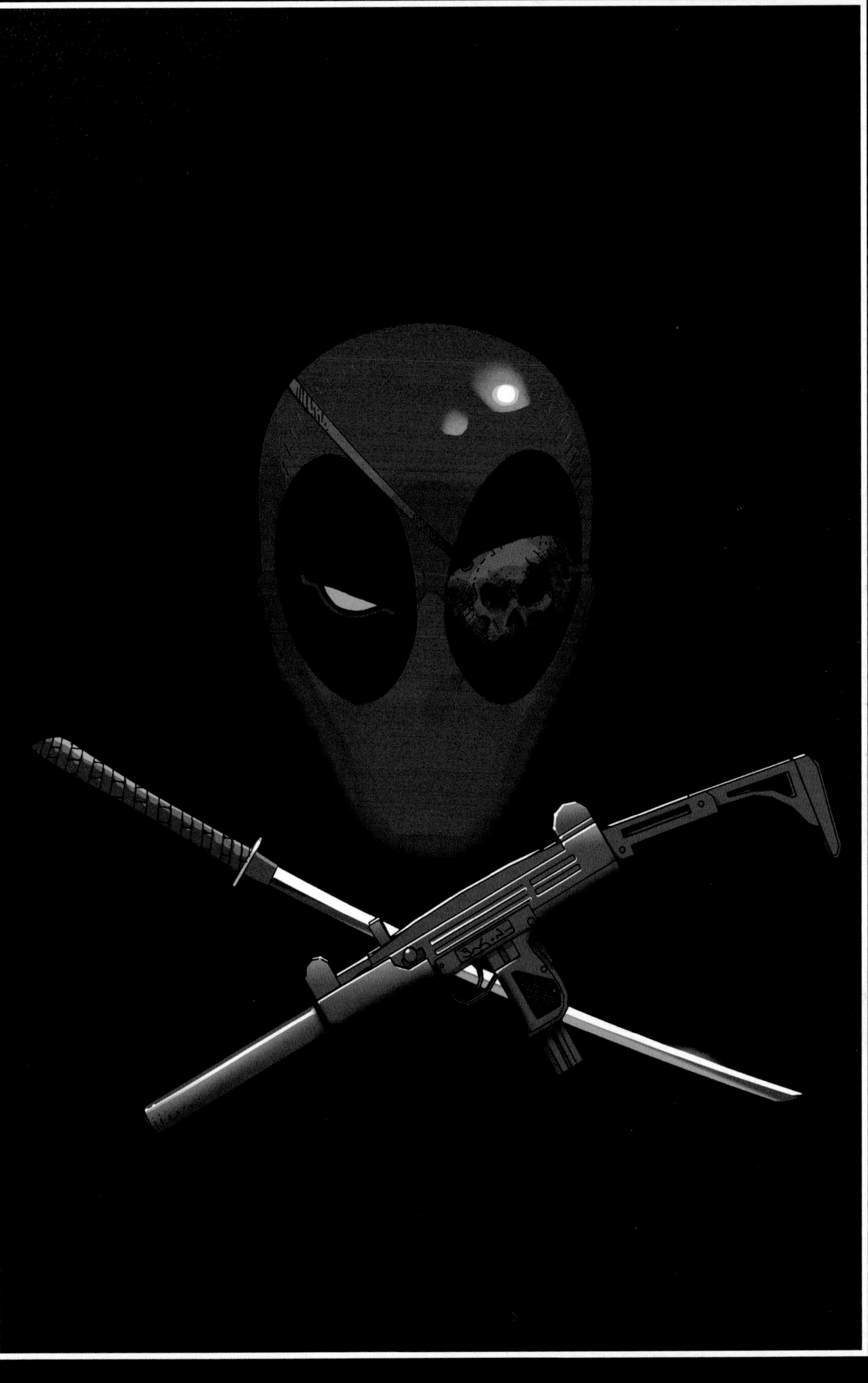

DEADPOOL #13

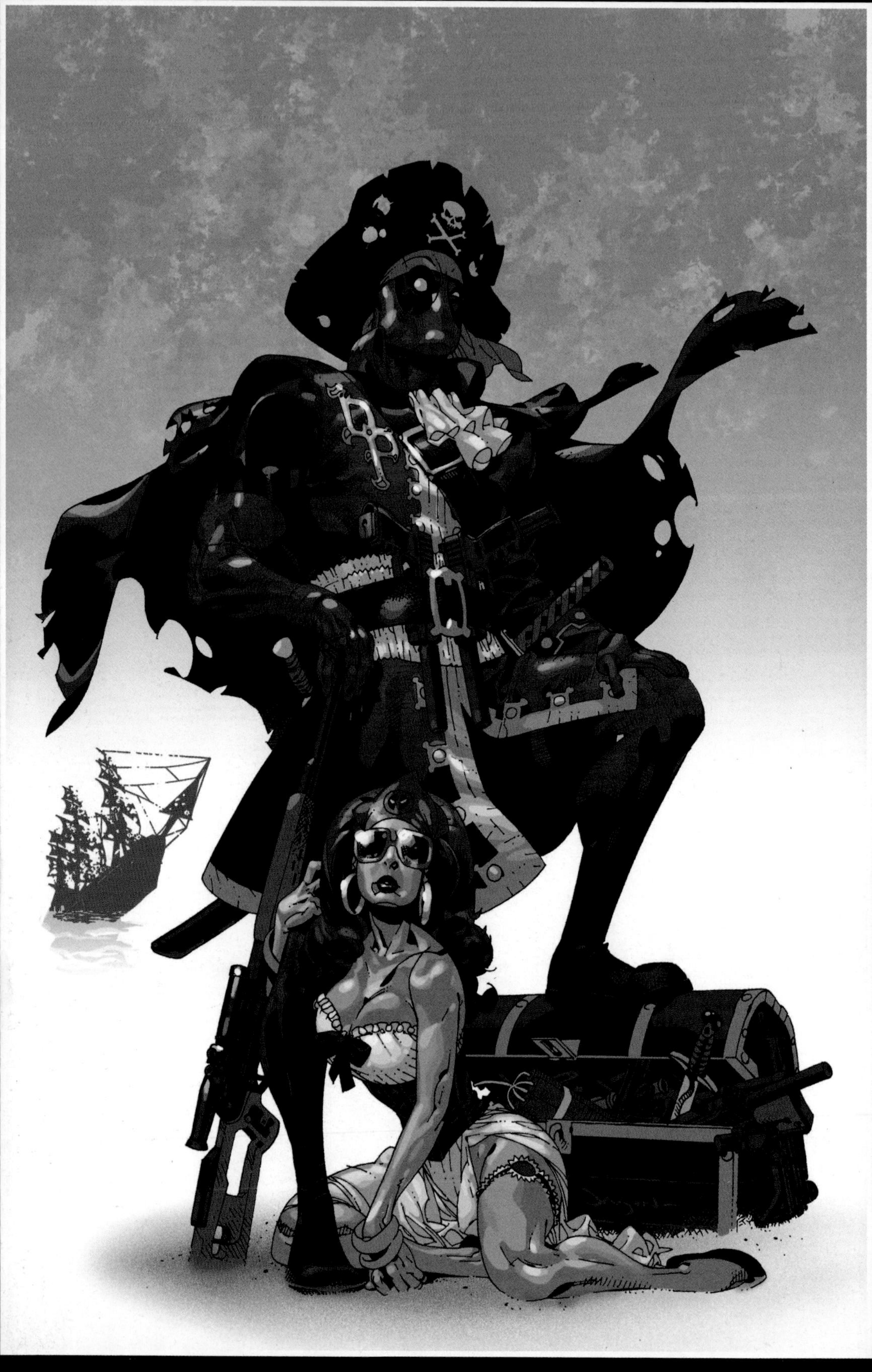

DEADPOOL #14

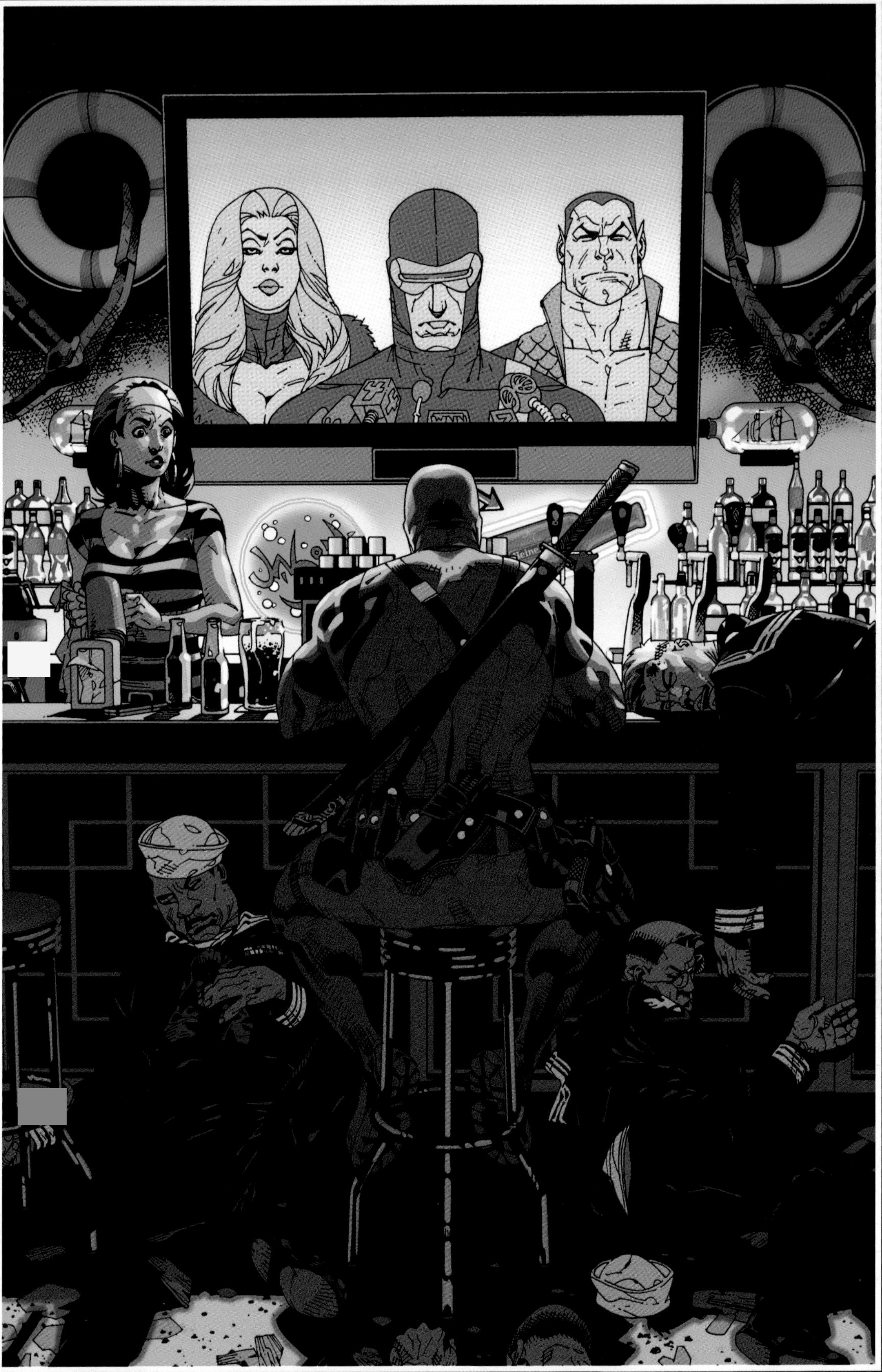

DEADPOOL #15

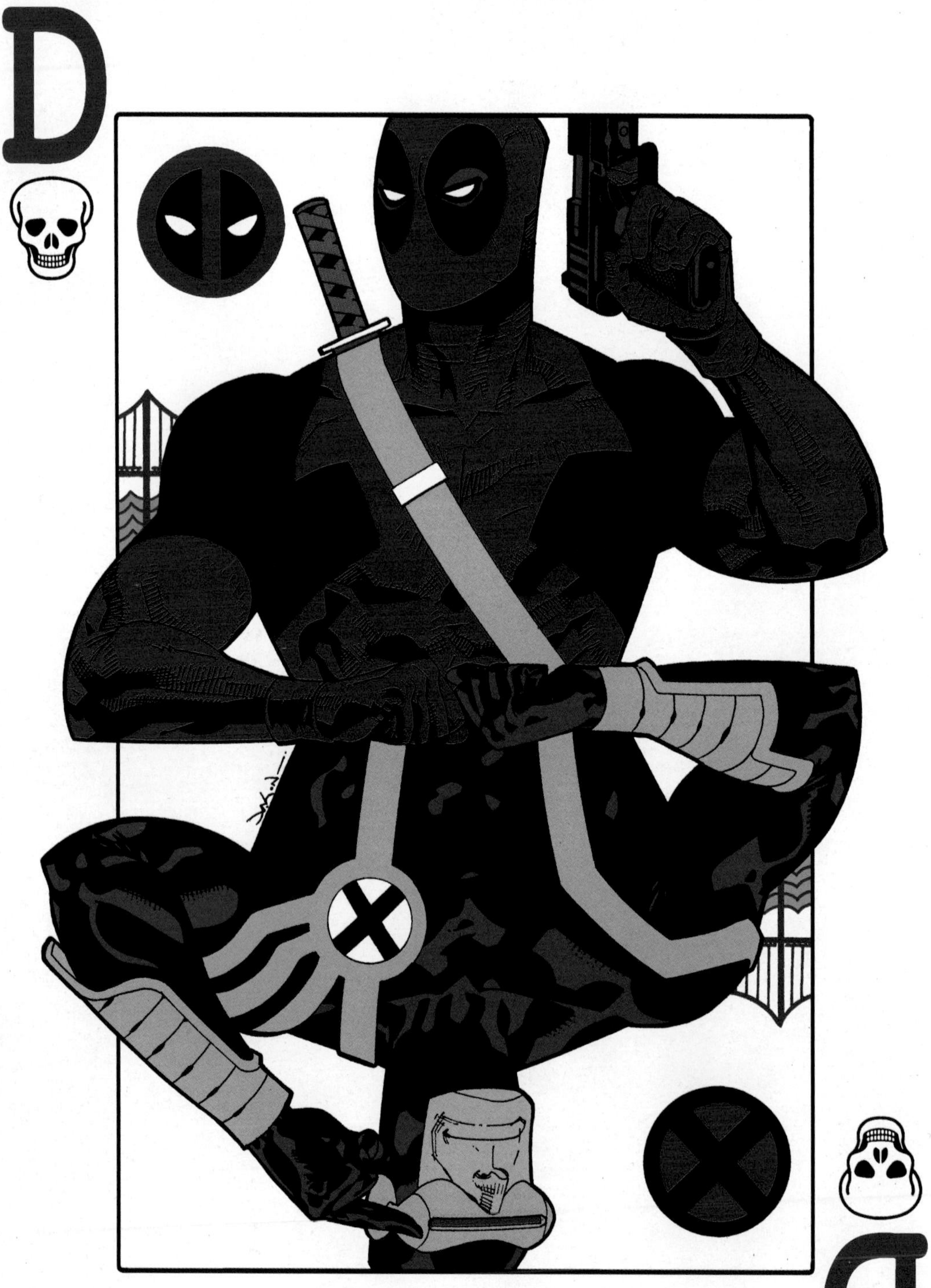
D
D

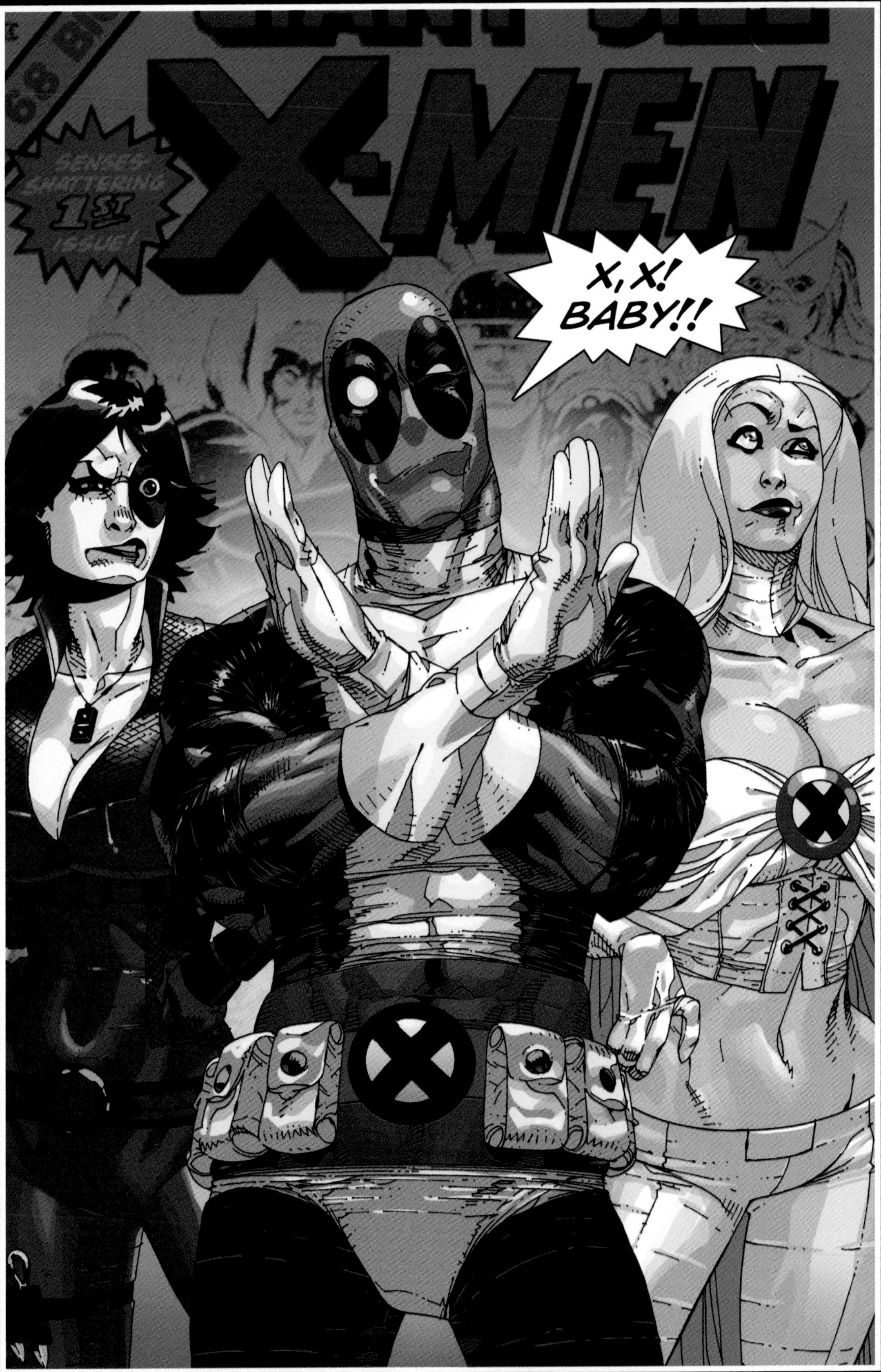
SENSES-SHATTERING 1ST ISSUE!
X-MEN
X, X! BABY!!

DEADPOOL #17

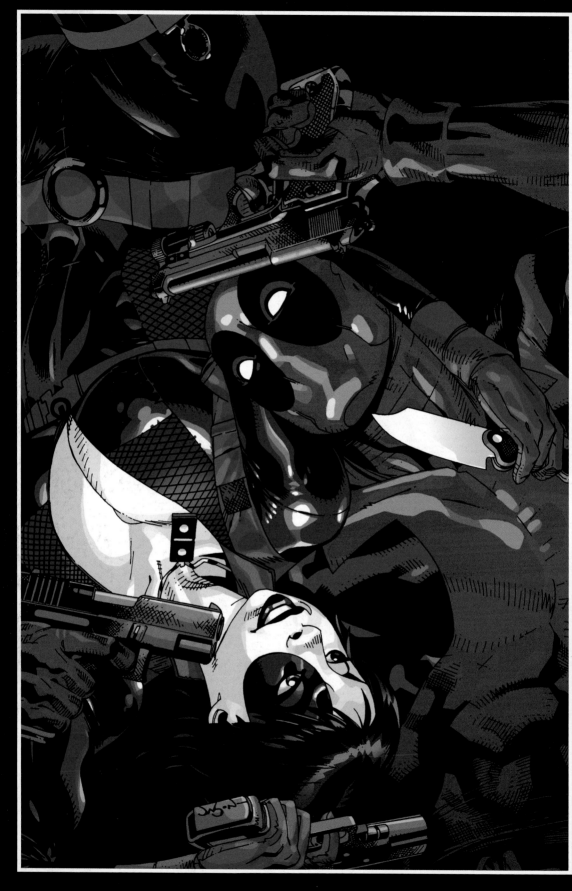

DEADPOOL #18

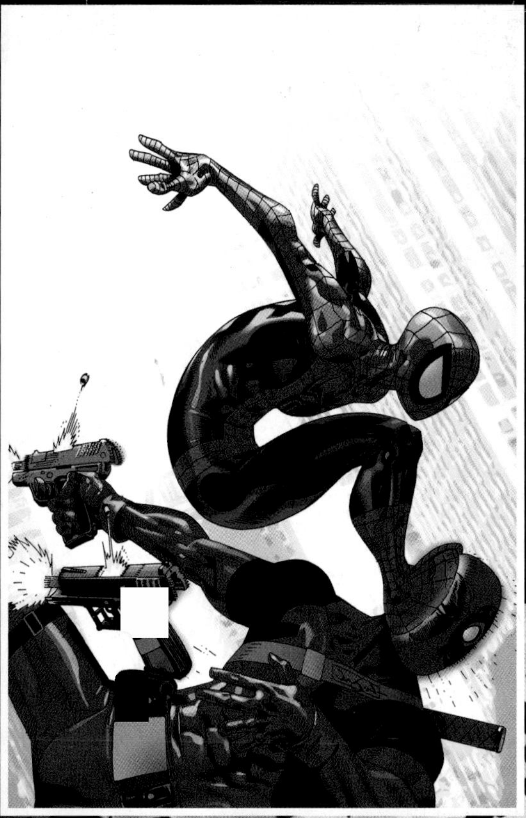

DEADPOOL #19

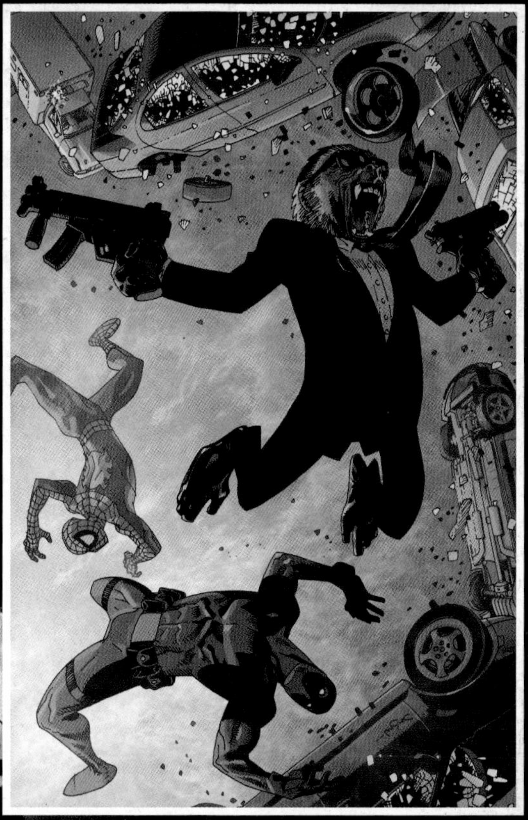

DEADPOOL #20

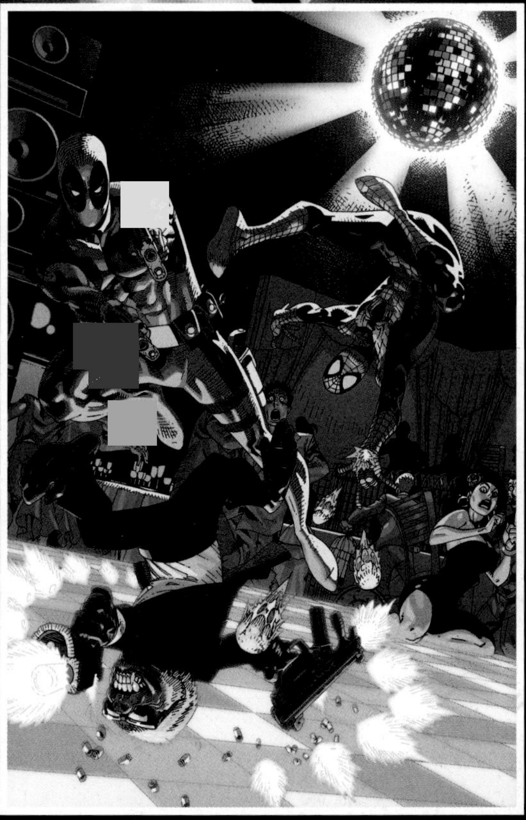

DEADPOOL #21

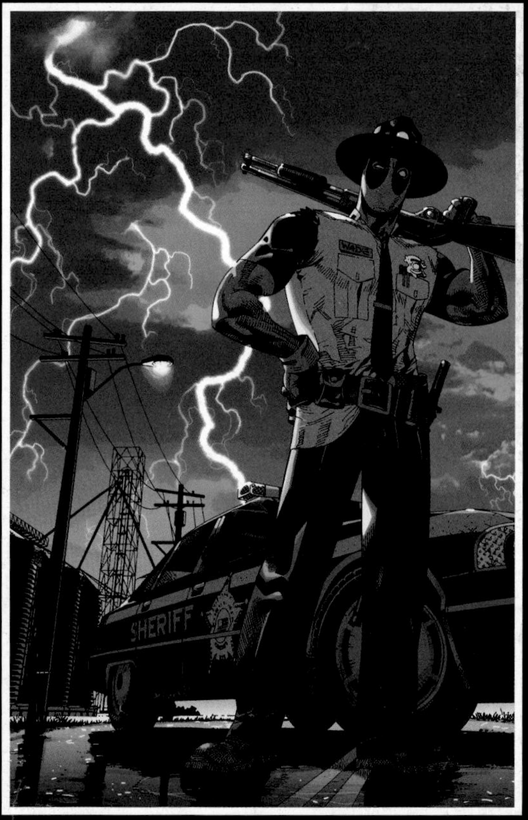
SHERIFF

DEADPOOL #22

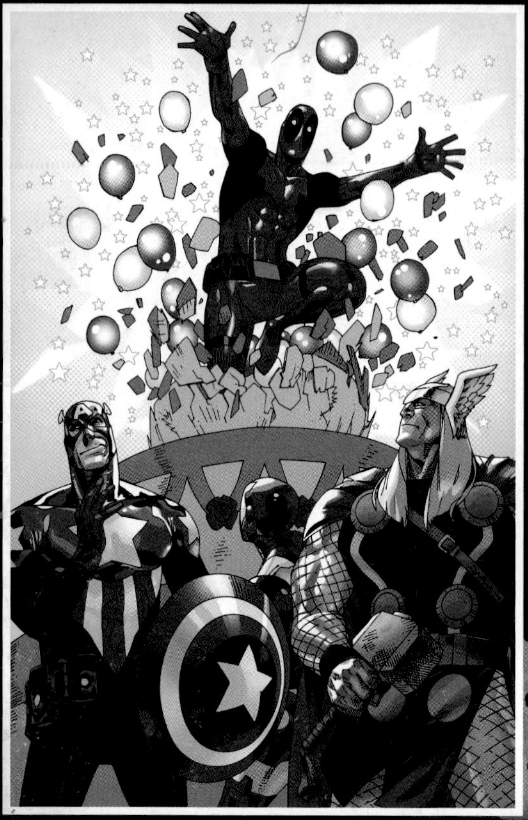

DEADPOOL #23

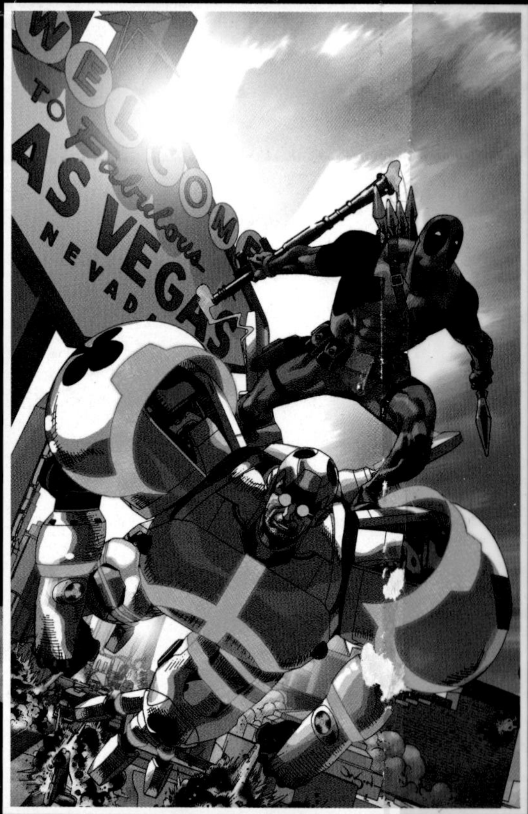
WELCOME
TO Fabulous
AS VEGAS
NEVAD

DEADPOOL #24

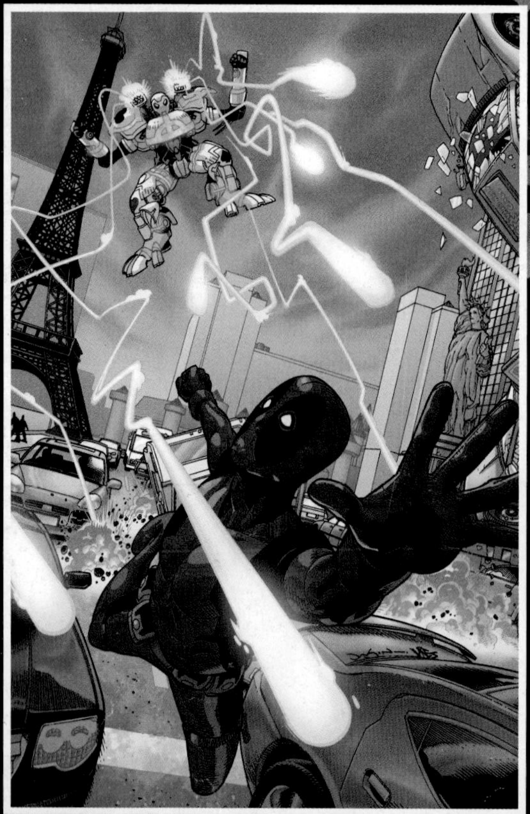

DEADPOOL #25